W9-BYZ-890

Secrets to
SPIRITUAL
POWER

Secrets to SPIRITUAL POWER

WATCHMAN NEE

compiled by Sentinel Kulp

 Whitaker House

Unless otherwise indicated, all Scripture quotations are from the *New King James Version*, © 1979, 1980, 1982 by Thomas Nelson, Inc. Used by permission. All rights reserved. Scripture quotations marked (KJV) are taken from the *King James Version* of the Bible.

Excerpts from *Changed into His Likeness,* by Watchman Nee, used by permission. Copyrighted in 1967 by Angus I. Kinnear. American edition published in 1978 by Tyndale House Publishers, Inc., Wheaton, IL 60189. Used by permission of Kingsway Publications, Ltd., Eastbourne, Sussex, England. All rights reserved. Excerpts from *Love Not the World,* by Watchman Nee, used by permission. Copyrighted by Angus I. Kinnear; first published in 1968. Excerpts from *The Normal Christian Life,* by Watchman Nee, used by permission. Copyrighted in 1957 by Angus I. Kinnear. First published by Gospel Literature Service, India. American edition published in 1977 by Tyndale House Publishers, Inc., Wheaton, IL 60189. Used by permission of Kingsway Publications, Ltd., Eastbourne, Sussex, England. All rights reserved. Excerpts from *Sit, Walk, Stand,* by Watchman Nee, used by permission. Copyrighted by Angus I. Kinnear. First published in 1957 by Gospel Literature Service, Bombay, India. American edition published in 1977 by Tyndale House Publishers, Inc., Wheaton, IL 60189. Used by permission of Kingsway Publications, Ltd., Eastbourne, Sussex, England. All rights reserved. Excerpts from *What Shall This Man Do?* by Watchman Nee, used by permission. Copyrighted by Angus I. Kinnear; first published in 1961.

All of the views stated by Watchman Nee are not necessarily those of the publisher.

SECRETS TO SPIRITUAL POWER: FROM THE WRITINGS OF WATCHMAN NEE

Sentinel Kulp
P.O. Box 129
Sunneytown, PA 18084
sentinelkulp@juno.com
www.wellofoath.com

ISBN: 0-88368-498-5
Printed in the United States of America
© 1998 by Whitaker House

Whitaker House
30 Hunt Valley Circle
New Kensington, PA 15068

Library of Congress Cataloging-in-Publication Data

Nee, Watchman.
  Secrets to spiritual power / Watchman Nee ; compiled by Sentinel Kulp.
     p. cm.
  Includes bibliographical references (p. 291–294) and index.
  ISBN: 0-88365-498-5
   1. Christian life. I. Kulp, Randal W., 1956– II. Title.
  BV4501.2 .N415 1998
  248.4—dc21   98-047850

No part of this book may be reproduced or transmitted in any form or by any means, electronic or mechanical, including photocopying, recording, or by any information storage and retrieval system, without permission in writing from the publisher.

3 4 5 6 7 8 9 10 11 12 13 14 /10 09 08 07 06 05 04 03 02 01

Contents

A reverence of the LORD
is but the beginning of wisdom;
a full knowledge of all the Holy One's ways
is a complete understanding.

—Proverbs 9:10,
compiler's paraphrase

Who Was Watchman Nee?

Watchman Nee was born in China on November 4, 1903, and given the name Ni (Nee) Shu-Tsu. He was an answer to his mother's prayer. Having previously had two daughters, and fearing she would bear only daughters like her sister-in-law who had given birth to six, she offered a petition to the Lord: if He would be gracious in providing her a son, she would offer him back in service to Him. And so, a year later, her first boy was born. However, it was not until some years later, when the boy had reached manhood, that God was pleased to take that which had been offered. Perhaps this was why, when the call of the Lord did come upon his life, Watchman Nee treated it with all solemnity and seriousness. He contemplated the issue of salvation, knowing that it had to be all or nothing in his devotion to the Lord. So after heavily weighing the decision, in the year 1920, he accepted Jesus Christ into his heart at the age of seventeen. And in looking back upon his life, the record of service he gave to the Lord was proof that he gave his all.

Two incidents come to mind that show the intense consecration and zeal that Watchman Nee had for the Lord. In 1922, after he had been seeking the power of the Holy Spirit for quite some time, God showed him the obstacle to his receiving that power. It was his longtime sweetheart Charity, who was unsaved. Although he was pierced to the heart and even begged God to let him be with her, eventually he yielded to God's will. When he let her go, the power came. But God was not finished working, for several years later Charity was saved. She and Watchmen Nee were reunited, and in 1934 they were married.

The other incident occurred in 1926. Watchman Nee fell ill with tuberculosis and was expected to die. He did not want to leave this world without putting on paper the wonderful truths that God had taught him from His Word. He worked zealously, in spite of his weakness and high fever, to write his three-volume work entitled *The Spiritual Man,* which he finished in 1928. Several months later, amazingly and miraculously, when the doctors had given up any hope for his survival, he was healed by God.

Having been blessed with a photographic memory, Watchman Nee felt it was the Lord's call upon him to be a watchman for brothers and sisters of the faith in China. To properly utilize his amazing memory, Watchman read everything he could that was written on the Christian faith, with the hope of sifting through the chaff. Although for Watchman Nee there was no difference in the path leading to spiritual growth and maturity than for any other Christian, it was his zeal to serve and to experience the fullness of what God offers to those He has redeemed that catapulted him far past what most Christians attain in their spiritual experience. As a result, it did not take too many years before his stature in spiritual matters became readily apparent to those who knew him. Furthermore, as word of his achievements spread, he became widely respected by Christian leaders the world over. As the years passed, he was greatly used by the Lord, not only for the conversion of many people into a saving knowledge of God, but also for planting numerous local fellowships throughout China and Southeast Asia.

Though Watchman Nee did not neglect the importance of salvation and the forgiveness of sin, the strength and authority he commanded stemmed from the fact that he did not stop there. Throughout his ministry he emphasized that redemption was merely the beginning of the Christian walk. He consistently exhorted people toward full sanctification—something that occurs in subjective experience as our self-life is done away with and replaced with the resurrection life of Christ. Thus, his message not only encompassed the saving of souls, but also encouraged people to move on to full maturity in their spiritual life and walk—something that can only be achieved when Christ, the risen Savior, lives out His life through us.

The Lord was gracious in raising up this man to serve His people during a difficult period of time. It was a period of transition and turmoil, not only for China, but also for the world at large. Watchman Nee continued faithfully in the service of His Lord until the Communists imprisoned him in 1952. Though he died in prison in 1972, after twenty years of confinement, the insights that were given to him from the Lord continue to enrich the lives of believers worldwide.

Preface

I was only thirteen years old at the time, and much too young at that point in my life to have a grasp on even the basics of what life was about. Nevertheless, there I was, sitting in the middle of a stadium filled with people, most of whom were intently listening to a preacher who was explaining the precious gift that a loving heavenly Father was pleased to offer to a lost world. Oh, I had heard the story many times before. And I had previously accepted that it was true. I knew in my heart that salvation was something I needed. But this time there was something different. This time something made the message speak to me, as if it was a personal invitation Christ was offering. It was at this moment that I came face to face with the reality that I had to make a decision. From this time forward, I was going to be held accountable and would have to answer to God for who and what I was before Him. Since I accepted that I did not fit the high standard of perfect righteousness that this Holy Creator of mine required, it was clear to me that I was lacking what was needed if I expected to stand before Him without fear of judgment. I needed the redemption that He offered. And further, it was something I wanted. Moreover, I knew it was something I could get. All I had to do was respond to the gracious gift that the Father was pleased to offer through the finished work of His Son. So I gave my answer to God's invitation as given through Billy Graham and went forward, in public, to make a profession of faith in Christ.

I will always be thankful for the opportunity that was provided for me by Brother Graham at Shea Stadium, because it was at that time that the Lord convinced me to accept His open invitation to eternal life through salvation. But I am also thankful to my pastor, a small town evangelistic-style Lutheran who had been called home from a mission field in Africa for health reasons. It was his sermons that, over the years of my childhood, had been breaking up the hard ground in my heart, plowing furrows that would eventually receive the seed of God's Word. The Lord bless you, Brother Flothmeier.

Now I was saved. And somehow I was different—I knew it—though I could not explain it. I could feel it! And what a joy filled my heart to confirm this fact. I had accepted Christ! I had eternal life, and with it I had an intense desire to please the One who had given me such a wonderful gift. I had changed inside, in some way, and because of this change I was convinced that my outward walk in life would be different from now on. Furthermore, since I was now a child of God, I could serve Him. I could please the One who had so wonderfully blessed me.

These were my thoughts at that time—thoughts that have reoccurred in the minds of new believers since the time of Pentecost. And so, in a manner somewhat like Jacob who had received the blessing (Gen. 32:24–30), I set out to serve God, in my way, and as best as I knew how. And because of this, the next twenty-some years of my Christian walk consisted of what all too often could be compared to a roller coaster ride of faith. Why? Though I had the seed of the Spirit of life in me, I was unable to break out of the fruitless cycle that I was in, and into the freedom and victorious life that were available to me as described in the Scriptures. What was the reason? I was not told, nor did I realize, that I was still lacking a strong foundation in the first principles of Christ (Heb. 6:1–3).

In the midst of all those years of struggle and frustration, of ups and downs, little did I know that the grace of God had never left me. However, because of my ignorance as to the conflict that existed within me, there were many times when I even doubted my salvation experience. It was not until later in my life that God revealed to me the truth that it was, in fact, His grace that was still with me, patiently waiting and working toward the time when I would learn the next lesson of faith—the lesson I had been so reluctant to learn since that day, years ago, when I became saved. And no wonder that it took so long for me to see this truth. Throughout the entire course of our spiritual lives, this lesson is probably the most difficult lesson we, as Christians, have to learn.

At the beginning of our Christian lives, and as a result of our new inborn sense, we are overwhelmed with the feelings of ecstasy and joy that usually accompany those who have been forgiven of their sins. Though on the one hand these feelings are the confirmation we have in our hearts that we are accepted before God, on the other hand we actually stumble in the face of this newfound approval. We assume that because we are saved we are fully accepted before God, and that He will be pleased with whatever we offer to Him, so long as it appears to stem from our good intentions. However, at this point in our spiritual lives, we are still ignorant of the fact that God makes distinctions that we are not yet mature enough, nor discerning enough, to make. You see, He still rejects all that emanates from our flesh, just as He did before we were saved. The change that has taken place upon our receiving Christ has only touched our spirits, and as of yet it has not entered into the realm of our souls, not to mention our bodies. And yet, in our ignorance, with our desire to return the favor that has been bestowed on us, we set out to serve Him with some of the very things He came to deliver us from. And so, we offer up to Him the works of our flesh.

This was the spiritual lesson that took me over twenty years of my life to learn. And it is the most crucial lesson we, as believers, have to learn. Why? Because God through the Holy Spirit has the task of attempting to teach us something we do not want to see or recognize about ourselves. It is very similar to the people of Israel as they journeyed in the wilderness. Why was God testing them? What was He trying to teach them all those years? He was making repeated attempts at revealing something to a people ignorant of who and what they really were. They were a people who made repeated promises, and yet a people who were not equipped to follow through with their word—a people who murmured and grumbled at every test God placed in their path. Hence, the lesson of their wilderness trials was "that they may know themselves." (See Deuteronomy 8:2.) Like His people of old, I did not know myself very well. As a result, it was not until after years of making repeated attempts at pleasing God, and inevitably failing, that in desperation I finally gave up. I had reached the end of myself. I threw in the towel and admitted total defeat. This was seven years ago, but what I did not know at the time was that the end of myself is the very place where God begins.

Thus, since I was now ready to learn what I had been so reluctant to learn in the past, God began to make drastic changes in my life, both external and internal. Though at times I felt more like I was clinging on for dear life rather than just learning to follow the leading of the Spirit, the results slowly began to be manifest. Over the period of the next few years, I entered into what I had yearned for: growth and maturity in spirit. I must admit, this growth was not without cost. But what price can be put on things of an eternal value? What is too high a price for that which is pleasing to the Lord?

It was during this time that the Lord brought a brother to me to assist in laying the foundation that was needed for my growth in the Lord. He also tutored me on the importance of daily devotions in the Word and the need for quiet times. And as these began to have an effect on my walk and fellowship with the Lord, they also kindled a strong inward desire to read and learn more. After a few years, when these disciplines that I would need to carry me forward throughout the rest of my spiritual life were thoroughly instilled in me, the Lord was gracious in bringing before me a number of saints who took notice of what had now become an intense desire to know and understand more of the Lord. A few of these dear saints counseled me to read the works of someone I had never heard of: a man named Watchman Nee. It was explained to me that his understanding of the Lord and spiritual matters went very deep. So after having had his name confirmed by a number of witnesses, I purchased a few of his books at the local bookstore.

As I began reading, I could sense in my spirit that this man had come to know God in a very intimate way. However, his work was not what I would consider quick reading, and much of it was difficult to grasp. Actually, it was not until a year or two later that I fully came to understand why: it is difficult for the flesh to grasp the things of the spirit. Nonetheless, at the time I was not about to let that deter me. So I continued to consume as much as I could of the writings of Watchman Nee. That was in 1994. By the end of 1996, I was finishing the last of what was available through the local bookstore, which amounted to over sixty books. And I have not ceased in being thankful to the Lord for this servant and for having access to the insights he was given.

Though I have read the works of about a hundred authors, there are few who come close to Watchman Nee in their depth of understanding and in their expounding upon the subjective, practical experience of Christian spiritual life. No matter what stage a Christian is in as far as his walk and maturity, the strengths and weaknesses of each are examined in detail throughout Nee's writings—which leads us to the reason you have this book before you.

As I was nearing the end of what was available by Watchman Nee, the Lord laid a burden on my heart to share some of the many wonderful insights that had been so helpful to me in my spiritual walk and growth. And though I had the desire to share, it grieved me that the average Christian would never have the time and opportunity to be fed with the meat of the Word as I had been by all these books. For this reason, I set about to extract many of those powerful insights, combining them into a book that would facilitate their being made readily available to the body of Christ—and in a format that was easy to consume.

The result is before you. It is my prayer that the Lord would bless you through this compilation as much as I was blessed through my reading of the original works of this humble and faithful servant of the Lord.

Acknowledgments

Most of the excerpts contained in this book are a paraphrase in my own words. However, it was appropriate and necessary to obtain permission from those who hold the copyrights on Nee's materials. The following organizations hold the rights to these works and have been gracious in granting their use.

The majority of the works of Nee used as sources for this book are available through Christian Fellowship Publishers, New York. A complete list of their books can be requested by contacting them at Christian Fellowship Publishers, 11515 Allecingie Parkway, Richmond, VA 23235.

The Normal Christian Life; Changed into His Likeness; Sit, Walk, Stand; Love Not the World; and *What Shall This Man Do?* are under copyright by Kingsway Publications, Lottbridge Drove, Eastbourne, East Sussex, England BN23 6NT. Three of these books—*The Normal Christian Life; Changed into His Likeness;* and *Sit, Walk, Stand*—are published in the United States by Tyndale House Publishers, Inc., P.O. Box 80, Wheaton, IL 60189-0080.

The Release of the Spirit is under copyright by Sure Foundation, Inc., 2522 Colony Court, Indianapolis, IN 46280. *Song of Songs* is under copyright by Christian Literature Crusade, P.O. Box 1449, Fort Washington, PA 19034.

To these organizations, and especially to the people behind them, I express my heartfelt thanks for their consideration and approval. Writing this book was only a task assigned to and completed by a faithful servant, but seeing that others have the opportunity to be blessed by it is cause for rejoicing.

Introduction

I would like to make a few points in order to help you better understand the purpose behind the work set before you, so that you can view it from the perspective that was intended.

But first, an explanation of what this is not. This is not meant to be a compilation of the best of Watchman Nee's material. If one wishes to view the best of what is available by Watchman Nee, one would have to repeat what I have done—purchase and read all the materials of his that are available in print. For of the insights that were given to this man by God, most were of such spiritual depth that there would be few, if any, shortcuts on the road to attaining an understanding of all of them.

This is intended to be a tool whereby many of the powerful insights that were given to this man during his life of service and sacrifice might be gathered together and compiled into a concise form—a form that could be useful in feeding a body that is in desperate need of a sound spiritual diet. Where it was possible, direct quotations from the author were used. In most places, though, it was not possible to take certain precepts out of the context of an overall discussion and still retain the same emphasis and meaning without changing the wording. For this reason, great care was taken in these areas so as to adhere to two main objectives: to maintain the integrity of scriptural truths, and to convey the thoughts and spiritual insights of the author as clearly as possible while maintaining the potency with which they were given in his materials. It is my prayer that I have been able to do this in a way that would not displease the One who gave this man his insights.

Having now made available, for the first time on one table, choice selections that the Lord revealed to this man, and in portions that believers are well able to consume, I desire and pray that the Lord would use this book to bless and feed thousands more than this man's works have already fed. Also, I pray that He would stir the spirits of many with a thirst and a hunger for more of the same—that they would take a further and closer look at some of the many delicacies the Lord has made available through Watchman Nee. It is with this in mind that I designed the overall outline of the book—to facilitate an easy reference to the particular work used by consulting the reference index.

I pray that Christ would have preeminence even in the legacy of the spiritual nourishment this servant of God has left us.

One

The Normal Christian Life

God's normal for a Christian can be summarized as follows: I no longer live! Now it is Christ who lives His life in me (Gal. 2:20).

There are two aspects of salvation that should be manifest in a Christian's life: the first is the forgiveness of sin; the second is his deliverance from sinning. Anyone who is not experiencing both of these aspects in his life is living beneath the privileges that God has accomplished for us in Christ.

Because of our limited comprehension of the state of our fallen nature, we do not have a true appreciation of how helpless the natural man really is. Thus, we still have some expectations in ourselves. And as a result of this faulty line of thought, we think that we can please God.

The blood can wash away my sins, but it cannot wash away my *"old man"* (Rom. 6:6). For this we are in need of the Cross, that the old man may be crucified. Though the blood deals with sins, it is the Cross that deals with the sinner.

At the beginning of the Christian life, we are concerned with our doing and not with our being; we are distressed more by what we have done than by what we are. We think that if only we could rectify certain things we would be good Christians; therefore, we set out to change our actions. We try to please the Lord, but we find that something within us does not want to please Him. And the more we try to rectify matters externally, the more we realize how deep-seated the problem really is.

Since we came into the world by birth, we must go out by death. To do away with our sinfulness, we must do away with our life. But how do we die? It is not by trying to kill ourselves. Rather, we die by recognizing that God has already dealt with us in Christ. This is summed up in the apostle's statement, *"As many of us as were baptized into Christ Jesus were baptized into His death"* (Rom. 6:3).

The Cross terminates the first creation, and out of death there is brought in a new creation in Christ: the Second Man.

The conditions of living the Christian life are fourfold: (1) knowing—revelation from God of what Christ has done for us, (2) reckoning—experiencing what He has revealed to us in our lives, (3) presenting ourselves to God—consecration to God of that which pertains to the new life He has placed in us, and (4) walking in the Spirit—maturing in our spirits to be sensitive to His every leading. The experience of every believer should encompass these four conditions.

God's way of deliverance is altogether different from man's way. Man's way is to try to suppress sin by seeking to overcome it; God's way is to remove the sinner. Many Christians mourn over their weakness, thinking that if only they were stronger all would be well. But God's means of delivering us from sin is not by making us stronger and stronger; rather, it is by making us weaker and weaker. God sets us free from the dominion of sin, not by strengthening our old man, but by crucifying him; not by helping him to do anything, but by entirely removing him from the scene of action.

It is not an intellectual knowledge at all, but an opening of the eyes of the heart—to see what we have in Christ.

For the written Word of God to become a living Word from God to you, He has to give you *"the spirit of wisdom and revelation in the knowledge of him"* (Eph. 1:17 KJV).

We are the factory, and our actions are the products. The blood of the Lord Jesus has dealt with the question of the products, namely, our sins, and the Cross has made a clean sweep of the factory that produces the goods.

22

What is "in Christ" cannot sin; what is "in Adam" can sin and will sin whenever Satan is given a chance to exert his power over it.

Faith is the substantiation of things hoped for (Heb. 11:1). This means making them real in experience. Substance is an object I possess—something before me. Substantiating means that I have the power or faculty to make that substance be real to me.

The promises of God are revealed to us by His Spirit so that we may lay hold of them.

We, as Christians, are never told by God to struggle to get into Christ. We are not told to get there, because we are already there. However, we are told to remain where God has placed us.

In dealing with Christ, God has dealt with the Christian; in dealing with the Head, He has dealt with all the members. It is altogether wrong for us to think that we can experience anything pertaining to spiritual life merely in ourselves, apart from Him.

Every true spiritual experience means that we have discovered a certain fact in Christ, and have entered into His experience.

The greatest negative in the universe is the Cross, for with it God wiped out everything that was not of Himself; the greatest positive in the universe is the Resurrection, for through it God brought into being all He will have in the new order of things. The Cross is God's declaration that everything within us from the old creation must die, because nothing of the first Adam can pass beyond the Cross.

There is an old world and a new world, and between the two there is the tomb. And although God has already crucified me with Christ, I must still consent to be consigned to the tomb.

That which has not passed through death can never be consecrated to God, because God will only accept that which is of the new order of things—that which pertains to His Spirit.

Presenting myself to God implies a recognition that I am already altogether His.

How can we ever expect the Lord to live out His life in us if we do not offer our lives to Him?

If we give ourselves unreservedly to God, many adjustments may have to be made. God will not let anything of our old selves remain. His finger will touch, point by point, those things that are not of Him until everything from our old nature has been removed.

God will always break what is offered to Him. First He breaks what He takes; but—after the breaking—He blesses, and then uses it to meet the needs of others (Mark 6:41).

We must all go to the Cross, because what is in us by nature is a self-life. Adam chose a self-life rather than a divine life; therefore, God had to gather up all that was "in Adam" and do away with it.

If we lack the experience of the outpouring of the Holy Spirit, we should ask Him for a revelation of the eternal fact that it is a gift of the exalted Lord to His church. Then, upon our having seen this fact, our efforts will give way to praises.

The Christians in Corinth had become preoccupied with the visible signs of the Holy Spirit's outpouring. At the same time, their lives were full of contradictions and were a reproach to the Lord's name. Though they did not lack the indwelling Spirit, they did lack a knowledge of His presence. Hence, a revelation of the indwelling Spirit was the remedy Paul offered to the Corinthian Christians for their unspirituality (1 Cor. 2).

In order to experience the life of Christ in a practical way, a day must come, as definite as the day of our conversion, when we give up all rights to ourselves and submit to the absolute lordship of Jesus Christ in every area of our lives. A revelation of this requirement is the first step to holiness; consecration (the offering of our whole lives) is the second step.

Until the lordship of Christ is a settled thing in our hearts, the Spirit cannot operate effectively in us. If we do not give Christ absolute authority in our lives, though He may be present, He cannot be powerful. The power of the Spirit is held back.

A forgiven sinner is quite different from an ordinary sinner, and a consecrated Christian is quite different from an ordinary Christian.

Grace means that God has done something for me; law means that I must do something for God.

The trouble with the law is not that the law's demands are unjust, but that I, as a sinner, am unable to meet them.

The law makes our weakness manifest. Had it not been for the law, we would never have known how weak we are. The law is what exposes our true nature.

The law was not given with the expectation that we would keep it; it was given in the full knowledge that we would break it. And when we have broken it so completely as to be convinced of our utter need, then the law has served its full purpose. It has been our schoolmaster to bring us to Christ, that in us He Himself may fulfill it (Gal. 3:24).

What does it mean to be delivered from the law? It means that I am henceforth no longer going to try to do anything to please God; for if I do, then I immediately place myself under the law. Therefore, I have no alternative; I must allow Christ to fulfill the law in me. And finally, I see that this alone is what is pleasing to God (Matt. 5:17). This is deliverance from the law!

It is only after having reached the point of utter despair in ourselves—so that we cease even to try—that we put our trust in the Lord to manifest His resurrection life in us. The sooner we give up trying, the better. For it is only by ceasing in ourselves that we give place to the Holy Spirit. And then, we will see a power stronger than ourselves carrying us through.

As long as we are trying to do anything, He can do nothing. It is because of our trying that we fail.

We all need to come to the point where we say, "Lord, I am unable to do anything for You, but I trust You to do everything in me."

One faulty line of thinking that is prevalent among Christians is this: we know that justification is ours through the Lord Jesus and that it requires no work on our part, but we think sanctification is dependent on our own efforts. We know we can receive forgiveness only by our entire reliance on the Lord, yet we believe we can obtain deliverance by doing something ourselves. After salvation, the old habit of "doing" reasserts itself, and we begin our old self-efforts again. However, the Bible declares that, in both justification and sanctification, He is the doer. *"It is God who works in you"* (Phil. 2:13).

Living in the Spirit means that I trust the Holy Spirit to do in me what I cannot do myself. It is not a case of trying, but of trusting; not a case of struggling, but of resting in Him.

The Cross has been given to procure salvation for us; the Spirit has been given to produce salvation in us.

We think of the Christian life as a "changed life," but it is not. What God offers us is an "exchanged life," a "substituted life," and Christ is our substitute within.

Many believers have a wrong understanding of sanctification. It is commonly conceived that every item of our lives should be holy. But that is not holiness; rather, it is the fruit of holiness. Holiness is Christ.

I cannot please God, but there is no "I cannot" in Christ. *"I can do all things through Christ who strengthens me"* (Phil. 4:13).

If we let go of our own will and wholly trust Him, we will not fall to the ground and break; rather, we will fall into *"the law of the Spirit of life"* (Rom. 8:2). For God has not only given us life, but He has also given us a law of life.

Revelation always precedes faith.

One of God's greatest problems in the church today is not the outward denominations and divisions of the body that man has made; rather, it is our own individualistic hearts that create and continue to sanction these divisions.

What God desires more than anything else is a man who will desire after His own heart.

The trouble with many of us as Christians is that we have changed the channel into which our energies are directed, but we have not changed the source of those energies. We tend to forget that in the matter of handling the things of God, it is not a question of comparative value, but of *origin*. Where does the resource originate from? Our flesh? Or the resurrection life of Christ!

The Holy Spirit has been given the task of teaching us (John 14:26). He does this by delicately putting His finger on something of the old nature that He sees in us and saying, "This is natural; this has its source in the old creation and did not originate with Me. This cannot abide." Until He does so, we may agree in principle, but we can never really see the truth. We may assent to and even enjoy the teaching, but we will never truly loathe ourselves.

Light has only one law: it shines wherever it is admitted.

We can know neither the hatefulness of sin nor the treachery of our self-nature until we experience the flash of revelation from God upon us that allows us to see as He does.

There is so little evidence of spiritual life, where life is present in us, because the soul is enveloping and confining that life so that it cannot find an outlet. If we are living in the soul, we are working and serving in our natural strength, rather than drawing from God.

God desires to bring us to the point where our natural strength is touched and fundamentally weakened (Gen. 32:24–25), so that we dare no longer trust ourselves.

True satisfaction is brought to the heart of God when we are really "wasting" ourselves upon Him (Matt. 26:7–8).

We cannot inject spiritual appetite forcibly into others; we cannot compel others to be hungry. Hunger has to be created, and it can be created in others only by those who carry with them the impressions of God. But there must also be something in us that gives release to the fragrance we have of Christ and that produces in others an awareness of need. And that something is a willingness to yield, a breaking and a pouring out of everything to God. This is what draws others out and on to know the Lord.

Two

Changed into His Likeness

God cuts short our old, self-willed nature to make way for our new nature in Christ, which works in willing cooperation with Him. Thus, the Spirit moves to attain God's ends by His own means. This is the goal of all God's dealings with His own.

Our salvation (justification) is entirely from God. And if this is true of the beginning of our salvation, it is also true of all that follows as we are sanctified. If the source of our life is in God, so also is everything that follows. Nothing starts from us.

All knowledge is the outcome of obedience. It is when we do His will that we are able to see more of His will. If any man determines to do His will, he shall know what that will is (John 7:17).

Those who know God have no need to protect their rights. Because they believe in Him, they learn to rely on Him for the outcome—knowing that whatever His will should be, it will be to their benefit in one way or another.

It is the death of Christ working in a man's life that produces purity of spirit. And it is this purity of spirit that brings further light or revelation from God.

Whether we can bring Christ into the situation to be God's vessel of recovery depends on whether we can get out of the way to make room for Him.

The difference between man's work and God's work is a question of source and a question of time.

The sign of the covenant was circumcision. We are to be a people who put no confidence in the flesh (Phil. 3:3), for it is when we are in the flesh that we are spiritually helpless.

What is true faith? It is when we are defeated and at the end of ourselves—when we must put our complete trust in Him. This is faith.

We never worked for our salvation, gradually scaling heights until we attained it. The Lord both sought and saved us. And victory over sin is the same; it is received, not worked for.

If we submit to His work in us, the life of our old nature will progressively be reduced to zero, so that the life of Christ may be fully displayed.

The distinctive feature of true Christianity is that it compels people to receive.

God does not say, "The soul who sins must get his sins cleansed"; He says, *"The soul who sins shall die"* (Ezek. 18:4).

The Christian life is the Christ-life. Christ in me has become my life and is living my life instead of me. God gives Him to me to be my life.

The daily life of the Christian can be summed up in one word: *receive.*

Just as God once opened our eyes to see our sins laid upon Christ, so once again He must open our eyes to see our own selves in Christ. And this is something that He delights to do.

It is when our thigh (natural strength) has been touched that we can hold God the closest (Gen. 32:25–26). We are strongest when we are weakest (2 Cor. 12:10).

With an abundance of natural strength, we are useless to God. With no strength at all, we can hold on to Him. And with His strength flowing through us, *"we are more than conquerors"* (Rom. 8:37). (See Genesis 32:24–28.)

Three

Sit, Walk, Stand

Every new spiritual experience begins with an acceptance, by faith, of what God has already done.

God is waiting for you to cease doing! And once you have done this, He will begin.

The operation of His life through us is truly spontaneous—it is without our own efforts. The all-important rule is not to try, but to trust; not to depend on our own strength, but on His.

Nothing is so blessed as when our outward efforts cease and our attitudes become unforced—when our words, our prayers, and our very lives all become spontaneous and sincere expressions of the life of Christ within us.

Too many Christians have all the doctrine but live lives that are a contradiction of it.

God will perfect every man who has faith in Him. We are *"confident of this very thing, that he which hath begun a good work in you will perform it until the day of Jesus Christ"* (Phil. 1:6 KJV).

Just as David and his armies fought before the rise of the kingdom of Solomon, so it is now. There must first be a period of spiritual warfare, as represented by David and the work he accomplished with his armies, before the glorious reign of the True Solomon. And God is seeking those who will cooperate with Him today, as David did, in preparatory warfare.

All work that is going to be effective must be conceived by God. If we plan the work and then ask God to bless it, we need not expect God to commit Himself to it. God's name is not a rubber stamp to authorize work that is ours in conception. True, there may be blessing upon such work, but it will only be partial, not full. There can be no "in His name" on it; alas, there will be only our name.

The abiding principle of all true Christian work is *"In the beginning God"* (Gen. 1:1).

God never asks us to do anything that we *can* do. He asks us to live a life that we can never live and to do a work that we can never do. Oh, how Christians need to see this truth!

Four

Love Not the World

Since the day Adam opened the door for evil to enter God's creation, the natural tendency of the world order is toward Satan and away from God.

A sentence of death is not passed on the dead, but on the living. And in one sense, the world is a living force today, relentlessly pursuing and seeking out its subjects. It is true that when the sentence is pronounced, death still lies in the future, but it is nevertheless certain. A person under sentence of death has no future beyond the confines of a condemned cell. Likewise, the world, being under such a sentence, has no future. When we realize that the world is under the death sentence, it begins to lose its grip on us.

Show the world the fruits of Christianity, and it will applaud; but show the world Christianity, and it will oppose it vigorously.

The so-called Christian nations are the outcome of a futile attempt to reconcile the world and Christ.

Religious people attempt to overcome the world by removing themselves from it. Christians overcome the world by being otherworldly.

There was a time when the church rejected the world's ways. Now she not only uses these ways, but she also abuses them.

The Christian way to solve the problem of loving the world is not by removing worldly things, but by delivering the heart from the grip of worldly things.

Give yourself to God; live for Him wholly and utterly. Why? Because *"the world passeth away, and the lust thereof: but he that doeth the will of God abideth for ever"* (1 John 2:17 KJV).

Five

Back to the Cross

If the effect of the Cross were limited to the substitutional side —that is to say, the side that causes people not to perish but have eternal life—the salvation God gives would still be incomplete. Though this would save people from the penalty of sin, it would not save them from the power sin has over their lives. For this reason, the Savior completed a twofold work: He saved people from the penalty of sin, and He saved them from the power and control sin has over them. Sadly, many only take advantage of the former!

God's Word does not say that the old man needs to be washed. This old man—the sin factor—is corrupted beyond repair. Therefore, God's way of dealing with the old man is to put it to death. This is accomplished through a union of the old man with the Lord Jesus in crucifixion. An ignorance of this fact explains why so many live in defeat. Apart from dying with Christ, there is no other way to put the old man to death (Gal. 2:20). And apart from putting the old man to death, there is no way to live in victory.

What is the consequence of having this sin factor—the old man—crucified? The *"body of sin"* is *"done away with"* (Rom. 6:6). And *"done away with"* means "rendered powerless."

The way you obtain the substitutionary death of the Lord Jesus is the way you enter into co-death with Him—by believing! All who believe in the substitutionary death of Christ are saved; all who believe in the co-death with Christ overcome sin.

The old man is not crucified by "touch" or "feel"; he is crucified by "reckoning" (Rom. 6:11). Whenever a believer fails to reckon, his old man is revived; but if he truly reckons, there will be supernatural power coming to him.

Satan is always looking for an opportunity to reactivate the old man. Whenever we are careless or unwatchful, whenever we do not stand on the death-ground of Calvary, our old man will revive its activities and resume its position.

When the Lord Jesus was on the cross, He had authority to come down if He so wished. By the same token, those who are crucified with the Lord can let their old man come down from the cross, if they so choose.

Many of the children of God often wonder why their old man is resurrected. They have failed to see that the death of the cross is a prolonged one.

To die to self is, in experience, deeper and more advanced than dying to sin.

It is during the middle stage of the Christian's spiritual life that he becomes capable of distinguishing between what is sin and what is self. This discernment is the result of having experienced victory over sin (Rom. 6:11), but not victory over self. When a believer possesses the experience of overcoming self completely, he has the mature life that the apostles had. From the viewpoint of those who have advanced this far, it is much easier to overcome sin than self.

Apart from the Lord we can do nothing (John 15:5)! Only He has shown us and accomplished for us the way to the death of self. And it is none other than the Cross. However, it is not a single or sole crucifixion; it is actually a co-crucifixion (Gal. 2:20).

The moment our self comes down off the cross, self returns to its old position. And a believer, in and of himself, has neither the power nor the method to control this self.

To deny self is a daily matter that should never cease. Paul said, *"I die daily"* (1 Cor. 15:31).

"He that loveth his life [soul] *shall lose it* [no fruit in eternity]; *and he that hateth his life* [soul] *in this world shall keep it* [he will

not be without fruit] *unto life eternal* [spiritual life]" (John 12:25 KJV). If a believer allows this non-spiritual self-life to be the main driving force of all his earthly activities, then—though this one may be saved—he will lose his life in the age to come (the Millennium) and suffer eternal loss of reward in terms of fruit. (See Matthew 6:1-6; 1 Corinthians 3:8.)

For the Christian, death to self is the door to life. It is the only way to fruitfulness. Hence, death is absolutely necessary. But how many of us are really dead? Death to self is the cessation of all self's activity!

Christ is not only the Savior who saves us from our sins, but He is also the Savior who saves us from ourselves. To die to the self-life is the only pathway to spiritual life. The turning point in experiencing God's full salvation lies in being delivered from self. And only God can cause us to die to self; no one else is able to do so.

If you have not experienced the death of self, your spiritual life will have little real progress.

Though, as Christians, we have the fact of our inheritance, this does not necessarily mean that we have come into the experience of enjoying our inheritance. Hence, fact and experience are vastly different from one another.

In order to possess and enjoy an inheritance, the inheritor must take two steps: first, he must believe that there is such an inheritance; second, he must singularly arise to take possession of this inheritance.

It is our responsibility to take the step of exercising our faith to take hold of the inheritance we have in the Lord Jesus, by using it and managing it as though this spiritual property were ours. It is a lack of faith that prevents us from going and taking possession of what God has already given to us as an inheritance. (See Numbers 13:30.)

Fact is God's work; faith is our trust in what God has worked; and experience is having God's work lived out through our lives in a practical way.

A believer becomes more spiritual simply, and only, as he possesses more spiritual experiences. These experiences are not self-created but are based on spiritual facts.

In spiritual progression, fact is the foundation, faith is the process, and experience is the consequence. In other words, fact is the cause, faith is the way, and experience is the effect.

To know Christ is to know the power of resurrection, and to know the power of the resurrection of Christ means we have a deeper knowledge of Christ Himself. Knowing (experiencing) the power of the resurrection of the Lord helps us to come into a true knowledge of Him. How do we know this? Because without His resurrection life there can be no power of the Holy Spirit.

That which stems from the first Adam does not live after going through death, because only the resurrection life of the Lord comes out of death. The sad situation today is that many try to testify of Christ with their natural life. There are so few who witness out of their experiential knowledge of the power of His resurrection life.

In the Bible, we see three distinct classes among God's people: (1) the children of Israel, who were chosen from among the people of the world; (2) the Levites, who were chosen from among the children of Israel; and (3) Aaron and his sons, who were chosen from among the Levites.

Today, there is a class of workers who have such an intimate fellowship with Jesus Christ that they are called to the highest work with the Lord—the work of intercession that our Lord Jesus Himself is doing (Rom. 8:34).

It is the Christian's calling to be a priest unto God. Sadly, though this is the calling, many forsake this high privilege and degenerate into the lower classes.

The more humble one is at God's feet, the more useful he is in God's hand.

Those Christians who take hold of Christ as their sanctification are today's Levites. These are Christians who have separated themselves from the world and have drawn near to God. Hence, they are acting as today's Levites.

To serve in the sanctuary is something seldom seen by men. Except for God, no one sees those who serve. They receive neither glory nor praise from men. They shut the door and pray in secret. They are rewarded in secret. In a place that is unknown to men, they see God's face, hear His voice, and walk with Him. They serve in that dark and lonely place within the veil.

I beseech you this day to seek for the higher life, which is the priestly life, and for the higher service, which is the priestly service. Be willing to put your hand on the plow and not look back at the world (Luke 9:62). Count all the things of the world as loss in order to gain Christ (Phil. 3:7–8).

There is no truth that is not found in the Word of God, because all truths are recorded in the Scriptures. However, though they all are documented in the Bible, many of them have nonetheless been buried in God's Word and hidden from mankind because of the foolishness, unfaithfulness, irresponsibility, and disobedience of men.

The deadness and feebleness of the saints today is largely due to their receiving and following the truth with their minds. This is nothing but the law. In spite of the exactness of the letter, it is absolutely not of the Holy Spirit.

Herein lies the reason for the lack of life in the assemblies of today: the human hand has substituted itself for the sovereignty of the Holy Spirit.

A person's attitude before God has much to do with his interpretation of God's Word. Many come to His Word with the hope of finding some rule that will justify their own walk. Their motive is to transform the Word of God into a law that suits them. This is a common occurrence among those who have not been dealt with by the Cross. Hence, only those who have gone through the Cross are able and equipped to interpret the Bible correctly.

God wants us to live according to the manna principle: he who gathered much had nothing left over, and he who gathered little had no lack. (See Exodus 16:18; 2 Corinthians 8:15.) If in an assembly some of the believers have no means to maintain their living, either the church or some of those individuals within the assembly should help them. The local church cannot look upon the plight of unemployed believers without its helping them the best it can. This does not, of course, include those who refuse to work.

Victory is not due to our depending on self. On the contrary, victory is due to our standing in the finished work of Calvary.

Satan's strategy against the saved is to cause them to have an incomplete consecration (Acts 5:1–3). And one of Satan's greatest fears is a saved person with total consecration.

The Lord has appointed the way to victory for us: it is the Cross (1 Thess. 3:3). The defeat of Satan is at the Cross. Therefore, he is most fearful of people going to the Cross and obtaining the victory of Calvary in their daily lives.

With real death, there comes real resurrection. This is what Satan hates the most, because he has no foothold on those who have died.

The secret of maintaining victory against the Enemy is found in Psalm 25:15: *"My eyes are ever toward the LORD, for He shall pluck my feet out of the net."* Thus, we must look to God continually, because He knows where the nets are, and He alone is able to pluck our feet out of these nets. He will watch over our every step until we reach the goal.

What our Enemy has is a power stronger than ours, but what we have is authority over his power (Luke 10:19).

Always stand firm on the teachings of Romans 6:11 by reckoning yourself to be dead to sin and alive to God. In this way, you can triumph today and reign in the age to come.

Six

Let Us Pray

God's people must pray before God Himself will rise up and work. This is a principle for God's working.

Prayer is not an expression of our wishes for God to yield to our petitions and fill up our selfish desires. Prayer is the union of the believer's thoughts with the will of God. It is simply the believer's speaking out through his mouth the will of God.

Prayer does not alter that which God has determined. It never changes anything; it merely achieves what He has already foreordained. Prayerlessness, though, does bring about a change. God will let many of His resolutions go suspended due to a lack of prayerful cooperation from His people.

"Verily I say unto you, Whatsoever ye shall bind on earth shall be bound in heaven: and whatsoever ye shall loose on earth shall be loosed in heaven" (Matt. 18:18 KJV). Earth must bind first before heaven will bind, and earth must loose first before heaven will loose. However, God never does anything against His will. It is not because the earth has bound something that the Lord is then forced to bind that which He has not wished to bind. Not so. He binds in heaven what has been bound on earth simply because His original will has always been to bind what the earth has eventually bound. He waits until His people on earth bind what heaven has aspired to bind, and then He listens to their command and binds for them what they have asked.

If the people of God fail to show sympathy toward God by yielding their will to Him, He would rather stand by and postpone His work.

Because believers mind too much of their own affairs and fail to work together with God, many enemies and much lawlessness are not bound, and many sinners and much grace are not released. How greatly restricted is heaven by earth! Knowing God respects us so much, why can we not trust Him enough to pray?

How many of our prayers truly express the will of God? How often in our prayers is self completely forgotten and the will of the Lord completely sought?

We often think of prayer as an outlet for expressing what we need—as our cry to God for help. What we do not see is that prayer is the asking of God to fulfill His needs or purposes.

Whenever a believer is in need, he should first inquire: Will such lack affect God? Does He want me to be in need? Or is it His will to supply my need?

We should pray that God fulfills His will. Then it no longer becomes a question of whether our needs are met, but rather, whether God's will is done.

To ask the Lord to supply our needs, whatever such needs may be, cannot be considered prayer of the highest level. God's purpose is for us to be so filled with His will that we forget our own interests. He calls us to work together with Him to accomplish His will.

Prayer for God's work can be compared to rails for a train. Prayer is the rails; His work is the train. There are many things that God wills to do and would like to do, but His hands are bound because His children do not sympathize with Him and have not prayed so as to prepare ways for Him.

One who really prays not only is a person who often approaches God, but also is a person whose will frequently enters into God's will—that is to say, his thought often enters into God's thought.

We should draw near to God, allowing Him to impress in us that which He desires to do, so that we ourselves may intercede with groanings (Rom. 8:26). When we pray according to this kind of burden, we will have a sense that we are divulging the very will of God. Whatever the will or burden that the Lord puts in us, whenever it is reproduced in a person's heart, that person is able to make the Lord's will his own will and pray it out accordingly.

When we pray as we ought to, our prayer will shake up hell and affect Satan. For this reason, Satan will rise up to hinder such prayer. All prayers that come from God touch the powers of darkness.

Nothing of the will of God is ever released without passing through man. Moreover, the will of God, when released through man, is never free from an encounter with Satan.

Since the time of the founding of the church, there is nothing God does on earth without the prayers of His children.

When you sense a burden to pray, this indicates that there is an item in God's will that requires your prayer. Pray when you feel the burden of prayer; this is praying according to God's will. Each time God puts a prayer thought into us, the Holy Spirit burdens us to pray for that particular matter. As soon as we receive such a feeling, we should immediately give ourselves to prayer.

What a pity that so many people quench the Holy Spirit in this area. They stifle the very sensation the Holy Spirit gives to move them to pray. If there is no response given to the prompting of the Spirit, after a while, few of such sensations will be received. For this reason, we must be extra careful in dealing with the feeling that the Holy Spirit gives to us.

If the burden grows so heavy that it cannot be discharged by prayer, we should fast. When prayer cannot discharge a burden, fasting must follow.

In prayer meetings, we should not allow our prayer to jump around from one matter to another before the first one is thoroughly prayed through. If this is the case, it is apparent that the people praying are only interested in their own specific concerns.

When more than one person gathers for prayer, the burden for each matter must first be discharged before moving on to another issue. It is important to pray until the burden is discharged. This is the secret of success in prayer meetings.

Every brother or sister who comes to a prayer meeting ought to have a prayer burden, so as to pray. He or she should learn to touch the spirit of the entire gathering and must learn to enter into the feeling of the whole assembly.

Corporate prayer does not come automatically; it has to be learned. We should learn how to sense the feeling of others, learn how to touch what is called the prayer of the church, and learn how to recognize the release of the prayer burden.

In true prayer, we should not simply ask concerning things that pertain to our own welfare; we should also pray for the glory of God and for heaven's rule over the earth.

It is the case with carnal Christians that their prayers lay stress solely on the aspect of their own welfare.

Our wrestling is not *"against flesh and blood"* (Eph. 6:12). Therefore, we should be inwardly exercised and have spiritual insight so that we gain a knowledge of the spiritual realm and can observe much of Satan's "hidden" work.

Since *"the weapons of our warfare are not carnal* [of the flesh]" (2 Cor. 10:4), we should not employ any earthly means against the fleshly, earthly instruments used by Satan.

Prayer is the best offensive weapon against our Enemy. In our prayers, we should ask God to bind Satan and render him powerless. If first we bind Satan in prayer, our victory is assured.

To *"destroy the works of the devil"* (1 John 3:8) is God's intention. To avenge believers is undoubtedly His will. Nevertheless, He waits for His children's prayers.

A spirit of trust is essential to prayer and to the total Christian life. If our relationship with the Lord continually fluctuates—with our having neither assurance nor confidence—our entire lives will be wounded fatally.

Our weakness is most easily manifested in prayer. Nothing in the spiritual realm reveals our weakness more than prayer. Yet, thank God, we have the almighty Holy Spirit to help us.

The tactic of Satan is to wear out the saints. (See Daniel 7:25.) Wearing out has in it the idea of reducing—a little here, a little there—thus, the wearing out is virtually imperceptible. We must ask God to open our eyes so that we may discern how Satan desires to wear us out and how we should combat this tactic.

A loss of consecration means the loss of power. And a loss of testimony signifies the loss of the presence of God (Judg. 16:16–21).

Seven

The Messenger of the Cross

We, as workers of the Lord, ought to know why the Gospel we preach fails to gain more followers. What you and I have is all too often mere eloquence of words. There is no power behind the spoken word to cut to the heart.

We should not strive to be orators praised by the people; we ought to be mere channels through which His life will flow into human hearts (1 Cor. 2:1-4).

To preach the Cross is relatively easy, but to be a crucified person preaching the Cross is not so easy.

A person who desires to preach the Cross should adopt the way of the Cross.

So often what we preach is indeed the Cross; but our attitudes, our words, and our feelings do not seem to bear witness to what we preach. This is because much of the preaching of the Cross is not done in the spirit of the Cross. Only a crucified person preaches the message of the Cross in the spirit of the Cross.

The Cross is the wisdom of God manifested in such a way that it appears as foolishness to an unbelieving world (1 Cor. 1:18). Thus, if we are to be "fools" for Christ, we should proclaim the "foolish" message while assuming the "foolish" way, adopting the "foolish" attitude, and using the "foolish" words.

The failure of people to receive life must be a failure of those who preach! It is not that the Word has lost its power; it is men who have failed. Men have hindered the outflow of the life of God.

How can we give to other people what we ourselves do not have? Unless the Cross becomes our life, we cannot impart that life to others. The failure of our work is due to the fact that we are eager to preach the Cross without that Cross being within us.

The Cross we preach to others should first crucify us.

We cannot give what we do not have. If all we have is thoughts, we can give only thoughts. However, what people lack is not thoughts, but life!

If the Holy Spirit is not working with His authority and power behind the words we speak, the hearers will not undergo any change in their lives.

The "do" of the Scriptures is not the doing with our own strength; it is instead allowing the Holy Spirit to live out the Word of the Lord through us.

The Lord Jesus was lifted up on the cross for the sake of giving spiritual life to men; likewise, if we desire to cause people to have spiritual life, we, too, must be lifted up on the cross so that the Holy Spirit may flow out of us as well.

Whoever does not know the death of the Cross does not have the life of the Cross for other people.

We must know the life of the Cross as well as its death. Having the death of the Cross, we die to sin and our old nature; but having the life of the Cross, we daily live in the spirit of the Cross.

It is only as the Cross is allowed to burn into our own hearts through the fire of sufferings and adversities that we will be able to see it reproduced in the hearts of other people.

In the eyes of the world, the Cross is something humble, lowly, foolish, and despicable. To preach it with excellent speech and the wisdom of the world is totally contradictory to its spirit and can therefore be of no avail (1 Cor. 2:1).

Before we reach a mature spiritual walk, we usually view our natural talents as harmless and profitable in kingdom service, even though the work done by relying on our natural abilities does not impart the life of the Holy Spirit to others. Usually it is not until after we discover this fact—that all our natural efforts are futile in spiritual matters—that we are finally willing to acknowledge how inadequate our natural abilities are, and how necessary it is that we seek greater divine power. How many there are who proclaim the Cross in their own natural strength!

In short, crucifixion spells death. And the crucifixion of our old nature will be expressed in helplessness, weakness, fear, and trembling.

Whatever work is done by depending on our natural life is mostly in vain, but work performed in the power of supernatural life bears much fruit. Death is the indispensable process of fruit-bearing. In fact, death is the only way to bear fruit (John 12:24–25).

Frequently, in our attempt to achieve Pentecost, we bypass Calvary. We do not realize that without our being crucified—thus shedding all the trappings of the natural man—the Holy Spirit cannot work through us to gain many people. Here, then, is the spiritual principle: die, and then bear much fruit.

Until we have exhausted the natural strength in our bodies, we cannot even begin to rely on the power of the Spirit. If we really know how to die to our natural strength and to depend wholly on the power of the spirit life that God has put in us, we will never work in the strength of the soul life, whether we have natural strength or not.

The Lord Jesus has taught us that our soul life, or natural life, like a grain of wheat, should fall into the ground and die (John 12:24).

If we always maintain an attitude of uncompromisingly hating our soul life, we will learn experientially how to depend on the power of the spirit life and thus bear fruit to the glory of God.

What comes merely out of the mind can reach only the minds of other people. It can never touch their spirits and give life.

We must let the Cross work in us to make us willing to deliver ourselves daily to death for the Lord's sake, abhorring the strength that belongs to our natural life and placing no confidence in ourselves or anything that proceeds from self. Only in this way will we see the life of God and His power flowing into other people's spirits through our words.

We need to realize that Satan is already a defeated foe.

The way of salvation is not in God making us good, but in His saving us out of Adam and putting us into Christ. This is our reality today. For when we are in Adam—in the flesh—we practice sin; and when we are in Christ—in the spirit—we practice righteousness.

In the minds and hearts of many believers lies an important error: the expectation that God will change us. God does not and will not ever do anything in us; instead, He will put us in Christ.

The works of God have been accomplished in Christ. Today we can only receive what He has already done in Christ. By believing it, you will have it. You can only possess it by taking hold of it "in Christ." May God grant us such a revelation that we may see everything that we already have in Christ.

If we are in Christ, all that is Christ's is ours.

The victorious life that I seek in Christ is actually something I already possess.

"All righteousness" (Matt. 3:15) is fulfilled only when we choose the baptism of the Jordan (death).

Without the obedience in Gethsemane, there would not have been the death at Calvary. Many people flee from the face of the Cross because they have not done well in their consecration at the Garden.

God wants to lead us to the place where we live entirely by His Spirit, because outside of the Holy Spirit there is no life. All that is outside of God's Spirit is dead.

Christians should not only refrain from sinning, but they should also overcome death and be filled with life. Whatever is of the flesh is death, and whatever is of the Spirit is life (John 6:63).

Whoever contacts God's Word without contacting the Holy Spirit will not see the power of God's Word. For without the Spirit of God, the Word is no more than a dead letter.

For some, the Word of God becomes life when they read it; for others, it is only words on paper. What is the reason? Some receive the Word of God in the power of His Spirit, while others try to understand the same words with the wisdom of their natural minds. The Word of God is quick and powerful and has life (Heb. 4:12). But when a person receives the Word solely with his mind, he will not experience the power and the life in God's Word.

The acceptance of the truth in the power of the mind means receiving it directly from a book, teacher, or the Bible—while bypassing the Holy Spirit. The Pharisees knew the Scriptures directly in this way; hence, what they possessed was something dead, something void of any living experience with God. The result was that they did not recognize the Author of the Book, though He stood in front of them.

Whatever emanates from the Holy Spirit is of faith, and whatever emanates from the flesh is dead works.

Just as the disciples could not really understand and experience Christ before they received God's Spirit, so believers today are not able to genuinely know and experience the Word of God except by the power of the Holy Spirit.

Is it not better to wait for the Lord's command through the Spirit and obtain a net full of fish in one casting than to work all night in the flesh and accomplish nothing? (See John 21:1–6.)

The most perilous situation in the church today is that so many of its leaders are in high places because of their natural talents, rather than their spirituality.

God needs individuals who are full of the Holy Spirit more than He needs any other kind of person.

When we realize that man can be saved only by the Holy Spirit, that truth can be comprehended only in the Holy Spirit, that prayer can be heard only through the Holy Spirit, and that our spiritual life can be advanced only by the Holy Spirit, then we will truly believe and depend on the Holy Spirit.

Many people in the church think they can bypass the Spirit and be *"more than conquerors"* (Rom. 8:37) by knowing many truths. Yet, in experience, they are defeated again and again because the power is lacking. This can be likened to David's trying to use Saul's armor to fight Goliath (1 Sam. 17:38–39). The weapons of the flesh will not work in spiritual warfare. But when the Spirit uses His sword (the Word), it is very powerful.

A dividing of the soul and spirit (Heb. 4:12) is exceedingly essential, since it concerns spiritual growth. Why? Because a Christian cannot seek that which is spiritual if he does not even know the distinctions between what is of the spirit and what is of the soul.

What is a spiritual person like? If a person can neither speak before God speaks, nor move unless God moves first—if he must look to God, wait on God, and depend on Him for everything—that person is spiritual.

When doing God's work, it is not a question of what is being done, but rather, from where did the work originate—our flesh or the Holy Spirit?

If you touch God, you can cause other people to touch Him also; but if you touch only the soul, you cause people to touch only you. How vast is the difference!

As soon as the Word of God enters, you can immediately distinguish between what is soulish and what is spiritual. There is a judgment within you that is sharper than any human judgment.

The flesh has become so corrupted that even what you think and feel is not very trustworthy.

This is the lesson of the journey in the wilderness: that we may know ourselves (Deut. 8:2). God allows us to be defeated to bring us to the place where we realize that we are corrupt, undependable, and beyond repair.

God's intent for us, after we are saved, is that step by step we come into a deeper knowledge of our corruption, as well as into a greater rejection of our own self-righteousness. He wants to continue to work in us until we are completely delivered from self. This is the first work of the Holy Spirit in a believer—to lead him to know self.

How difficult is the lesson of seeing self as it really is! To know one's self is to be deprived of glory; to deny one's self is to make one's self suffer.

Because of the believer's unwillingness to have such self-knowledge, the Holy Spirit is not able to reveal to him his true character. As a result, the Lord is forced to use some painful means to make the believer know himself.

In God's eyes, there is nothing more unclean than self. It is the mother of all sins. Self is God's greatest enemy, because self always declares independence from Him. What is self? Whatever man possesses or is able to do without seeking, waiting on, or depending on God.

God has no other aim than to lead you to the end of yourself, so that you may know yourself.

God allows His children to struggle and struggle in the flesh, until they realize how futile their efforts are. Why? Because it is only after much struggling that we come to see the helplessness and hopelessness of struggling in our flesh.

God led the children of Israel through the wilderness for forty long years. And He let them fall and sin many times, with this one purpose in view: that they might know themselves.

If you insist on clinging to your precious self, God is compelled to keep you in the wilderness longer. You will then experience more wilderness defeats to take you to the end of yourself.

God has always known how corrupt man is. Additionally, He knows that we do not realize this ourselves. He therefore employs ways and means to teach us, so that we may know about ourselves what He has always known. For it is only after we have recognized our corruption that we will ever accept all the grace He makes available to us.

The Cross is a principle. This principle is to deny self and depend on God.

Romans 6 speaks of our co-death with Christ; Romans 7 speaks of the battle between the new and old natures; and Romans 8 speaks of the victory that is already ours in the Holy Spirit.

Wherever sin is, there is the activity of self. And wherever self is active, there will be sin before God.

The fruit of the Holy Spirit is determined by one principle alone: the total loss of self.

Selflessness is the source of all virtue in man. In the same way, selfishness is the source of all sin in man.

Whatever is done out of one's self will be burned up on that Day at the judgment seat of Christ, and what is done out of God will remain (1 Cor. 3:12–15).

Just as our flesh cannot live if separated from its created life, so our spiritual life is not viable apart from the life of the Creator.

God wants us to have no activity outside of Him. He wishes us to die to ourselves and be dependent on Him as though we cannot move without Him.

The Lord will not ask how good your work is; He will only ask who does the work: His Spirit or your flesh?

Let me tell you that except by leaning on God and trusting in Him moment by moment, I do not know of any way to live a sanctified life. Without depending on God, we can do nothing—we cannot even live as a Christian for a single day.

Self-reliance is the cause of all defeats.

The first subjective effect upon man in the Fall was that his mind was enlarged in its capacity to function. Before the Fall, man had a certain kind of mind; but after the Fall, his mind began to contain a large portion of things that were originally God's purpose for him to have eventually—but not in the way he obtained those things at that time. For this reason, Paul mentioned in Ephesians 6:17 that the believer is to *"take the helmet of salvation."* This verse helps to show the need for the deliverance of the human mind.

We are responsible for doing the will of God, and it is God who is responsible for seeing to it that we experience the right consequences after we have done His will.

What kind of person may know God's will? One whom God has delivered from his own brain power. Your mind must be renewed before you may prove what God's will is (Rom. 12:2).

A person may continually confess how wrong his flesh or natural life is and yet all the while cherish his thoughts and opinions. Though he admits his weakness with his mouth, in his heart he is still full of his own thoughts and cleverness. He considers his view to be superior to that of others and his way to be better than that of others. These are people whose lips are full of God's will, but in actuality they know little of it.

As your natural life is dealt with by God, you will begin to be clear on His will.

We are not sure if a worldly brain is effective in other matters, but we are sure of this one thing: a worldly brain is absolutely useless in spiritual matters.

Eight

From Faith to Faith

"For *therein is the righteousness of God revealed from faith to faith: as it is written, The just shall live by faith"* (Rom. 1:17 KJV). The more our faith makes progress, the deeper the revelation we have of God's righteousness.

Doctrine is something people try to explain on earth; truth is what I become before God as I am transformed into the image of Christ and experience the realities of what the Lord Jesus has accomplished. What is reality? Truth is reality. Jesus is the truth (John 14:6); this should be our reality.

Often we do not know what truth really is. As we approach God, we rely on our own feelings rather than the truth of God, and on our own experiences rather than His truth. We should realize that sometimes God's truth opposes our feelings and our experiences. The solution is learning to recognize what is true. Which is true: that which the Lord Jesus has accomplished before God for me or that which I feel or experience?

May we always remember that we do not obtain freedom by our feelings; the one and only thing that makes us free is the reality, or truth, of God.

We should not be deceived but should always remember that salvation is a matter of truth, not a matter of feelings.

What can make a person free? Only the truth can make a person free, and only reality can set a person free. If anyone relies on his own feelings and experiences, he will constantly be defeated. (See John 8:32; 14:6.)

Truth is not obtained through preaching; it comes from the enlightenment of God.

Having revelation is possessing truth. All who have doctrines without enlightenment have their minds full of ideas; only those who have revelation have life and reality.

When you receive revelation, you will neither think of your own experience nor pay attention to your own feelings. Instead, you will believe that what is from God is absolutely certain and sure.

Only those who receive revelation from the Holy Spirit enter into reality.

Why is it that in the Scriptures God seems to always choose the second person? Ishmael was the older son, yet God chose Isaac, the younger son. Esau was the older brother, but God chose Jacob, the younger brother. Why does God accept the second but reject the first? What comes first in this world is not what is spiritual, but what is natural—then comes what is spiritual (1 Cor. 15:46). This is the principle or law of the second, which can be found throughout Scripture.

"Unless one is born again, he cannot see the kingdom of God" (John 3:3). In this verse, our Lord implied that being born once is not good enough; one must be born again. *"That which is born of the flesh is flesh, and that which is born of the Spirit is spirit"* (v. 6). Whatever is born of the flesh—whatever is given to us naturally by our parents—belongs to the first. But whatever does not come by means of the flesh but comes by being born of the Holy Spirit belongs to the second. Today, Christians must learn to distinguish between the first and the second, between what is given to us by our parents and what is given to us by God through the Holy Spirit.

God never looks at good works per se; He only looks at the source of those good works. What is the source of your good works? Do they come from self or the Holy Spirit? What is the underlying principle in asking such questions? It revolves, quite plainly, around this issue of the first or the second: God always rejects the first, but approves the second.

In practice, Christians usually eliminate the bad of the first but use the good of the first. Hence, God is displeased with this mixture of the natural with the spiritual.

If the One who came from heaven would not rely on His perfect flesh but relied instead on the Holy Spirit, how much more ought we to depend on the Holy Spirit?

May we daily put the natural life to death by the life of God until the day of the Lord's return. May God's new creation swallow up the old creation.

It is not that God does something for you today. No, He has already done everything in Christ. If you believe this, the accomplished fact becomes your experience today.

Most young believers attempt to hold on to victory with their own strength; but as soon as they are tempted, they fall. The lesson we need to learn is that we do not even need to struggle to hold on. God cares for the faithfulness of His Word far more than you or I can care for the victory. Just believe, and God will take care of the result.

If you do not overcome, it is because you do not believe. For as soon as one believes, one instantly overcomes. (See Matthew 17:19–20.)

Something is very definitely wrong if we do not know the will of God for our lives, because *"He who follows Me shall not walk in darkness"* (John 8:12).

God's will is outside of us, but Christ's mind is inside of us. Consequently, if we seek it, He will give us understanding into His will.

The Cross is not only a doctrine; it is also an experience. If there has really been death, there will really be fruit. If there is no death, there will be no fruit. The degree of death determines the amount of life; the number of *"stripes"* (Prov. 20:30) measures the totality of life overflowing.

A grain of wheat needs to fall to the ground and die before it can bear fruit (John 12:24). Whether it is soft or hard, the outer shell of the natural self-life blocks the outflow of the divine life within. Only through the working of the Cross will this outer shell be broken.

How difficult it is to touch the real person inside if his outer shell remains unbroken.

The law of fruit-bearing is death. May we fall to the ground and die, that God may reap much fruit.

Here is a spiritual law or principle: where there is no pressure, there is no power; but pressure can and does produce power. For a Christian to know what power is, he first needs to know what pressure is. Pressure was always with the New Testament apostles. They were daily pressed and heavily burdened. Because the apostles were weighed down exceedingly, there was no one else who had such power as they—for the pressure caused them to look to God.

What does the Bible teach us on the relationship between pressure and power? One is directly proportional to the other. Only those who have experienced being weighed down under pressure know what power is, and the greater the pressure, the more the power.

Many brothers and sisters fail to be delivered from sin because they faint under the pressure. They have not learned how to properly utilize the pressure sin has placed on them. They have not wholly rejected their natural strength and wholly depended on His strength to carry them through.

Any prayer that does not move us cannot move God. It is all a matter of power. Furthermore, as power is determined by pressure, all pressure comes with a purpose.

Resurrection is the life that passes through death and yet exists. What is natural cannot be resurrected after passing through death. All that belongs to God will live after going through death. God allows death to come upon us so that we might know what can pass through death and what cannot pass through death, and what is natural and what is of Christ, or what is natural and what is supernatural.

May God grant us the grace to press on like Paul, so that we all *"may know* [experience] *Him and the **power** of His resurrection"* (Phil. 3:10), not just the *fact* of His resurrection.

Whenever we encounter new pressure, we should convert it into power. If we do this, our power will grow with each new encounter. For when we are *"pressed on every side, yet not crushed;...perplexed, but not in despair; persecuted, but not forsaken; struck down, but not destroyed; always carrying about in the body the dying of the Lord Jesus"* (2 Cor. 4:8–10)—only then is Jesus' life manifested through us.

What a shame that today Christians view the good life as a life having few difficulties and little distress. Whenever they encounter anything painful, they ask God to remove it.

Each time a person sins, it produces two effects: first, it gives him the pleasure of sin; and second, it creates in him a craving for more sin.

One believer has observed that the experience of a Christian is chainlike: it is the chain links of death, resurrection, and rapture, repeated over and over again, until the Christian reaches glory.

Nine

Take Heed

Satan wants man's soul. Oh, how willing people are to sell their souls without compensation!

If in the church people strive to be great, this is bringing the values of the world into the church.

The value of righteousness far exceeds all other things.

What things are of gain to us in this world are counted as loss by Christ in His work. Yes, all things are of no true value, and are even as refuse, when looked at in comparison with the exceptional privilege of intimately knowing and serving Jesus Christ (Phil. 3:7–8).

What is the Gospel? It is God giving grace to men according to His own good pleasure. It is abundant forgiveness bestowed upon sinners, yet not according to the need of sinners, but according to the riches of God.

The Lord forgives us for two reasons: first, He forgives our debt so that we may be free; second, He wants us also to have the power to forgive. Thus, He puts us under the discipline of the Holy Spirit until we are filled with a spirit of forgiveness.

When a spirit of criticism and unforgiveness increases in the church, many problems arise. Let us submit ourselves under God's authority, for the kingdom of heaven is full of forgiveness.

The Father said to the Son, *"Sit thou at my right hand, until I make thine enemies thy footstool"* (Ps. 110:1 KJV). On earth, in the church age of grace, Jesus does not directly manage the affairs of the world. He will wait until His enemies have become His footstool. Hence, the Father is continuing His work in this day of grace, to build a new kingdom for His Son.

Christians should have only one aim: maintaining the grace of God in this age by living a spiritual life.

To be listed as the last of all men—as men doomed to death (1 Cor. 4:9)—should be the goal of believers.

During the martyrdom of the early church, many exhibited such courage and serenity that the spectators were deeply moved. There are even some stories of Roman soldiers who, after they had killed Christians, believed in the Lord Jesus and asked to be killed.

The Gentiles did not have the law before they were saved, and they are not required to keep it after they are saved, for God has not given the law to the Gentiles.

The function of the law is to fulfill the promise. The end is grace, and the means is law. The law must be used to bring people into grace.

The law has its demand upon the flesh, but we are in the Spirit. Having begun our new life in the Spirit, should we expect that life to be mature if we are in the flesh (Gal. 3:3)?

That which violates the law is the flesh, and that which attempts to keep the law is also the flesh. The life and fruit of the Spirit are not of the flesh; rather, they are of the Spirit. Thus, they are beyond the reach of the law. If you try to keep the law, it is your flesh that attempts it. And as the law enters in, the Holy Spirit ceases to be active.

When we receive our new life, *"the righteous requirement of the law"* (Rom. 8:4) is already fulfilled in us. There is no need for us to keep it, for the ordinances of the law are fulfilled in those who walk not after their flesh, but after the Spirit (v. 4).

We do not need to keep the law, yet we have the righteousness required by the law. This is the Gospel.

God has used a means other than the law to produce righteousness in us. The righteousness of God comes to us through faith in the finished work of Christ on the cross. We have been joined with Christ. Whoever would go back to the law in an attempt to try to please God becomes an adulteress.

Many believers make no progress in their spiritual lives because either they do not walk in God's will, or they do not know how to walk in God's will.

Today, many Christians treat God as their servant, expecting Him to grant their desires—rather than being His servant, waiting on Him, and seeking His desires.

God has a definite plan for the lifework and daily activities of every believer. Violation of God's will and plan for the believer's life is the root of all the failures of believers.

If we do not know God's will for our lives, it is not because of anything lacking on God's part. On the contrary, we do not hear Him because we do not have our hearts open to His will (John 10:27).

In order to know God's will in a matter, it is vital that we first cast aside our own opinions. Why? Because such prejudice shuts out the will of God from our hearts.

This matter of getting rid of our own ideas as a prerequisite for knowing God's will is so essential that it can never be over-emphasized.

How many times do we kneel and pray with our lips, "O Lord, reveal Your will to me, for I am willing to do Your will"? Yet, though we may say it with our lips, our hearts neither approve of, nor desire to do, His will.

If there is already secret desire in us, it is futile to seek the Lord's will.

It is lamentable that most believers generally are ignorant of the life of the Holy Spirit, as well as the experience of the Holy Spirit, in their lives. As a result, they are unable to distinguish between the inspiration of the Holy Spirit and the motivation of the soul.

Satan is not afraid of Christians doing good things; he is only fearful of their doing the will of God. As long as he is able to entice believers away from doing God's will, he is fully satisfied.

Only those who have received "little grace" tend to boast of what has been given to them.

Humility is not looking less at oneself; humility is not looking at oneself at all.

The reward we get for obeying the Lord is having more power to deny self and to obey the Lord the next time we are tested. Similarly, disobeying the Lord has its punishment—yielding more to self and rebelling more against the Lord the next time we are tested.

In this life, the Lord manifests more of Himself to us through our obedience. And our joy increases through the suffering that results from that obedience. How rare is absolute obedience; and yet, how sweet it is.

Most Christians tend to dwell on the things in which they have obeyed, thus priding themselves on how tenderly they have loved the Lord—without recognizing how much there is that they have not obeyed.

People usually let what they have been faithful in fill their thoughts, and they regard the things they have been unfaithful in as unnecessary, legalistic, extreme, or exclusive. People also tend to be more rigid in those areas where they have been faithful, and very compromising in areas where they have been unfaithful.

To be righteous toward self and lenient toward others involves great loss, yet this is the road that leads to our reigning with Christ. Christians should learn to be strictly righteous toward themselves and extremely lenient toward other people.

Contentment is a Christian virtue; offering up all to God is the first step in acquiring this virtue. Believers who long for the world cannot help but seek vainglory.

If we are not enlightened by the Holy Spirit, who alone can cause us to understand that all we have in Christ is eternal and real, we will surely covet earthly things.

Unless we allow the Holy Spirit to work the spirit of the Cross into us, we will not be exempt from possessing the evil desire for fame. Only those who have come to love the Lord in this way will not seek greatness in the world.

It is only when saints are joined to the Lord in His death that they are truly dead to the world in heart.

There is a lack of quietness among today's believers; they talk too much and fail to *"study to be quiet"* (1 Thess. 4:11 KJV).

Those who have received much grace from God usually have their heads bowed. Only those who are not deeply rooted in Christ tend to be flippant. (See Proverbs 18:2.)

A quiet life is usually a fragrant life. If we speak less, what we speak will be more powerful. Talkativeness is a point of leakage in one's spirituality.

A man full of the Holy Spirit will not tell anything that is not received from the Lord. Not a single word will be spoken out of self. If we truly learn to obey the Holy Spirit in this area, our daily speech will be reduced by half! This will glorify God.

To grit one's teeth as a means to not speak is not quietness before the Lord, because the heart has already spoken.

How often we experience dryness in our spiritual walk. We feel unsatisfied and lacking. Yet this is due to our unbelief! For if we truly believe His Word, we will not be thirsty (John 4:14).

The healthier and stronger a saint's spiritual life is, the less he joins the crowd (Jer. 15:17).

God is always patient. Hence, when He inspires us by the Holy Spirit, He takes His time. *"He that believeth shall not make haste"* (Isa. 28:16 KJV). Sudden urges and feelings are, nine times out of ten, not from the Lord.

The principle at work in us, as Christians, should always be: *"So then death worketh in us, but life in you"* (2 Cor. 4:12 KJV). The spirit of the Cross must indeed be our standard.

Most saints fall into the trap of thinking we needed God's grace only when we were yet sinners. We forget that throughout our lives, even after we are saved, we are still in need of the grace of God. Indeed, there is not a moment in our Christian walk when we are not under His grace.

Except for the grace of God, we would have been consumed long ago (Lam. 3:22). Hallelujah, the Lord has given us grace!

Troublesome to the faithful saints of God are those who do not treat sin as sin but instead invent new ways to cover up sin. Even more disturbing are the many believers who take sin so lightly. How sad it is that these have gradually lost their sensitivity to sin.

As a result of more defeats than victories in their lives, some believers begin to excuse themselves by thinking that it is impossible to overcome sin. Then, as these sins prevail over their lives, the accusing voice of conscience grows dimmer and dimmer. How pitiful! What a fall!

Spiritual sensitivity and physical sensation are alike in one respect: if we are wounded often, and exposed to the wind and frost too frequently, we become numb. And if spiritual sensitivity is lost, spiritual life will soon dry up.

Many times we think ourselves too busy in our lives. But is it not just a matter of priority? We are "too busy," yet we still find time to eat three meals a day.

Ten

Grace for Grace

What is *"grace for grace"* (John 1:16)? It is the blessed portion that God gives to all who receive Christ—grace upon grace, grace after grace, and then more grace because we have already been given grace. Each blessing, when we take hold of it, becomes the foundation that God uses for giving an even greater blessing.

We are all sick people. How then will God deal with us? He has two steps: first, He causes us to know that we are sick; and second, He induces us to ask for a physician.

God sends us the law so that we might know that we are sinners. Then He sends the Lord Jesus so that we might be healed. People must receive the truth of the first before they can receive the help of the second. If they are not willing to accept the witness of the law, they will not be able to receive the benefits of grace and truth.

When a physician examines a patient, he first diagnoses the disease before he writes out a prescription. Originally, I think I am in good health; but the physician, after he has felt my pulse, measured my temperature, and carefully examined me, tells me I am a sick man. Previously, I considered myself a good man; but now I meet the law, which tells me I am a sinner. The work of the law is to show people that they are sick within. The work of the Physician is to heal the sickness.

The Gospel of God includes two aspects. The first makes Christ our righteousness, so that we can live before God with His righteousness. The second causes Christ to live out His life in us, so that we may live a good testimony before the world.

Salvation has a double aspect: the objective, which is before God, and the subjective, which is within us. There is justification on the one hand and regeneration on the other. Justification is our new position before God; regeneration gives us the new life in us.

The old covenant is inscribed on stone tablets—the words of which we, in ourselves, have no power to keep. But the new covenant is written on the heart (Jer. 31:33), with His Spirit living in us to give us the power to keep it. God has not commanded us to keep the outward law, but He has commanded us to keep the inward law.

The salvation of God that the sinner usually conceives of is this: I give You work, and You give me wages. According to the measure of how much I work, that much will I receive in wages— yet not as a son, but as a hired servant. How sad!

We are in bondage to sin because the body is in bondage to sin. Unless, and until, the body is dealt with by the Cross, the entire body will be under the bondage of sin.

In the eyes of God, the human body is truly *"the body of sin"* (Rom. 6:6), because sin is the master of the body.

If sin reigns in our mortal bodies, it is not because we must obey it, but rather, because we want sin to reign over us.

If we do not exercise our will to choose that which the Lord has accomplished for us, then, even though the Lord has already crucified the old man, we, in our experience, will still be in bondage to sin.

If a Christian believes in co-death yet does not exercise his will to resist sin, his faith is dead and ineffective. Our will must yield to God; otherwise, victory is impossible. We must not only determine not to sin; we must also determine to practice righteousness.

Sin has two sides. On the outside, and before God, our sin needs to be forgiven and washed away by Him. Meanwhile, within us, sin must be overcome so that we might be delivered from it.

Just as sin has two sides, deliverance has two sides. The Lord not only saves us from the penalty of sin, but He also delivers us from the power of sin. And it is only when both have been accomplished in us that our salvation is complete.

What is the aim of having our old man crucified? That our body of sin might be disemployed or disabled—done away with (Rom. 6:6).

Why is it that so few experience the life of victory that the Lord Jesus has obtained for us? Because in spite of what the Lord has accomplished for us, we have not accepted His work, believed in what He has accomplished, or taken His victory by faith.

"He that loveth me shall be loved of my Father, and I will love him, and will manifest myself to him" (John 14:21 KJV). I have met many renowned persons in Christianity, but I am afraid relatively few of them really know God. Many people know how to study the Bible, but they do not know God. They know the Scriptures, yet they do not know the power of God. Some of them can even preach what they do not experience. Why is this so? Because the Lord has not revealed it to them, signifying that they have not loved the Lord and kept His commandment.

What God has prepared for those who believe in Him is eternal life, but what He has prepared for those who love Him is to be revealed in the future (1 Cor. 2:9–10).

Eleven

From Glory to Glory

Why did God not declare Himself as the God of Adam when He spoke to Moses? Because He is the God of the seed of faith, not the God of the seed of the flesh.

What is meant by resurrection? It means the natural has passed away and the supernatural has come.

The most basic sin, according to the Word of God, is unbelief. This is the root of all sin. How sad that we pay so little attention to the one sin that the Bible emphasizes the most.

Today, people look at many fragmentary sins instead of at the root of sin. In doing so, they overturn the work of Christ and pursue psychological salvation, which is merely a moral improvement and change of lifestyle but not the receiving of life itself.

To be baptized means that one has come out of all of the things of the world; it means that one has come out of Adam. Yet how can we come out of the world and Adam? The only way is to die. And once dead, all is finished. To be buried in baptism is to write the final page in a man's old biography. Death is not the last thing, but burial by means of baptism is—it is the final act and concludes all that is in Adam.

From God's view, the shed blood of Jesus on the cross has completely solved the sin problem of the world. But from humanity's standpoint, man still needs to add one ingredient—faith.

Just as the beginning of salvation is by grace, so the keeping of salvation is likewise by grace. The condition for obtaining salvation is the same as the condition for preserving salvation.

We should know what baptism truly expresses before we are ever baptized. We should know what baptism is stating: that we are not only saved, but that we have also been delivered from the world. Baptism is the act that declares to the entire world that we are no longer joined to it. Why? Because we have been emancipated from it.

Baptism is turning our backs toward the world and turning our faces toward Christ. And between the two—between the world and Christ—there is no middle ground. (See Matthew 6:24.)

We often think of how we may change this world. However, God's intent is not to change this world, but to judge this world, and then to give us a new one.

The problem with many Christians today is that they have sprinkled the blood of the lamb on their doorposts and lintel, but they have not sat down to eat of the flesh of the lamb (Exod. 12:7–8). Hence, they have been delivered from the penalty of sin, but not from the bondage of the world (Egypt). Our understanding of this should be clear: for one to have deliverance from sin in a daily, practical way, it is required that he eat of the flesh of the Lord Jesus Christ.

Twelve

Gospel Dialogue

Just as no inverted cup can receive water, so no proud person is able or willing to accept the salvation of God.

People conceive an incorrect idea: that though we are saved by grace, we must keep this salvation by our own efforts. A Christian should serve God with faithfulness, but the only proper motive behind his service is the love of Christ. And the power for doing such things is the Holy Spirit.

How many there are who do not understand the grace of God clearly! They think that after they are saved, they have to do good or else God will withdraw His salvation. This is like a purchase that is made on an installment plan. But God does not ask us to pay Him back by installments, nor will He take His salvation back, even if we perform no good deeds after receiving it.

The old man stands between sin and the body, accepting the instigation of sin on the one hand, and directing the body to sin on the other.

It is only when we reckon ourselves to be dead to sin that we will no longer be under the dominion of sin. Though sin is still alive, it cannot tempt a dead person, because he who is dead is freed from sin.

At the beginning of your faith, you believed that the Lord died for you. But today, you should reckon His death as your death.

The first step in salvation gives us peace and satisfaction and causes us to experience much joy. The second step in salvation gives us the power to overcome sin and to walk in His way. Overcoming the power of sin within you is deliverance and emancipation, not forgiveness. Since the master within you has been changed, you are no longer under the rule of the old master.

As Adam is the head and we all are parts of him, so likewise is Christ our Head, and we are the members of Him.

There is one point many believers do not clearly understand: every believer has eternal life (John 3:15–16), but not all believers will enter the millennial kingdom. Eternal life is obtained through the gift God gives of His righteousness to us; whereas the millennial kingdom is entered by means of one's own righteousness. Eternal life is obtained by faith and will never be lost, but the millennial kingdom is prepared for those who, through victorious living, overcome. (See Revelation 2:26–27; 3:11.) Eternal life is possessed in this age; the millennial kingdom will be set up at the Lord's second coming.

Had the Lord not died on the cross, we would still be sinners. If He had died but had not been resurrected, we might not be sinners any longer, but we would still be dead men. Only the power of resurrection breaks the power of death.

Christ's death has cleared my old debts, but His death does not guarantee my not incurring new ones. Christ must be resurrected, and His new life put in me, before I can live a different life from the former one. Death is what has cleared my sinful case; resurrection is what empowers me to sin no more. Consequently, the Lord Jesus not only died and atoned for our sins before God, but He was also resurrected to live within us, so that He could bear our burdens and enable us to overcome temptations and sins.

Death solves the problem of sin; whereas resurrection gives us a new life so that we may not sin.

God puts us in very difficult situations for two reasons. One is to prove to us the reality of the power of the Christ who indwells us. The other is to cause us to declare to others, with abundant satisfaction, that the indwelling Christ is truly real.

Christ, by His death, concludes the old creation and, by His resurrection, commences the new one.

Resurrection is not real to us unless it is more than objective fact; it must also be subjective experience.

Position and experience, though they are different, cannot be separated. According to position, believers are already justified and sanctified; but according to experience, they may not be living out their position before God. The more we look into our own experience, the less experience of Christ we will have. But if our eyes are kept on Christ, we will be transformed into His image. This is true experience!

Those who are familiar with the grace of God realize that they are not one bit worthier today than they were on that first day they believed. Why? Because the qualification for entry into heaven is entirely founded upon the Lord and His work.

God uses the blood to cleanse us from our sins, but He uses the Cross to crucify the flesh.

If one truly believes that he was crucified with Christ, his body of sin is dead and therefore unemployed. Only then can he present his members to God for His use *as instruments of righteousness* (Rom. 6:13). This is God's requirement: that your body first be unemployed.

Romans proves to us that a sinner cannot be justified by the works of the law. Galatians shows us that a believer cannot be sanctified by the works of the law. We are both justified and sanctified by faith.

Faith and works are inseparable; they are the two sides of one coin. Works are the expression of faith; whereas faith is the source of works. This is the reason that the writer of Hebrews used the word *faith* while James used the word *works*.

Christ accomplishes redemption, the Holy Spirit enlightens, and God the Father receives us with His love.

The salvation God offers to man reaches into the three main areas of each believer and includes the following: eternal salvation, or the salvation of the spirit; the salvation of the body; and the salvation of the soul. The salvation of our spirits occurs at the time of regeneration, when we believe in the Lord (John 3:16). The salvation of our bodies will take place when we receive new ones from the Lord in the future. (See Romans 8:23.) The salvation of the soul is referred to as the end of our faith (1 Pet. 1:9). It pertains to the denial of our self-life and is a prerequisite to entering into the millennial reign of the Lord (Matt. 16:25; 25:21–23).

Hell is where the thirst for sin and the burning fire of lusts will never be satisfied.

We know that the daily life and work of a Christian on earth will be judged in the future. But this is not a judging for the salvation of a Christian. Rather, it is the judging of his fitness for the millennial kingdom, and his position in it. (See 1 Corinthians 3:13–15.) Thus, there are two perils for us as we stand before the judgment seat: first, we may be completely barred from the millennial kingdom, or second, we may receive a low position in the millennial kingdom if we are allowed to enter.

The way you judge your fellow believers now will be the way that you will be judged by God in the future (Matt. 7:1–2).

God is testing us now to see if we are fit to be kings in His kingdom, to see if we are worthy to minister as priests in His kingdom. Serving in the church is great, but serving in the kingdom is even greater. May we all be found worthy.

Thirteen

Full of Grace and Truth
(Volume One)

I have yet to meet an atheist who lives somewhat morally.

How few there are today who keep their bodies morally clean, yet there are fewer still who keep their minds pure.

The righteousness of man cannot satisfy God. It is only when God sees His own righteousness that He saves.

The Pharisee, in his theory of salvation, failed on two points: first, he thought he needed to do good in order to be saved; second, he deemed himself already good enough to be saved.

As far as the sinner himself is concerned, he is destined by God to perish. Yet he might still be saved, if he relies on a third party who can save him. That third party is Christ.

Applying the blood of the slain lamb to the doorposts and lintel is something objective; whereas eating the flesh of the lamb is subjective. (See Exodus 12:7–8.) If you have put the blood on the outside, but have not eaten the flesh of the Lamb, there will be little transformation in your life, and you will not have the strength to be an overcoming believer.

Without the application of the blood, the purging out of the leaven will not save and justify anyone. (See Exodus 12:15.) Furthermore, putting on the blood without purging out the leaven will not sanctify. What is so sad today is that although all Christians have the blood applied, so few are submitting to having the leaven purged!

Refusing to purge out the leaven will not result in perishing with the rest of the world, that is true; nonetheless, it will affect our entering the millennial kingdom (as typified by Canaan). With the blood applied, one has eternal life; with the leaven purged, one gains the kingdom. (See 1 Corinthians 5:7–8.)

"For you were bought at a price; therefore glorify God in your body and in your spirit, which are God's" (1 Cor. 6:20). A servant is hired for employment; a slave is purchased with money. One who has been hired does have liberty; whereas one who has been bought by the blood of Christ has no liberty. We are God's bondslaves, not His servants.

Never believe the mistaken notion that salvation is reserved only for those who are worthy, for there is no one in the world who is worthy to be saved. Yet according to the mercy of God, none in the world is unfit for salvation.

We should all do as Christ has done. Before He came into this world to accomplish His mission, He sat down and counted the cost. (See Luke 14:28.)

Fourteen

Full of Grace and Truth
(Volume Two)

God's heart's desire toward mankind is one of love. Throughout the times of old, by His servants, God repeatedly revealed this
to us in various ways (Heb. 1:1–2). But mankind still did not comprehend His love for us; so God sent His Son.

The God of glory Himself condescends to be a man. This is
humility!

Let God be praised, for He does not save people because they
do good. Instead, He saves according to this principle: *"Where sin
abounded, grace did much more abound"* (Rom. 5:20 KJV).

Many people have the idea that salvation is not only by God's
grace, but also by our works: God's grace—plus our works—equals
salvation. The natural man is always seeking to get saved by his
own efforts.

Not only can one not be saved by doing good, but he who seeks
to be saved by doing good is to be cursed (Gal. 3:10).

Sadly, many people, after a while, begin to doubt their salvation. They say that they do not feel like they did when they first
got saved. But the problem lies in themselves, not in God. For
they have trusted in their feelings rather than in what God has
done. We must learn from the Passover experience: the firstborn
did not see the blood on the doorposts, yet the death angel passed
over. For God had said, *"When I see the blood, I will pass over"*
(Exod. 12:13).

The Bible does not say, "If you feel saved, you are saved" and "If you do not feel saved, you will perish." It simply states that when God sees the blood, He will save you. For this reason, you should not rely on your vacillating feelings.

The children of Israel were saved, not because of their own merits, but because of the blood of the lamb. And the Egyptians perished, not because of their evil deeds, but because they did not have the blood of the lamb.

We must remember that on Passover night in Egypt, there was one dead in every house. The one that died in the house of an Israelite was a lamb; whereas the one that died in the house of an Egyptian was a person. There will always be one dead in every house.

To the unsaved person I say, either you die or He dies! If you do not trust Him who died, you yourself must also die.

Only when Christians have learned to be satisfied with all of their portion in Christ will they be able to overcome those things that the world has to offer. As long as they are satisfied with those things that the world offers, they are not satisfied with Christ.

According to the Word of God, whoever sets his mind on the things of the flesh is at enmity with God (Rom. 8:7), and whoever has the friendship of the world is also at enmity with God (James 4:4).

What is pride? Pride means to exalt oneself above a position he has actually attained. Claiming a name beyond the reality of what one has achieved—that is pride.

Man is forever trying to gradually reform himself by accumulating more merits and hoping for salvation at the last. But that is not glad tidings; that is woeful tidings.

If we are saved, we are given new life. And if that life is given place to grow, it will spontaneously flow out.

We should know the difference between the old and new covenants. Under the old covenant, men must advance step by step until they attain the right position. Under the new covenant, men proceed step by step from the position they have already obtained.

The new covenant is totally different from the old. During the time of the old covenant, man had absolutely no position before God; but under the new covenant a position is first given to man—a position that never changes. This truly is great news!

Faith is not expectation. It neither waits for the future nor requires the performance of any work. It merely accepts as fact in reality and experience what God has declared and accomplished.

Fifteen

Gleanings in the Fields of Boaz

This is the secret of the victorious life: we do nothing; He does it all. When we cease, He flows out. The more we cease, the greater He flows.

If one is not experiencing the victorious Christian life, it is either because he is not born again or because he has not been well taught in the full Gospel of Jesus Christ. Either what he knows is only an imperfect Gospel, or he does not really believe in God's Word due to the lack of revelation. For His Word says that *"the law of the Spirit of life in Christ Jesus has made* [us] *free from the law of sin and death"* (Rom. 8:2). If this is not our experience, it is not that there is anything lacking on God's part.

How do we know what part of our thoughts or decisions is from God and what part is our own? We cannot know by looking within ourselves. This is the work of the Word. For the Word of God is sharper than a two-edged sword and alone is able to divide between what is of the soul and of the spirit, and to discern between the thoughts and intents of the heart (Heb. 4:12).

We lack discernment with respect to other people's situations because we have not allowed God to give us light about ourselves in that area. We need to discern our own self first—only then can we help others.

When we live in the flesh, everything we have from Adam is present; but when we live in the Spirit, all that is in Christ becomes ours.

How many of us convince ourselves that if we could just change this habit or that aspect of ourselves, we would then be all right? However, this is not so. There must be a complete exchange of life—we must be displaced and replaced with Christ.

If we look within ourselves, we cannot see how we are in Adam, nor can we believe it. Likewise, if we look within ourselves, we cannot see how we are in Christ, nor can we believe it. Accordingly, we must stop looking within ourselves and look only to Christ. Then we will begin to see ourselves in Him and will begin to experience what He has already accomplished for us.

We can never know what sin really is until God's light shines in. Only then is our conscience awakened so that it can begin to feel the awfulness of sin.

Many people have only experienced a half-salvation. They know that God has forgiven their sins, but they do not know that He has also broken the power that sin has in their lives.

To be baptized means to be included in Christ's death. Have you truly been baptized?

The minding of the flesh is death (Rom. 8:6). Hence, whenever and wherever the flesh is given place, there death is found.

God puts a representative symbol before us—the Cross—and we, too, put a representative symbol before Him as our answer— baptism. Baptism is our response to God, embodied in an act. Though we say nothing, God understands.

Many Christians are of the opinion that it was only our sins that were nailed to the cross. They fail to see that our old nature was also nailed to the cross. In Adam, we are altogether rotten and sinful. Therefore, insofar as God is concerned, we can do nothing with the flesh, except finish it on the cross.

Baptism is like the second edition of Calvary. That is, it is one's own personal version of Calvary.

Baptism is burial. But what is the condition for burial? Death! We are not baptized in order to produce death; no, we must die first—thereafter we can be buried in baptism.

Only that which comes forth from the Spirit is life. Whatever emanates from the flesh is death.

We must learn to recognize and distinguish between the workings of the flesh and the workings of the Cross. Unless we have been dealt with deeply by the Cross in our own flesh, we will not be able to recognize what is of the flesh in others.

In our labors for the Lord, the person who builds with gold, silver, and precious stones knows God as Father; he knows the Cross subjectively as well as objectively, so that all he is has been brought through death. He also knows that everything done by him must be done through the Holy Spirit.

Man looks at the use of a vessel, but God looks at its value. Wooden and earthen vessels in a house may appear more useful than the gold and silver vessels, but the gold and silver vessels are far more valuable. God's point of view—God's regard—is not for use; it is for value.

Truth preached without light becomes doctrine, but truth preached with light becomes revelation. When truth is received as doctrine, it gives us a big head; but when truth is received as light or revelation, it becomes life experience.

How does God use the Spirit of Truth to lead us into the Word of Truth? By having the light of God shine upon the Word. When this occurs, we are at once brought by the Spirit of Truth into a living experience of the reality of that truth.

The gifts that God has given to the church are not for this age alone. They are even more for the next age—the kingdom age. Though they are to be received and fully developed by us now, it is with an eye toward using them in the kingdom. Moreover, how well we have received and developed them in this age is the determining factor of what we will be accounted worthy to receive in the kingdom age.

God's children make so many errors in their spiritual pursuits because they do not know the Scriptures and the power of God (Matt. 22:29).

Those who are under the deception of evil spirits tend to be self-confident. They will not easily accept others' advice, nor will they trust in the feelings of other brothers and sisters in Christ.

God has given the church on earth two great treasures: one is the Bible; the other is the Holy Spirit.

We may delay the growth of the life of God's Son in us, but we have no way of accelerating it. Because of this, it is of utmost importance that we accept God's orderings of circumstances in our lives, for it is by these circumstances that we receive the disciplines we need from the Holy Spirit to strengthen us as we grow.

We must learn to accept the discipline of the Holy Spirit and allow Him to enlarge our capacity, for our spiritual maturity is the sum total of the discipline we have received from the Holy Spirit.

The measure of one's life is based on the degree of one's death.

In spiritual matters, do not be afraid of people's opposition. If things are of God, eventually people will acknowledge them to be right.

Doctrine is always limited; whereas life is unlimited.

Since the kingdom is related to authority, one must first be subject to God's authority and be an obedient person before the authority of the kingdom can pass through him.

If a person in official authority and position has spiritual authority as well (which means his having the reality of life, with the inner anointing as well as outward supplying), it is quite natural for people to submit to him. But if what he possesses is only positional authority, without the reality of spiritual life, it is a hardship for people ever to submit. Nevertheless, people still need to learn to submit in order to cultivate submission and obedience.

A brother once asked me, "How should I seek the crown of glory?" My answer was, "Do not seek it, for seeking it is futile. Accept the thorny crown today, and the crown of glory will be yours in the future. Reject the thorny crown today, and you will not have the crown of glory in the future."

The chief lesson of today is learning to take up the Cross and die daily (Luke 9:23). Without death there can be no resurrection; without suffering there can be no glory.

How pitiful that so many works done "for the Lord," "in the name of God," "for the kingdom of God," or "for the church of Christ" are but the activities of man's corrupted flesh! These are done without seeking God's will, without receiving God's order, and without depending on God's power. The children of God simply do what they think is best! Everything is there, except God.

What we see in the church of God today is a great lack of knowing *"Christ and Him crucified"* (1 Cor. 2:2).

Formerly, people were baptized into the death of Christ; now baptism has become a sacrament. Formerly, the laying on of hands was for identification; now it has become a ritual. What was formerly filled with life and spiritual reality has now become a kind of empty ceremony. When life truly comes, all these lifeless terms and rituals that are in use become living realities.

Sixteen

Whom Shall I Send?

How well we learn to serve today is only the preparation to determine the capacity in which we will serve for all eternity.

Many people are not being drawn into the kingdom. But it is not because God lacks the desire to have the Gospel preached, nor is it that He has no intention of saving men. Rather, so many people remain unsaved because He does not have the man or men whom He can use. It is because we, the saved, do not cooperate with Him that they are not set free from their captivity.

If you read the Bible carefully, you will discover that God gives His spiritual riches, life, and light to only one class of people. Who are among this class of people? Those who yearn to be used by the Lord with all their hearts.

In ministry, real power is based on the measure of your heart toward God. Real power is based on how much you love the Lord.

The measure of your consecration will be the measure of the power that God gives you.

To the degree that our hearts are toward God, to that degree will our eyes be opened. The reason we, as the children of God, have so little light is that we have no heart for the Lord. And the reason for the lack of power among us is our inadequate consecration.

Man, in his ignorance, deems himself capable of doing God's work. But the work of God is not a matter for man and has not been given to man to do. God Himself does the work, because it is

God's work and not man's. The only requirement given to man is to believe on Him whom God has sent (John 6:29).

Working with God is not a matter of our proceeding to work for Him; rather, it is our allowing God to first work Christ in us, and then our going out to tell people of the Christ we know through revelation and experience. The work is actually done by God; we merely report to others what God has done in us.

The Holy Spirit works along these two lines: on the negative side, He eliminates the old creation in the believer by the means of the Cross; and on the positive side, He establishes the new creation in the believer by incorporating Christ in him through revelation.

The highest responsibility of man is simply to cooperate with God and not hinder His working.

Only a born-again person can testify of how the Lord saved him. Without such an experience of new birth, no one can do this work. Yet the same rule applies to victory, sanctification, fullness of the Spirit, Christ reigning within, and so forth. Only those who have received the grace and actually experienced these things can be proper witnesses of them.

Fullness of stature in our spiritual life is reached through both the complete elimination of the self-life and Christ wholly possessing the man.

One of the great difficulties man has is that he cannot be quiet before God. A disquieted person has great difficulty in receiving revelation. A wandering mind and uncontrolled thoughts are like waves on the face of a lake whose waters move unceasingly, thus blurring on its surface the reflection of the trees and the flowers along its banks.

The Cross alone deals with our natural life, mind, and emotions. Those who desire to learn to live in the spirit before God must learn to accept the dealings of the Cross. If our natural mind and emotions are not dealt with, we can hardly live a life in the spirit.

If we have a lack of life in our service to the Lord, our labors will be only activities, and we will not be able to meet the needs of God's children. Why? Because only life can truly meet the needs of His children.

If we learn to serve Him well today, He will entrust us with many greater things at His return.

The measure of our usefulness to God will be found in the measure of His life that is in us. As the measure of God increases in us, so our usefulness to Him also increases.

Our usefulness before the Lord is nothing less than His nature being developed in us. Through it, God imparts His life; and as this life in us is released, we become useful in ministering to others.

Many brothers and sisters in Christ make no spiritual progress before the Lord. All they have is mental knowledge; there is no true light.

True authority is exemplified in love, so that the children of God will learn to obey from their hearts. Though one may be in authority in the church, he should never lord it over the flock; rather, through serving, he should be an example to the flock (1 Pet. 5:3). The Bible always stresses this fact.

Seventeen

The Prayer Ministry of the Church

Here is the principle of God's working, the secret of His action: whatever He wills to do, if man does not will it, He will not do it. We cannot make God do what He does not want to do, but we can hinder Him from doing what He does wish to do.

Heaven desires to do but will not act right away; heaven waits for someone on earth to desire first and then will act.

Today the church stands on earth to accomplish the will of God. If she is able to meet His will, God will not be restricted. But if she is unable to rise up to that will, God will be restricted.

The measure of the power of God within the church today determines the measure of the manifestation of that power.

What is the prayer ministry of the church? It is God telling the church what He wishes to do, so that the church on earth will pray out its accomplishment.

Prayer is not asking God to do what *we* want, but asking Him to do what *He* wants. Oh, let us see that the church is to declare on earth the will of God in heaven. The church is to pronounce on earth that this will of God is what she wants. If she fails on this point, she will be of very little value in God's hands. The highest use of the church to God is to facilitate His will being done on earth.

Many matters are piled up in heaven, many transactions remain undone, simply because God is unable to find an outlet for His will on earth.

The manifestation of God's power may not exceed the prayer of the church. Today, the greatness of God's power on earth is circumscribed by the greatness of the church's prayer. In heaven God's power is unlimited, but on earth today the manifestation of His power is dependent on how much the church prays.

If prayer is always centered on self, on our personal problems and our small gain or loss, where is the way for the eternal purpose of God to get through?

Many people come to a church meeting with the attitude of observing or attending, and consequently they get nothing out of it. But thank God that when the brothers and sisters are gathered together in the name of the Lord, there is agreement; there is harmony.

If a church meeting is as it should be, then after the gathering the people know whether the Lord was there.

If our prayer is in accordance with the mind of God, not only will it be answered, but it will also be remembered and rewarded at the judgment seat of Christ.

How foolish for some people to say they do not need to pray since God knows all their needs! The purpose of prayer is not to notify God, but to express our trust and our faith in Him, and our expectation and hearts' desire of Him.

The name *Father* is a new way for men to address God. Formerly, men called Him "the Almighty God," "the Most High God," "the Everlasting God," or "Jehovah God." None dared call Him "Father."

Originally, the Lord Jesus Christ alone could call God "Father." But now, the Lord invites us also to call Him "Father."

Prayer is this: God desires to do a certain thing, yet He will not do it alone. He waits until men on earth pray for this thing, and only then will He do it. Though He has His own will and mind and strongly desires to meet our needs, He waits for men to pray. It is not that God does not know our need, but rather, that He will supply our need only after we have prayed.

Though the will of God is already formed, He will not perform it until His children's minds are stirred and they express His will through prayer.

In the New Testament, the name of the Lord usually represents authority, while the Holy Spirit represents power; all authority is in the name of the Lord, and all power is in the Holy Spirit.

As soon as one believes in the Lord Jesus and is saved, he is commanded by God to be baptized. Why? Because we are baptized into the name of the Lord Jesus (Acts 19:5). When I receive baptism, I receive a share in His name. The church cannot obtain a greater authority on earth than the authority vested in the name of the Lord Jesus. Our relationship with the name of the Lord Jesus begins at baptism, for we are baptized into that name.

Baptism is an assurance that all we are needs to go through death daily; only what little is left after going through death has any spiritual usefulness. What is destroyed upon passing through death is that which cannot stand before God. That which passes through death is called resurrection. Only those who stand on resurrection ground are able to use the authority of the Lord Jesus.

There must be a day when the backbone of our natural life is broken by the Lord; only after this has occurred will we be useful to Him. This is not a doctrine; this is life.

To know the name of the Lord is a revelation, not a doctrine. There ought to be a day when God opens our eyes to see the power and the majesty of His name.

The Bible presents a kind of prayer that is the highest and most spiritual, yet few people notice or offer up such utterance. What is it? It is "authoritative prayer." We know the prayer of praise, the prayer of thanksgiving, the prayer of asking, and the prayer of intercession, but we know very little of the prayer of authority.

In our day, where does the prayer of command have its origin? At the ascension of our Lord. Ascension gives us victory through a new position before the face of Satan. This is not a new position before God—we obtained that position before Him through the resurrection of our Lord—but it is a new position before our Adversary. It is one of authority!

The significance of ascension is quite different from that of death and resurrection. While the latter is wholly for the sake of redemption, the former is for warfare—to execute what His death and resurrection have accomplished. Ascension makes manifest a new position for us, for in ascension He has raised us up and made us to sit with Him (Eph. 2:6).

Authoritative prayer begins in heaven and ends on earth. In spiritual warfare, this kind of praying downward is exceedingly important. What is praying downward? It is standing upon the heavenly position Christ has given us and using authority to resist all the works of Satan by commanding that whatever God has commanded must be done.

The meaning of *amen* is not "let it be so," but "thus it shall be."

Satan commences his work by causing us, if he can, to lose our heavenly position—for heaven is the position of victory. He knows that as long as we stand in and maintain that position, *"we are more than conquerors"* (Rom. 8:37). However, if we are removed from that high position, we are defeated. Thus, all victories are gained by our standing in that heavenly, triumphant position.

Those who would be overcomers must learn to remove mountains. What is a mountain? It represents a difficulty that is blocking the way the Lord would have us to go; it stands in our path so that we cannot get through. What should we do? We should command it to move! To ask God to remove the mountain and to command the mountain to move are two entirely opposite things. Yet it is very rare that we take the authority of God and speak directly to the difficulty.

Authoritative prayer is not asking God directly; it is applying God's authority directly on the difficulty. The principal work of overcomers is to bring the authority of the heavenly throne down to earth.

Ordinary prayer is asking God to bind and loose, but authoritative prayer is using His authority to bind and loose.

Unless we are in subjection to God's authority, which means that we are faithful to the leading of the Holy Spirit, we cannot exercise authoritative prayer. Why? Because we must first be willing to subject ourselves to His authority before we can exercise the rights of His authority.

Since creation was originally placed under the control of man, why then does the creation not listen to man's command today? Because man has failed to listen to God's Word. The man of God was slain by the lion because he had been disobedient to God's command (1 Kings 13:20–25). But on the other hand, Daniel was not hurt by the lions because he was innocent before God and had done no harm to the king (Dan. 6:22).

The Bible reveals a close relationship between prayer, fasting, and authority. Prayer speaks of our desire before God, while fasting illustrates our self-denial. The first privilege that God granted Adam was food. Fasting, therefore, signifies a denial of man's first legal right. When prayer and fasting are joined, faith will instantly be sparked. And with faith comes authority.

We see in Ephesians 6:18 that we are to watch and pray. What does this mean? It means we need to be watchful on the one hand and prayerful on the other—watching to prevent any danger or emergency, while praying *"with all prayer and supplication"* (v. 18). It means having both the spiritual insight to discern the schemes of Satan and the authority to thwart his ends and means.

Someone who knows the Lord deeply once said that we have all committed the sin of neglecting prayer and that we should tell ourselves, *"Thou art the man"* (2 Sam. 12:7 KJV).

Eighteen

Practical Issues of This Life

In the Lord's work, a dry eye reveals a dry and hard heart. It is only as the tears flow that the heart is opened up. How strange that what is in the heart finds its exit through the eyes.

Some regard tears as a sign of weakness; but quite the contrary, the one who has no tears to shed has buried his humanity.

Tears have a cleansing effect not only in the physical realm, but also in the spiritual realm. In the physical realm, a few tears will help you to see more clearly. Similarly, without a few tears your spiritual eyes would soon lose their function.

Anyone who fails to cry for sin fails to experience the joy of forsaking sin.

The expression of a Christian should be one of love, not hate. The attitude of a Christian should be one of meekness, not arrogance. And the life of a Christian should be one of denial, not pleasure.

The Lord exhorts us to deny ourselves. Those who choose to deny themselves forfeit their personal rights. Having given up any claim to personal rights, these cannot be provoked to anger. This is denying self.

A subjective person is full of self. He has an opinion on every matter and a conviction on every subject.

If you are truly a humble person before God, you will eventually come to realize that the ridicule, despising, and slander that is directed at you from people is part of the discipline of the Holy Spirit, and you will accept such discipline.

One who rejoices at the failure of others and grieves at the success of others is a jealous person.

One who is pleased with his brother's fall and unhappy with his brother's progress is a person full of pride. This is the meanest of all attitudes. For if a person delights in another's fall, he shares in the attitude of Satan.

A person who truly knows the Lord expects other people to be raised up, as well as himself.

If you are one who exalts your own self, you will surely grow angry and take offense when you meet someone of greater spiritual stature.

The deeper one's self has been dealt with through the Cross, the greater one's deliverance from self will be. How is this manifested? The man who has been totally delivered from self cannot be provoked to rise to his own defense.

A Christian who loses his temper is simply revealing his resistance to the discipline of the Holy Spirit. He is unhappy and displeased with the arrangement of events the Holy Spirit has ordered for him.

Because our days on earth are limited, we need to learn how to number them so as to please God (Ps. 90:12), for some days are accredited and some rejected by God. May He be gracious to us all and teach us how to "redeem the time" so that our days will be counted to our favor and His glory (Eph. 5:15–17; Col. 4:5).

The day you receive the salvation of the Lord is the day you begin your spiritual history. Yet since the day you became a Christian, there have been days that have not been numbered. Even in the Bible we notice there are days like this that are ignored and go unrecorded. Why? Because God has looked upon them as wasted days and therefore has not credited them.

As Christians, we should realize that the days that we live according to our own human will—away from God, defeated and fallen—are not numbered by Him.

Let us, as Christians, be diligent day by day. For if we spend our days foolishly—if we rebel against God, commit sins, or walk after our own will—our days will be totally wasted as far as God is concerned. How dreadful this is!

If you have wasted many days, do not fret. Trust in Him to allow you to begin to credit each day to His glory. Then, if your service is done according to His will, one day in His sight may be reckoned as many days. For one day in His courts is better than a thousand wasted days (Ps. 84:10).

Why are so many Christians still thirsty? Why do they have to go back to get more water after drinking from the well? Because they are drinking from the wrong well. As long as our eyes are on the waters of this world, we will thirst again. The world could offer all that it had to Jesus, but He would neither enjoy it nor accept its offer. He refused to drink even a drop of the water of this world. Thus, He was fully satisfied.

Paul did not simply say that He gained the Lord as his treasure. He had something to lose as well. He counted all other things to be loss—he let go of all these things—so that he could know and gain the excellency of the Lord Jesus Christ (Phil. 3:8).

Meekness means flexibility. One who is meek is able to declare that he will have whatever God wants him to have. Meekness is maintaining an attitude whereby whatever you have decided on is subject to change according to God's will, because a meek heart is an obedient heart.

Humility means a person will accept whatever the Lord gives him, for his expectations are not focused on himself. He is able to shout "hallelujah" and offer thanks to the Lord concerning anything the Lord may be pleased to give.

Any person who has had some spiritual experience will agree that nothing is more joyous than consecration; nothing can surpass the joy of putting oneself in God's hands and allowing Him to manage one's life.

Those who do not know God well will complain that God is too hard, reaping where He does not sow and gathering where He does not scatter (Matt. 25:24). But those who truly know God will confess that indeed the Lord's yoke is easy, and His burden light (Matt. 11:30).

How many of God's children sing "hallelujah" when they hear of the love of God and His wisdom and power but are fearful when it comes to hearing the will of God for their own lives!

Frequently we ask for fish, and God seemingly gives us a serpent; we ask for bread, and He appears to be giving us a stone. (See Matthew 7:9–11.) So we inquire why this is so. The fact is that we often think we ask for fish, not knowing that what we are actually asking for is a serpent. Moreover, what God gives us may appear to be a stone, whereas in truth it is bread.

Praising God for His grace marks the beginning of praise, but praising Him for His will completes the lesson of praise. To praise God for what is gained initiates a person into praise, but to praise Him for what is lost is to perfect that person in praise.

The following is from a daily devotional called *Streams in the Desert:* "A bar of steel is worth five dollars; when wrought into horseshoes, it is worth ten dollars. If made into needles, it is worth three hundred and fifty dollars; if into penknife blades, it is worth thirty-two thousand dollars; if into springs for watches, it is worth two hundred and fifty thousand dollars." In order that we may become more valuable to Him, He causes us to undergo more refinings and beatings.

The Lord does not charge us not to engage in the necessary affairs of this life; He only commands us not to be anxious and troubled while we do them. Outwardly, we can be fully engrossed, while inwardly we maintain constant fellowship with God.

Maintaining the strength we need for our daily walk depends entirely on the communion that exists between our innermost life and God. Only those inwardly living in the Holy of Holies can see that God indeed permeates all things.

How can we obtain inner rest? The first condition is this: *"Be anxious for nothing, but in everything by prayer and supplication, with thanksgiving, let your requests be made known to God"* (Phil. 4:6). The second condition is this: *"Take my yoke upon you, and learn of me; for I am meek and lowly in heart: and ye shall find rest unto your souls"* (Matt. 11:29 KJV). The first condition is faith, the second is obedience. Rest comes from consecration. Partial consecration means partial rest. Total consecration means total rest.

May the Lord help us to see clearly that rest comes only by trust and obedience. While the heart of unbelief remains, rest can never be attained.

Outside of Christ, I am only a sinner; but in Christ, I am saved. Outside of Christ, I am empty; in Christ, I am full. Outside of Christ, I am weak; in Christ, I am strong. Outside of Christ, I cannot; in Christ, I am more than able. Outside of Christ, I have been defeated; in Christ, I am already victorious. How meaningful are the words *in Christ.*

There are many things that make the Lord glad, but only when Christians are in one accord is His joy full. Winning souls for Christ may give Him joy, living victoriously may also give Him joy, but only His people's having one mind will make His joy full.

Some people can only say with their mouths that they are one with their brothers and sisters, for their hearts and minds are far from unity.

Sometimes there arises dissension among believers. Now, if such dissension is not due to faction, it must be due to vainglory. Each aspires to be great, and none will prefer the other in honor.

Lowliness of mind means not leaving any room for oneself—it is when we count others as better than ourselves. This is the most difficult of all Christian virtues.

How can a person count another as more excellent than himself? One Christian has well said, "In looking at myself, I look at my old man; in looking at another, I look at the new man."

How frequently we think so little of others. Our expectations of them are even higher than the Lord's! This is because what we see are their obvious failures, but what the Lord sees are their hidden victories.

The Bible gives two titles to the Lord: "The Savior of sinners" (Acts 5:31) and "the Friend of sinners" (Matt. 11:19). As a Savior, He redeems sinners; as a Friend, He communicates with sinners and feels their pains and sorrows.

The Lord places burdens on us that are beyond our power to bear. Yet remember, these are for the purpose of teaching us that in every situation He is with us. He feels what we feel, and He is waiting to dispense grace to us.

Nineteen

A Living Sacrifice

According to the Bible, salvation is related primarily to the world, not to hell. The opposite of salvation is the world. And as long as we belong to the world, we are not saved from it.

Salvation is a matter of position. As long as a person is in Adam (walking according to the course of the world), he stands opposite to God, making him an enemy to God.

Salvation deals with what I have come out of, as well as what I enter into. Eternal life tells me what I have entered into.

As hell is a place for those under the judgment of God, the world is also a place under His judgment. Therefore, salvation means being saved not only out of hell, but also out of the world.

Baptism is a public announcement that declares, "I have come out of the world."

As it was with Noah and the Flood, so it is with baptism. For baptism includes both immersion and emergence. What cannot pass through the water is not saved, but is drowned. However, what has passed through the waters and emerged from them is saved.

The water of baptism serves as a tomb (Rom. 6:4). What is buried must be dead, but what emerges must be alive in resurrection. Now, having emerged from the water, let us therefore *"walk in newness of life"* (v. 4).

A person is buried only after he is dead. You would vigorously object to being buried before you were dead. Death is the prerequisite of burial. Having been crucified with Christ, I am dead. Hence, my baptism is a testimony to that fact.

Spiritual truth is even more real than physical fact. God has joined us to Christ; hence, His death is our death.

Once one has believed on the Lord, the Savior has dealt with his past. Hence, from this time forward, the point of emphasis should be on how Christ will live out His life through this one who has believed.

From the Epistles we can discover a marvelous truth: what God stresses most for the believer is the future. He is not concerned with the past life, nor does He labor over what we should do about the past—because our past is under the blood.

If longtime believers are not willing to sacrifice all they have in order to follow the Lord, what good is it to instruct young believers to do so? It is very confusing for young ones to be taught to walk one way while they are being shown another. If the church is not a consecrated church—if the church is not separated from the world—she is not entitled to mention baptism or separation. The only way to help young believers grow up and mature in the Lord is for the church herself to be living and walking in such a state. If most of the believers in a fellowship are wholly abandoned to God, it will be very easy for those around them who are young in the Lord to learn to be likewise.

Man's failure is not due to his weakness, but rather, his not accepting God's strength. It is not in man's inability, but in his not allowing God to enable him. Only God can enable us to do what we ourselves cannot do.

What is impossible with man is possible with God (Luke 18:27).

The Son of Man came to seek and to save those who are lost in the wealth of this world (Luke 19:10).

Love is the basis of total consecration. The more we love Him, the more we are consecrated to Him. The deeper our affection, the deeper our consecration. The greater our experience of His love for us, the greater our consecration will be toward a lost and dying world. It is only as we come to see that He abandoned all of His world for us that we will likewise abandon all we have in our world for Him.

One basis for consecration is responsive love, and the other basis is God's legal right. On the one hand, for the sake of love we choose to serve Him; on the other hand, by right we are not our own. Consecration is thus based on a love that surpasses human feeling, as well as a warrant according to the law.

Consecration is more than love. It is the action that follows love. One who has consecrated himself is separated from everything in this world—from all his former masters. Henceforth, he will do nothing but what his new Master commands.

Men do not choose to consecrate themselves to God; it is God who chooses men to be consecrated to Him. All who believe they are doing God a favor by forsaking everything to serve Him are actually strangers to consecration. Let them make a hasty retreat, for they are not the chosen.

The Old Testament high priest wore two garments, one for glory and one for beauty. But just as with the priests, it is God who selects us to serve Him. And it is in consecration that God then clothes us with glory, along with beauty.

Consecration aims not at preaching or working for God, but at serving God. The word *"service"* (Rom. 12:1) in the original Greek bears the sense of "waiting on"—waiting on God in order to serve Him.

What is the result of consecration? The result is holiness, for the fruit of consecration is holiness (Exod. 28).

Deliverance from the power of sin comes not from the blood but from the Cross, while forgiveness comes not from the Cross but from the blood.

What is faith? Faith is when you are brought to the place whereby you can claim from God that something has already been done even though it appears it has not. If faith precedes one's work, such work is living. If work precedes one's faith, it is dead.

The secret of prayer is in two parts: praying from no word to God's Word, and praising from having the promise until the promise is fulfilled.

Every believer ought to know there are four things to be done attentively before God each morning: communion, praise, Bible reading, and prayer. If one neglects any of these four, the day will declare it.

A well-known pianist once remarked, "If I do not practice for one day, I notice something wrong. If I do not practice for two days, my wife notices something wrong. And if I do not practice for three days, the whole world notices something wrong." How many Christians there are who wonder why the performance of their spiritual life is not worthy to be manifested before others, yet they are not willing to spend time with the Lord daily!

Cultivate the habit of rising early for daily devotions. Try it many times; do it again and again. Until that habit is formed, though, ask God to give you grace that this good habit of early rising may be developed.

Twenty

The Good Confession

The best opportunity we have to confess the Lord comes right at the beginning of our spiritual lives. If this is not done at the outset, it becomes almost impossible later on. Because many are inarticulate during the first and second week of their Christian lives, they remain so ever after.

Secret Christians have ten times as many temptations and troubles as open or professing Christians. Why? Because it is only when one is willing to make a public confession of his faith that he becomes a separated person. The advantage of public confession is that it will save a believer from many, many future troubles.

If, for fear of falling, you do not openly confess the Lord, you surely will fall. Why? Because you have left your back door open; you have already prepared for the day of your fall.

Who would ever buy something in order to throw it away? Not God. For God is the God who keeps us as well as the God who saves us! When God purchases us, He redeems us—to keep us. After all, redemption would be meaningless if it were without preservation.

Can a flower be ashamed of the sun? As a flower opens to the sunlight, so we should confess the Lord to the world. For it is the world, not us, who ought to be ashamed. If we think confessing the Lord is shameful, it is we who are deceived along with the world.

How wrong it is that people desire to heap shame on us! But theirs is the shame, not ours. Let us stand up boldly and be "fools" for Christ and follow in His footsteps, despising the shame. Then He will surely confess us before His Father (Matt. 10:32).

If we ever expect to be totally separated from the world, we must first separate our hearts and spirits from it. For even if we separate ourselves from a hundred of the things of the world, we are yet in the world. If we do not first separate our hearts and spirits from the world, we will never separate ourselves from all the things of the world.

It is virtually impossible to tell new believers everything that is permissible and everything that is not permissible as a Christian. But if they understand that they must be separate from the world, they can apply this principle to innumerable situations. And what is of the world? Each and every thing that tends to quench our spiritual life before the Lord is of the world.

It is only as we count all things as refuse and rid ourselves of them that God can come in as El Shaddai, our all-sufficient God, and provide for us out of His infinite supply (Phil. 3:8).

When one becomes a Christian, he must leave his national characteristics outside the church, for there is no such thing in the church.

If a new believer does not open his mouth during the first year of his new life, he will hardly be able to open his mouth later on. Furthermore, it is the responsibility of the older saints to instruct every new believer on the importance of witnessing during the first or second week of his salvation.

There should be two great days of rejoicing in every believer's life. The first is that day when he believes in the Lord. The second is the day when, for the first time, he leads another soul to Christ (Prov. 11:30).

Many do not have power before God or man because their lives are closed on either end. You see, a channel of life must have two ends open. One end must be open to the Lord, and the other end must be open to men.

An interest in men, void of a burden before God, is simply inadequate and is therefore ineffective. One must have a burden before God prior to going out and laboring among men.

The greatest test of one's faith is his prayer life. If after three or four months your prayers are still not answered, something must be wrong with your prayers. This reveals whether you are sick before God.

The amount of faith we have is based on our knowledge of God, because it is the depth of our knowledge of God that determines the depth of our faith. Hence, in order to have more faith, we need to know more of God. And our salvation from the daily trials God places before us is based on knowing.

Faith comes by the Word of God (Rom. 10:17). His Word is His promise to us, which reveals His work. Hence, God's promise reveals the goals of His work. By allowing Him to work in us, His promises are manifested to and through us.

Preaching well on doctrine may correct people's minds and yet fail to save their souls. Our aim should be to save their souls, not correct their minds.

Twenty-One

Assembling Together

God has a dwelling place, a habitation on earth. In the Bible, the first habitation of God was found in the tabernacle. Today, we as Christians are joined together as the habitation of God.

For a Christian, independence means certain death. Isolation from fellowship takes away life as well as fullness.

The Word of God contains so many aspects of truth that people tend to establish churches based on one special aspect. We can see abundant evidence of this all around us.

In the Bible, the only rule for a division or dividing line among the church is geographical location. Locality constitutes the basic unit of fellowship.

Christians cannot join a church. They are already part of the church. To join means that they are still outside. We are already in the church and are therefore already joined to one another. Yet we act as if we are not. How sad it must be for God to see His people live and act contrary to how the Word says we should!

The church is so special that it cannot be joined. The determining factor is whether one is born of God. If one is born of God, he is already in; if he is not born of God, there is no way to join.

Many prayers can be offered privately. However, there is another kind of prayer that must be offered in the assembly if it is to be heard. It must be prayed in the name of the Lord by two or more people. God's corporate grace is only granted in the assembly; it is not given to individuals.

In the reading of the Scriptures, certain verses will not be opened up to us except in the gathering of the saints. They cannot be understood individually; but in the meeting, special grace is given to understand them.

No one can forsake the assembling of the saints together without forfeiting grace.

"The called-out ones assembled," or *ecclesia* in the Greek, is the meaning for the word *church*.

How should we gather together? All gatherings must be in the name of the Lord. This means that we gather under the authority of the Lord and are centered on Him. If we gather to hear a certain preacher, we are not gathering to meet the Lord. If we gather because of tradition, we are not gathering to meet the Lord. If we gather because it is convenient, we are not gathering to meet the Lord. There are many reasons why some gather together, yet they are not the reason why the Lord wants us to assemble together.

Many Christians are alone when present at a meeting, though there are people all around them. This is because, even after many years, they still do not know how to meet. They come to the meeting with the thought of what they can get, rather than letting all their actions be for the benefit of others.

When we are truly concerned with others' needs and others' edification, the Holy Spirit is honored and will do the work of edification both in us and in others. But if even one person is out of order in a meeting, the whole assembly suffers.

Whenever people walk in our midst, they should instantly sense the presence of God. This is the work of the Holy Spirit. It will cause them to fall down on their faces and worship God, declaring that God is indeed among us.

There are five different types of meetings in the Bible: gospel meetings, breaking of bread meetings, prayer meetings, exercise of gifts or fellowship meetings, and ministry or preaching meetings.

The church today needs to have all of these various meetings if it expects to be strong before God.

In the early church, gospel meetings (meetings in which the Gospel was preached), rather than listening to sermons, occupied the foremost place. The reverse situation is a proof of the weakness present in today's church meetings. To have a strong church, the preaching of the Gospel should be restored to its original position of being the most basic of all the meetings.

In thanksgiving, we notice the Lord's work; in praise, we consider the Lord Himself. We thank Him for what He has done, and we praise Him for what He is. And at our breaking of bread meetings, when our thanks and praise have reached a peak, the time for the breaking of bread has arrived.

Our acceptance of the Son is only half the salvation God affords us; the Father's acceptance of us is the other half. The Father receives us only after we have become acceptable in His Son. Consequently, at a breaking of bread meeting, it is after the breaking of bread that we can come to the Father with praise.

The throne of God is established on the praises of His people (Ps. 22:3). When the church of God starts to praise, she begins to touch the throne. The more we learn to praise, the more we touch the throne.

Though public prayer is difficult—and tends to be false, long, and men-pleasing—prayers in prayer meetings are stronger than private prayers. Also, it is far easier for God to answer the prayers of the corporate church than personal prayers. One problem today, though, is that there are more answers to personal prayers than corporate prayers, because there is so much falsehood, confusion, and vain words in corporate prayers.

Our spirits can either help or hinder the release of the spirit of a prophet. If new believers learn the lesson here, they will contribute to the strength of the meeting. For if the spirit of the brothers and sisters does not come forth, neither will the spirit of the prophet who is in their midst.

If, in our day, we learn how to meet as the body of Christ, the next generation will become stronger.

The fulfillment of the meaning of the Sabbath comes by entering into God's rest. However, to enter into God's rest, we must accept His work. Here, then, is the guiding principle for our entire spiritual lives: we must enter into His rest before we can be a part of His work.

Only after entering into rest are we qualified in God's eyes to rise up and serve. And only those who listen to and heed God's Word enter into rest, not into work.

The highest manifestation of spiritual life is seen in men praising God. It is the loftiest expression believers can ever show the Lord. Praise can take you to the highest place in the universe: the throne of God.

Take special note of this: those who offered praise in the Old Testament were those whom God had purposely led through distressing situations. It was out of their wounded feelings that they composed the words of praise.

Remember this: whenever God's children are praising, Satan must flee. Frequently prayer is a battle, but praise is victory. Prayer is spiritual warfare, but praise is the shout of triumph. For this reason, it is the shout of praise that Satan hates the most.

In the book of Acts, prison doors were opened twice—once in answer to prayer and once in answer to praise. (See Acts 12:5-10; 16:25-26.) However, while prayer may not always open prison doors, praise does!

Why is praise also triumph? Because when you only pray, you are yet in your environment; but when you praise, you have risen above your environment. Therefore, what prayer alone may fail to accomplish, praise can.

When your spirit is pressed beyond measure so that you can hardly breathe, pray if you are able to pray, and praise when you are not able to pray.

When you offer *"the sacrifice of praise"* (Heb. 13:15), that is, praise as a sacrifice, you will quickly transcend everything so that nothing can bury you.

The children of God are often subjected to the temptation of rising up to fight. And many even assume that they are not able to overcome unless they fight. They fail to recognize the wonderful principle that victory is not dependent on fighting, but on praising (2 Chron. 20:20–22).

Every time you meet a problem, ask for God's mercy. He will keep your hands from making war preparations and keep your mind from conceiving methods to do battle.

Nothing causes the Lord to move His hand as much or as fast as praise does. Praise rises higher than prayer. Those who praise do not rest on expectations; they have already transcended. They have praised until the victory has been won.

Human thoughts are generally occupied with struggling and fighting, because man always has the enemy in sight. But divine thought is centered on faith and praise; it transcends man's sight and sees as God sees.

You should praise when you have no feeling until you do have feeling. Then, continue praising so that a little feeling becomes much feeling.

Victory does not lie in struggling with your flesh. It comes when you lower your head and praise the Lord, saying, "Lord, I praise Your way. What You have arranged for me cannot be wrong. Whatever You do is perfect." Only then will your spirit rise above your problems, above your own inner feelings and into victory.

Twenty-Two

Not I but Christ

We know the door of salvation is not open forever. Likewise, we should remember that the door of apology is also not open forever.

As God's child, you should realize that if you do not apologize and ask forgiveness from a person against whom you have sinned, your spiritual life will be adversely affected if that one mentions your name with sighing before God. The gifts you offer to God will not be accepted, and your prayers will not be heard. His sigh will render you useless, and your way before God will be blocked.

We need to have a right estimate of our own indebtedness to God so that we can generously forgive our brother's debt. In order to see how little people owe us, we need only bear in mind how much we owe God. And what we owe God infinitely exceeds what we can pay.

Our indebtedness to God is far beyond our ability to repay. The difference between what people owe us and what we owe God is exceedingly great.

The tax collector prayed in the temple, *"God, be merciful to me a sinner!"* (Luke 18:13). A sinner asks for mercy; he would never think of asking for justification. But God said that this man was justified (v. 14). Why? Because the salvation that the Lord accomplishes is not according to man's concepts—it is according to His own thought.

God expects the recipients of His grace to be gracious. Hence, He not only looks for righteousness in those who are His, but He also looks for graciousness.

The Lord expects you to treat others as He has treated you. He does not demand of you according to righteousness, so He expects you not to demand righteousness from others.

It is exceedingly ugly in the sight of God for the forgiven person to be unforgiving, for the one who has received mercy to be merciless, and for the one to whom He has given grace to not be gracious to others.

A sad, but common, occurrence among believers is that soon after a brother has sinned against another brother, the matter becomes known to everyone, except the one who has sinned. The offended brother has broadcast it everywhere, yet he has not the strength to tell the offender. (See Matthew 18:15.) This indicates how weak he is, for it is only the weak who tell tales.

God's children should learn to rid the church of problems, not add problems to the church.

If your motive in pointing out a fault to a brother is to gain him, you will know how to point out his fault. But if you do not really desire to restore him, you will probably quarrel.

To tell a brother his fault requires you to completely set aside yourself before you can confront him. Otherwise, if you yourself are involved, you will never be able to fulfill this task.

In allowing a brother to sin against you, the Lord has looked upon you and has chosen you to be a vessel for restoration.

Christians' reactions, as well as their lives, should be under the control of God. If God controls our reactions, we will not react freely. As He commands us, so will we react. It is His life within us, the life He has given us, that does the reacting.

Man's reactions to ordinary, everyday matters can be divided into three levels: first, the level of reason, which reacts temperamentally and angrily; second, the level of good conduct, which reacts patiently; and third, the level of God's life, which reacts transcendently.

Man only demands so much; but as a people who are before God, we should give much more than man demands. Why? Because God's life in us transcends man's demands.

The Lord's life shows us He has power so that when people mistreat us without a reason, we can do just the opposite—treat them well without a reason.

What is the life that transcends? It is turning the other cheek after the first one has been struck; it is giving your coat to the person who has taken your shirt; it is walking the second mile with one who has only asked you to walk the first mile (Matt. 5:39–41). This is God's children doing things according to the grace of God.

Why must we turn the left cheek after being struck on the right one? To do so indicates that when the Lord permits man's hand to treat us ill, our choice is to let the Lord increase His work in us, rather than lessen it. By adding the left cheek, our reaction in effect says that we accept what the Lord is doing through man and that we allow Him to increase His work in us. Hence, by means of a human hand, the Lord increases our capacity and thereby causes us to grow spiritually.

This should be our prayer: "May the Lord's hand be on me. If I still have something to lose, I have not lost enough. For only when I have lost all will I not be able to lose any more. And as long as I may yet die, I have not died enough. For only when I am totally dead will I not be able to die further. Thus, may the Lord increase His hand upon me, rather than lighten it."

Let us remember that each time people treat us in an ill manner, speak evil of us, or make unreasonable demands of us, they are giving us opportunity to react as Christians.

No loss can be greater than not being a Christian in action. To be struck is a great loss; to be deprived of things is a great loss; to suffer disgrace is a great loss; and to lose freedom is a great loss. But in allowing these things, the Lord shows His confidence in our ability to manifest His grace. If we fail in these things, how very great is the loss!

The Christian life is a surprising paradox. The more you are persecuted, troubled, and unreasonably treated, the happier you are before God.

Sin is a power that holds people. We cannot destroy its power or put it to death, but the Lord can remove it from us. That is why the Word of God does not tell us to overcome sin, though it does tell us that we can be freed, or delivered, from sin.

One cannot be delivered from sin by exercising his will, for when one is using his willpower, he is unable to trust God's way for deliverance. Hence, God is forced to wait for that day when this one can confess his utter inability and fully submit himself to God's ability. Only when one has come to the point where he stops trying in his own strength does God then have the opportunity of providing victory for him.

To overcome sin does not require an ounce of strength, for it is the work of the law. As there is one law that makes me sin without my effort, there is another law that sets me free from sin—also without any labor on my part. And only the victory that requires no exertion is true victory.

The way of deliverance can be learned step by step. The first step is to see that sin is a law to you; the second is to see that the will cannot overcome the law; and the third is to see that there is another law that overcomes the law of sin (Rom. 8:2).

According to the Bible, what should be the relationship between the Lord and us? The principal relationship is that Christ should be our life (Col. 3:4). Once Christ has become our life, we are able to imitate Him. If we are ignorant of this fact—that Christ is our life—we will not be able to experience the Lord's life on earth. For this alone is the way; this is the victory.

What is the secret of life? As Christ is our substitute in death, so also is He our substitute in life. Just as it is great news that we need not die, so it is great news that we need not live.

It is wrong for any Christian to attempt to live the Christian life. And we are not asked to do so. The Word of the Lord says *"it is no longer I who live, but Christ lives in me"* (Gal. 2:20). This is the secret of living the Christian life.

When you find believers who are tired of trying to live like Christians, you should tell them that there is something much better. Then, as they once thanked God upon hearing the Gospel that they have no need to die, now they can thank God as they hear Him say they have no need to live. What a deliverance this is from a tiring and exhausting Christian life!

Defeat is not caused by less work, but by too much work. When we are working, God's grace cannot come to us. Likewise, in our working too much, the life of the Lord cannot be manifested in us.

Twenty-Three

Do All to the Glory of God

How can the Gospel be spread over the whole earth if you lose those born to you? For then you have to try to recover your own children. Forgive me for saying this, for it is my own word, but the worst failure in the church is the parents.

To lead your children to God, you yourself must first walk with God.

One reason for the failure of many Christian families is that the parents expect their children to be better than they are. They expect their children not to love the world but to go on with the Lord, while they themselves stay behind.

The standard that you follow in spiritual things will eventually be the standard of your children.

Your children will learn to love what you love and to hate what you hate. They will treasure what you treasure and condemn what you condemn.

The greatest coward in the world is one who oppresses the weak and the small.

May we instill in our children's hearts the understanding that to suffer for the Lord is noble and to be a martyr is glorious.

It is unchristian to be puffed up in victory, and a virtue to acknowledge defeat in a good spirit.

I trust, if the Lord is gracious to the church, half of the people added to it will be the children of Christian parents, and the other half will be rescued from the world. A church cannot be strong if the increase comes only from the world and not from the children of Christian parents.

People who have the courage to sin ought to have the courage to accept the punishment.

If a new believer does not change his friends, his spiritual future is bound to be shallow and weak.

It is impossible for a Christian to have many worldly friends if he truly loves the Lord and serves Him faithfully.

Every time you have improper communication with unbelievers, you incur loss.

The Lord Jesus is the Friend of sinners, not the sinner's friend. He came to seek and to save those lost in trespasses and sin (Luke 19:10), not to join with them.

Man's speech represents his heart; it reveals what is there (Matt. 12:34). One's actions do not always declare the person, but his words often do.

By its fruit is the tree known, and by his speech the person is revealed.

Those who do not know how to control their words are easily manifested by their eagerness to teach others.

Whether or not one can bridle himself hinges on whether he is able to bridle his words. To judge if he has the fruit of the Spirit in self-control, one only needs to observe how he controls his words.

The reason there are so many inappropriate words in the church is that so many want to hear them. Since there is such a desire, there is such a source of supply (2 Tim. 4:3).

There is today a hearing lust, a lust to hear unsuitable words.

The world measures how much it will give by its income; a Christian measures how much his income will be by his giving. And the measure that we give will be the measure that we receive (Luke 6:38).

Many today try to lay hold of Philippians 4:19: *"My God shall supply all your need according to His riches in glory by Christ Jesus."* Do we see, though, that God supplies the givers, not the askers? Only the givers have the right to use this verse; those who do not give are not entitled to the privilege.

Twenty-Four

Love One Another

There are four kinds of forgiveness in the Bible. First is eternal forgiveness, second is borrowed forgiveness, third is communional forgiveness, and fourth is governmental forgiveness. Eternal forgiveness is what we receive when we are saved (John 3:16). Borrowed forgiveness is God's forgiveness being declared through the church (John 20:22–23). Communional forgiveness is what we receive after confession of sin; this restores our walk of fellowship with the Spirit of God (1 John 1:7–9). And governmental forgiveness is when God removes His hand of discipline from us and now deals with us after a different manner than when we had not yet learned to submit to Him (Matt. 6:14–15).

To be disciplined by God is a glorious experience.

All the discipline of God is educational. He chastens us *"for our profit, that we may be partakers of His holiness"* (Heb. 12:10). This is truly glorious, because holiness is God's nature.

Holiness, as it is spoken of in Hebrews 12:10, is what God gradually works into us or slowly incorporates into us through His discipline.

A prime characteristic of New Testament salvation is that God has not only given salvation to us, but after He has given it, He starts to build it in us through patient inworking. It is by the joining together of these two processes that we see full salvation. The one is a gift that comes from Christ; the other is incorporated through the discipline of the Holy Spirit.

In order for a Christian to walk well before God, he must learn how to resist Satan. And in order for him to do that, he must first discern what the work of Satan is.

The special field of Satan's work is found in man's mind or thought life. He surrounds man with strongholds so as to prevent him from obeying Christ.

When satanic temptations first invade the mind, they are relatively easy to deal with; but once they become "facts" in the mind, they are most difficult to get rid of.

If one is concentrating on his thoughts, his eyes will not be focusing on the Lord.

After a thought is first resisted, you should consider the matter closed. Should the thought present itself a second time, it now comes as a lie and not the truth. You can well afford to ignore it, and if you do, it will soon disappear. So the basic principle is this: resist the first time; ignore the second time.

To resist Satan a second time for the same temptation is to discredit the first resistance; to resist the third time is to refute the first and the second resistances. Each new resistance means one more distrust of your former resistance.

Many do not resist Satan for fear that it may be the reproof of the Holy Spirit. They cannot distinguish between satanic accusation and the reproach of the Holy Spirit. Hence, they accept Satan's accusation as a reproach of the Holy Spirit. How can one tell the difference? Accusation from Satan is never clear and sharp; whereas revelation from God through the Spirit is always distinct and to the point.

We, as Christians, should understand that the primary fields of satanic operation are not only in the mind and in the body, but also in the conscience.

Satan draws carnal Christians out of the battle by enticing them to sin, and he gets mature Christians out of the fight by using accusation. Hence, he disables the carnal Christian by sin and disarms the spiritual Christian by accusation.

Many of God's children neither submit to the discipline of the Holy Spirit nor resist Satan's attack in their lives. This is really a problem today—on the one hand, no submission, and on the other, no resistance.

Almost all of the circumstances around us are given to us by the Lord so that we may learn lessons from them and be built up by them. What is unfortunate is that there are so few who are learning from their circumstances and are thereby being built up in the stature of Christ.

Fear is Satan's knock. If you answer the knock, you will receive a visit from him. If fear is accepted, things will soon happen; if it is rejected, nothing will come of it.

What is resurrection? It is a realm beyond the touch of death. And Satan is fully aware that he can do nothing to this resurrection life.

The conflict between the church and Satan is intended to show forth the Lord's victory, not to win it. The Lord has already overcome and won the victory for us!

God's system of grace was added because of man's insubordination and rebellion under His system of government. Hence, grace is for the purpose of redeeming and restoring those who are insubordinate and rebellious, so that they once again may be placed under the subjection of God's governmental system.

God's grace can never nullify God's government; rather, God's grace enables people to obey God's government. The humbler a person is, the further he progresses in God's governmental system.

The oneness of the body of Christ is based on the forsaking of sin. Hence, the reason God's children today are so divided is their many sins. Where the unity of the body is, in that place there is the forsaking of sin—for fellowship is based on dealing with and for-saking sin (1 John 1:7).

In order to become a vessel of honor before God, one needs to purge himself from the vessel of dishonor.

People on the earth are divided into two groups: the children of God and the children of the Devil. Likewise, there are only two fa-thers: God is a father, and the Devil is a father.

If we render judgment toward fellow believers without tears, there is no knowledge of brotherly love. If there is condemnation without distress, there is no understanding of brotherhood. And if there is nothing but reproach and criticism, it is evident that there is no love.

To love your fellow believers is to sacrifice yourself for all of them in order to serve and perfect them.

Do not brag of your love for God, but rather, learn to love your brothers and sisters in Christ. Bragging of love is empty, but the love of God is manifested through the love of the brothers and sisters.

When you became a Christian, your profession underwent a complete change. Christians have but one profession, and that is to serve God. Outwardly I may be busily occupied in various things, but inwardly I am before God, serving Him.

To be saved by grace is relatively simple, but to serve by grace is much higher. It is grace that enables us to serve God—the most abundant grace that God has bestowed on us.

As God built Eve from what He took out of Adam, so He builds the church from what is taken out of Christ. Christ has given us not only His power, grace, nature, and will, but also His own body. He has given us His bones and His flesh. He has given Himself to us, just as Adam gave his bone to Eve.

The body of Christ has two basic principles: first, unless it comes out of Christ, it is not the body of Christ; second, unless there is the work of the Holy Spirit, it is not the body of Christ. We must be baptized in the Holy Spirit and be filled with the Holy Spirit in order to be joined into one.

The church exists for the purpose of upholding obedience, because obedience brings life. And no sin is more serious than disobedience, for it contradicts the very reason for the church's existence.

The characteristic mark of the Christian is obedience, not work. And the distinguishing mark of the mature Christian is his ability to recognize those who should lead him.

Twenty-Five

The Life That Wins

The life that wins is not attained, but obtained. It is not a life changed, but rather, a life exchanged. It is not suppression, only expression.

The secret of experiencing the power of Christ is to let go of yourself and let Christ live instead of you. This requires childlike faith. Only then will you be more than a conqueror through Him who loves you (Rom. 8:37).

We must humble ourselves before God in order that we may see our lack and receive from His abundance of grace.

Under the old covenant, the people were required to offer one-tenth to God; but under the new covenant, ten-tenths are required.

If—when people say their lives are miserable, sad, and falling apart—we acknowledge the same thing, we are not rivers of living water, but barren deserts that dry up the moisture and deaden the plants.

Victory should be the Christian's normal experience, and defeat should be abnormal. According to the biblical standard, it is deemed to be strange if you do not overcome, and reckoned as common when you do overcome.

If your experience is different from that spelled out in the Scriptures, then you are in need of full salvation. Your being saved is a fact, but you have not obtained salvation in fullness.

Victory is actually a remedial facet of salvation. At the time of our being saved, something was missing—yet not on God's part, for

He never gives us a salvation that lets us live a wandering life. He wants us to have full salvation. He wants us to experience His victory in our lives. Hence, it is the experience of victory that is the remedial facet of salvation.

May we not deceive ourselves by imagining that sinning is inevitable for a Christian. I think no thought hurts our Lord more than this kind of attitude.

Let us ever keep in mind that victory is Christ Himself and has nothing to do with you or me.

Victory is a gift, not a reward. What is a gift? It is something that is freely given to you. That which you earn through work is a reward. (See 1 Corinthians 15:57.)

Only when one comes to realize the vanity of his works and the failure of his life is one then ready to accept the victory that is already his in Christ.

Under the law, God requires man to work for Him. What, then, is being under grace? It denotes God working for man. If we work for God, sin will reign over us; but if we let Him work for us, we rest in His victory.

True victory in the Christian's walk is an expressed life, not a suppressed one. An expressed life shows forth what has already been obtained.

How do we obtain Christ as our victory? On the subtraction side, it is the experience—*"it is no longer I who live"* (Gal. 2:20). On the addition side, it is *"Christ lives in me"* (v. 20).

Let us realize that the Cross expresses God's despair of men. It announces His hopelessness toward men. It is God's way of saying that He can neither repair us nor improve us; He can only crucify us. What is surprising is that, though we already know this fact of our utter corruption, we nevertheless continue to claim that we are not so bad.

One brother asked me how he could enter into victory. My response was to "let go." Victory is God's business, not ours; ours is to simply experience what He has already done.

Using mathematics, we can illustrate how we can live in victory. Two minus one is one. If you take Adam from me, what is left is obviously Christ. This is one, and this is victory. But if there is more than one, all of Adam has not been removed.

As you fulfill the condition for victory by yielding and letting go of yourself, you should at once believe that you have the life that wins—for the Son is waiting to live out His victory in you.

If I feel, it is I who is living; but if I believe, it is the Son of God who is living.

From the ancient days to the present hour, there is only one Overcomer in the whole universe. Praise the Lord, for He is the victory!

The only condition in obtaining the life that wins is letting go. Upon relinquishing your hold, He will prevail.

It is good to thank God for your victory, but you should also thank Him for your weakness. For the power of Christ is made manifest only in our weaknesses.

Faith is not asking for what God has already promised. Faith is believing in the promises of God.

While feelings may be useful in certain other things, in knowing the Lord they are useless and untrustworthy. In spiritual matters, it is faith—not feelings—that is required to prove them.

Today, the greatest problem among the children of God is their failure to believe His Word. This unbelief reflects on God as though He were lying. He has said that we are the branches through which His life will live and flow (John 15:5). We must believe Him.

The Scriptures show us that victory comes through believing the Word of God. God has said that His Son is our life, our head, our victory, our sanctification, and our power. And those who have experienced Him in these ways know that He bears all our burdens, takes care of all our responsibilities, supplies us with patience and gentleness, and supports us from within.

Which is more trustworthy—the Word of God or our experience? Of course, the Word of God! And yet, how prone we are to believe in our experience and consider God's Word to be false.

A mountain and faith cannot coexist. Either the mountain is removed, or the faith is removed. And each test God gives us is for the sake of training us to remove mountains.

True faith is believing in God even when our feelings, our experience, and the environment around us tell us otherwise. If we hold fast to this faith, our feelings, our experience, and the environment around us will catch up to where our faith is.

Only little faith hides when it is tested. Big faith stands against the testing. It is false faith that falls in a trial, and genuine faith that stands throughout the trial. Hence, with genuine faith you can meet any test headlong and remain standing.

Most Christians expect to see the results of their faith as soon as they believe. They want to experience victory the very moment they believe. But the real test of faith is found among those who believe God long before the victory is manifested. How long can you believe God—for three hours, three days, three months? If not, where is your faith?

Each time a trial of faith comes our way, we should understand that it is not we who are being proven, but the Lord. When our faith is being proven, it is actually the Son of God who is being proven; it is God's faithfulness and not you that is being tested. Whatever trial descends on you, it is to test what Christ can do for you—if you let Him.

It is only after your faith has been tested and proven that you will be able to help and benefit other people. And in the process, God's heart will be satisfied, and His name will be glorified. This is the faith that is *"more precious than gold"* (1 Pet. 1:7).

Do you fight your battles to victory or from victory? If you fight to victory, you will never succeed; but if you fight from victory, you can never be defeated.

Whenever you are governed by your mind, your feelings, or your self-will, you immediately live in Adam. Whenever you are governed by faith, you instantly live in Christ. And when you are living in Christ, all that is in Him becomes your experience.

Unfortunately, before we can learn to live in victory, we need to fail. God, permit us to fail—and to fail miserably—so that we might come to know how powerless and weak we really are.

The people of God under the old covenant failed. Though they had the truth, they did not have grace. Though they had the law, they did not have the power to keep the law. We, today, not only have the truth unveiled, but also the power of His grace supplying us to keep it. These are the results and benefits of a new and better covenant.

Each time you glory in your weakness while in the midst of trial, the power of Christ will overshadow you (2 Cor. 12:9).

What is meant by growing in grace? It is when truth comes and causes you to see what you have not seen before—your sin—and then having grace supply you with the power to overcome that sin. (See John 1:17.)

The nature of Christ's victory is absolute and cannot be improved upon, but the scope of His victory is ever enlarging, as people allow Him to manifest it through them more and more.

Do we know the difference between victory and triumphing in victory? The first is that which is totally done by Christ; whereas the second is that which is done by us. Victory is the work of Christ; triumphing in victory is our work. Victory is the work that prevails; triumphing in victory is the boast we have in Christ after the victory has been secured.

You ask me, "Where is the victory?" I ask you, "Where is the hallelujah?" For "hallelujah" is the note of victory! The right note expresses genuine victory.

If you continually look only at yourself, you will not be able to praise. But if you look at Christ, immediately you can fill the air with a "hallelujah" and a "praise the Lord."

There is no need to wait until you are actually defeated, defiled, and have seriously sinned to acknowledge defeat. No, whenever you have lost the note of thanks and praise, you have already lost the victory. So confess your failure, and move on again into victory!

If we cry as the world cries, and laugh as the world laughs, where is our victory? And more importantly, where is God's victory? We ought to let the world see that we have joy and strength unspeakable, even in the midst of trials and tribulations. Then, if we continue to offer up praise and thanksgiving to our God, though the world may look at us as mad, they cannot help but admire the Christ in us who causes us to appear as such.

If we are living it, the victory the Lord grants us is of such magnitude that whoever smites us on the right cheek will be offered the left; and whoever sues us for our shirt will be offered our coat also; and whoever would ask us to go one mile will be seen with us going two (Matt. 5:39–41). A victory with leftovers is truly God's victory. To barely overcome is the result of man's own work.

God gives us the life that wins not only so that we obey His will, but also so that we may know His will. Never think that the victorious life is only a matter of not sinning. Positively speaking, it also enables us to commune with God and to enjoy Him as we obey His will. I repeat: God gives us this life not for the sake of fulfilling our purposes, but rather, for us to fulfill His purpose.

Until we have anointed Him with pure ointment (Mark 14:3), He is not pleased. Until we cast all that we have at His feet (Mark 12:44), He is not satisfied. Everything we have must be offered up to Him.

Twenty-Six

The Release of the Spirit

God's intent is for man's spirit to be His dwelling place, with the Holy Spirit—through a union with the human spirit—governing the soul. Thus, our spirits and souls would then use the body as the means of expression for God.

It is the independent actions of our souls that must be destroyed. The soul, instead of functioning independently, must become the organ or vessel for the spirit's use.

The self-strength and self-government of the soul have been dealt a fatal blow by the death of Christ. This is similar to the experience of Jacob, who, after the Angel had touched his thigh, went to the end of his life with a limp. (See Genesis 32:24–31.)

Until the soul has been broken of its strength, it wants to be master. Through the Cross, though, it can be broken and become a very useful servant. If we submit to the Lord's yoke—the symbol of union and service—we can appreciate how the soul finds its greatest value in service, rather than in ruling.

Anyone who serves God will discover, sooner or later, that the greatest hindrance to his work for the Lord is not others, but his own self.

Many of God's servants are not able to do even the most elementary works. Ordinarily, their spirits should enable them to know God's Word, discern the spiritual condition of another, send forth God's messages under the anointing, and receive God's revelations. However, because their outward man has never been dealt with, revival, zeal, pleading, and activity are a waste of time. There is just one basic dealing that can enable man to be useful before God, and it is this: brokenness.

The Lord wants to break the outward soul of man in order that the inward spirit of man may have a way out. Why? Because it is only when the inward man is released that both unbelievers and Christians are blessed.

There are mainly two distinct conditions that can be found among those who possess the life of the Lord. There are those in whom His life is confined, restricted, imprisoned, and unable to come forth; and there are those in whom He has forged a way so that His life can be released through them.

Without the breaking of the outward man, the inward man cannot come forth to bless others because Christ's life is imprisoned by us. It is not that the Lord cannot bless the church, but that the Lord's life is so confined within us that there is no flowing forth. If the outward man remains unbroken, we can never be a blessing to His church, and we cannot expect the Word of God to be blessed by Him through us!

The Lord longs to bless the world through those who belong to Him. And brokenness is that way of blessing, that way of fragrance, that way of fruitfulness—but it is also a path sprinkled with blood.

The motive behind all the orderings of God in our lives is this: to break the outward man. Our daily trials and testings are for our greatest profit. Sadly, before the Lord even raises a finger, many are already upset. We must begin to recognize that all the experiences, troubles, and trials that the Lord sends us are for our highest good. Everything that God gives us is His best for us, so that our outward man may be broken and the spirit can come forth.

As with Christ, after our outward man has been stricken, dealt with, and led through various trials, we have wounds upon us that allow the spirit to emerge.

In our labors for the Lord, there are two possibilities that may arise, neither of which brings the result God desires. One possibility is that the outward man remains unbroken, thus leaving one's spirit inert and unable to function. In this situation, if one is a clever person, his mind governs his work; if he is a compassionate person, his emotions control his actions. While on the surface such labors may appear successful, the result of such work cannot bring people to God. The other possibility is that the spirit may come forth clad in the person's own thoughts or emotions. In this case, the result is mixed and impure, and such work brings men in contact with a mixed and impure experience of Christ. Hence, either of these two conditions weakens our service to God.

It is the Spirit alone who gives life (John 6:63). When the Spirit is released, sinners may be born anew and saints may be established. When life is communicated through the channel of the spirit, those who receive it are born anew. When life is supplied through the Spirit to believers, it results in their being established. Without the Spirit, there can be no new birth and no establishment.

May God bring us to the place where the outward man is completely broken. For when this is the prevailing condition, we will not be working on the outside while we are inactive on the inside. We will not be composed on the outside while we are crying on the inside. We will not be silent on the outside while there is an abundance of thoughts on the inside. Though we will not be poor in thought, we will not use twenty sentences to express what can be said in two. And our thoughts will assist, rather than hinder, our spirits.

When the outward man is broken, the things of the flesh and the world will be kept outside, thus allowing the inward man to live before God continuously. Once this has occurred, though the outward man may be engaged in conversation, the inward man is in fellowship with God. Yet only those who have submitted to the merciful working of God in their lives have the outward man and the inward man separated in this way, thus preventing all that affects the outward man from being able to reach the inward man.

The *"righteous requirement of the law"* is fulfilled in those who walk *"according to the Spirit"* (Rom. 8:4). In other words, the *"law of the Spirit of life"* (v. 2) works effectively only for those who are spiritual—those who set their minds on the things of the Spirit. And who are they? Those who do not *"set their minds on the things of the flesh"* (v. 5)!

Only those who are not intent upon what is carnal will be attentive to what is spiritual. Those who are intent upon spiritual things come under the force of the law of life by the Holy Spirit.

In His dealings with man, God's Spirit never bypasses man's spirit. Moreover, our spirits can neither ignore nor bypass the outward man. In order to touch the lives of others, our spirits must pass through the outward man. To do this, the inward man must have the cooperation of the outward man.

It is our responsibility to submit to the work of the Spirit in our lives so that we can be transformed into a vessel fit for the Master's use (2 Tim. 2:21). However, this can only be accomplished by the breaking of the outward man. And if this is not accomplished, we will be like Balaam, the self-styled prophet of old, whose donkey could see the Angel of the Lord, though he could not. (See Numbers 22:21–35.)

When God's hand is upon you to break you, it is not according to your will, but His; not according to your thoughts, but His; and not according to your decision, but His. This is the immutable law of God that works in us: His specific purpose is to break our hard outer shell and thus release our spirits for free exercise.

Spiritual work is accomplished in God's coming out through our brokenness. This is the only way God has ordained.

We must undergo thorough training and strict discipline, because whatever is untouched by God in us will be left untouched in others as we minister. Hence, we cannot teach others lessons that we ourselves have not learned before God. The more thorough our training is before the Lord, the greater our usefulness to God will be in His work.

If we have covered things in ourselves, we cannot uncover them in others. The worker is first a patient; he must be healed before he can heal others. He cannot show what he has not seen, nor can he teach what he has not learned.

When the inward spirit and the outward man have not been divided (Heb. 4:12), our inward spirit will be clothed in whatever there is of our outward man that remains unbroken. Thus, the condition of the inward spirit becomes that of the outward man.

The secret of truly knowing another man is touching his spirit and sensing what clothes it. Let me repeat emphatically that this is the basic principle for knowing another man: sensing, or touching, his spirit.

The disciplinary measures of the Holy Spirit are God-given lessons by which, in one thing after another, we are broken bit by bit. Furthermore, it is only in those particular areas where we have been broken by the Lord that we can touch others.

This is an invariable spiritual fact! Our spirits are released only according to the degree of our brokenness. Wherever we desire to save ourselves and hold back certain areas from God, in those very areas we are spiritually useless. The degree of our service is determined by the degree of our discipline and brokenness. The more we have been dealt with by God, the keener our perception of other men. Thus, the more we learn, the more we can discern— and the more we have to give.

The absence of spiritual understanding among believers in our day is due to a lack of spiritual learning. Therefore, let us realize that the more we are dealt with by God, the more we will be equipped to supply others' needs. Make no mistake; other than by broadening the scope of our experiences, there is no way to enlarge the sphere of our service.

In our day, God commits Himself to the church. His power and His work are in the church. Just as in the Gospels we find all God's work given to the Son, so today God has entrusted all His works to the church and will not act apart from it.

The basic teaching of the Gospels is the presence of God in one Man, while that of the Epistles is the presence of God in the church.

The Gospel of grace and the Gospel of the kingdom should be joined together. In the Gospels, these two were never separated. It was only in later years that those who heard the Gospel of grace apparently knew little or nothing of the Gospel of the kingdom. Thus, the two, over time, became separated. But now the time is ripe for them to be reunited so that people may be thoroughly saved, forsaking everything and wholly consecrating themselves to the Lord.

Consecration is merely an expression of our willingness to be in the hands of God, and it can take place in just a few minutes. Though we are willing to offer ourselves completely to God, we are really just starting on the spiritual road—for after consecration there must be the discipline of the Holy Spirit. It takes consecration plus the discipline of the Holy Spirit to make us into vessels fit for the Master's use (2 Tim. 2:21).

We may be sure that all our outward circumstances are ordered by God. Nothing is accidental. How foolish are those who have murmurings in their mouths and rebellion in their hearts toward the very things the Holy Spirit has measured to them for their own good. Remember, whatever happens to us is measured by the hand of God for our supreme good.

Let us not forget that the greatest means of edification is not prayer, though that restores us; it is not reading the Word, though that refreshes us; it is not attending meetings and listening to messages, though this does comfort and encourage us. The greatest means of edification is the discipline of the Holy Spirit in our lives. Like nothing else, this will build us up in strength to be able to minister to others.

Strong-willed people are convinced that their feelings, ways, and judgments are always right. But Paul said in Philippians, "Do not trust your flesh." (See Philippians 3:3.) We must be led by God to such a place that we dare not trust our own judgment. The beginning of the destruction of the outward man is when you no longer dare to trust yourself.

Formerly, when the strength of my flesh had not yet been broken, the outward man and the inward man were not able to join hands; but now, after having been broken, the outward man waits meekly, in fear and trembling before God.

While God is breaking our hard outer shell, He is also refining us. Thus, we see His twofold dealings with us: breaking down the outward man, and dividing it from the spirit. The first is done through the discipline of the Holy Spirit, while the latter is done through the Spirit's revelation.

The day that a discipline from the Father accomplishes its purpose is the day you really see the truth and enter into its reality. The work of the Holy Spirit is intended to break you down in the flesh on the one hand and, on the other, to build you up in the spirit.

As it was with Paul, when the Lord enlightens, He delivers. Enlightenment is deliverance, and seeing is freedom. Such enlightenment, such self-abhorrence, such shame and humiliation, such repentance delivers us from the bondage of long years. Only in this way does our flesh cease to operate, and our outward shell is broken.

So often, when the Lord deals with us, we see only the hand of man. Sadly, for many saints, even after years of the Holy Spirit's work of discipline, no noticeable effect has been produced. Though the Lord has struck once and again, they remain ignorant of the meaning. Hence, discipline is plentiful in the lives of many, but recognizing the hand of the Lord and His purpose in that discipline is rare indeed.

There is one common feature that marks those who have been enlightened and disciplined: they become meek. Meekness is a sign of brokenness. All who are broken by God are characterized by meekness. Formerly, we could afford to be obstinate because we were like a house well-supported by many pillars. But as God removed the pillars, one after another, soon the house was bound to collapse. Then, after the outward supports were all demolished, the self had to fall.

Without meekness, believers are hardly ready for participating in the corporate life and expression of the body of Christ, because only those who are broken have a true sense of the body. Sadly, many Christians miss out on the supply that God has placed into the church because they refuse to be broken. The greatest advantage of brokenness is that it enables us to receive the supply of all the body.

There is something quite remarkable about one who is broken. If you are one who is indeed broken, you will find that in your giving you are also helped. Moreover, you are able to receive help from every spiritual contact you make. After a while, you begin to marvel that the body is supplying you as a member.

Twenty-Seven

A Balanced Christian Life

In reading the New Testament, you should see that everything in Christ is already yours. If you have not possessed anything, it is because you have not experienced the crisis of faith. To live in the victories of Canaan, one must pass through the crisis or the threshold of the Jordan. Without passing through the threshold of faith, you will never be able to traverse the way of faith, and your spiritual life will make little progress.

It is as you pass through a crisis of faith that God shows you His riches in Christ. And after passing through the crisis of faith, you will experience more and more of the grace that is in Christ.

May I remind you that the Devil is as stubborn today as were the Canaanites in their day. He will resist you at every step of your way. Unless you stand in the victory of Christ, you will see defeat.

Crossing the Jordan River but not encircling the city of Jericho is like entering the gate of faith without walking in the way of faith. Crossing the Jordan alone without next encircling Jericho will never cause the walls to fall. Entering the gate of faith without walking in the way of faith will not result in spiritual progress. Hence, each time we are given faith, it is our continuance in that faith that actually brings victory into our experience—thus causing the walls to fall.

After the victory of Jericho, the children of Israel suffered defeat at Ai. Such is our natural inclination. No sooner do we experience a wonderful victory in Christ than we again begin to trust in ourselves—and fail. This is typical of one who is just beginning to live in victory.

The path of righteousness is as the dawning light, which shines more and more unto that perfect day (Prov. 4:18).

God gives His Son to the world so that people may be saved by Him; He gives the Holy Spirit to believers so that they may have the power to overcome. The accomplishments outside of me, by the Son, are objective truths; the accomplishments in me, by the Holy Spirit, are subjective truths. Hence, the Holy Spirit works into us the reality of that which the Lord has accomplished outside of us.

Faith is like *"an anchor of the soul"* (Heb. 6:19), but an anchor becomes effective only when it is cast forth. Faith is not operative until it is cast forth in Christ.

Crucifixion is that which is already done in Christ; mortification—putting to death the deeds of the body—is that which is yet to be done by the Holy Spirit.

As I willingly obey God in each task He places before me, the Holy Spirit works out God's salvation for me to do them, one by one (Phil. 2:12–13).

As you learn to believe in the truth outside of you, the Holy Spirit makes it operative within you. As you believe in the finished work of Calvary, the Holy Spirit will make it real in you.

God wants us to notice the following about resurrection: on the objective side, there is already resurrection, because Christ has already arisen; but on the subjective side, there is still the need to experience the power of resurrection in our lives. And God wants us not only to know Him but also to know the power of Christ's resurrection (Phil. 3:10). However, this is an element that is regretfully missing from the lives of many Christians.

Faith is based on the finished work of Christ, while obedience is based on the current work of the Holy Spirit in our lives.

If your life is hidden in Christ (Col. 3:3), you cannot help but experience aspects of death, resurrection, and ascension in your spiritual life. Likewise, if you are not hidden in Him, you will not experience any of these.

What Christ has accomplished gives us position; what the Holy Spirit commands causes us to have experience. What Christ has accomplished is fact that must be received; what the Holy Spirit leads us into is principle that requires our obedience.

Whether or not a Christian lives to please the Lord depends on his having a good balance between the objective and the subjective. Some believers place more emphasis on the one, while many emphasize the other. But according to the principle of the Bible, the order is first the objective, then the subjective. First comes the fact of Christ; then follows the leading of the Holy Spirit. And the end result of this proper balance is bearing much fruit.

The Bible divides the matter of salvation into three periods. The first is the past, in which God saved us from the penalty of sin. The second is the present, in which God saves us from the power of sin in our daily lives. The third is the future, in which God will save us from the presence of sin in His kingdom, as we reign with Christ. And yet, a mature Christian is one who has had experiences in all three of these areas. (See 2 Timothy 1:9; Hebrews 7:25; 9:28, respectively.)

We should tell those who are not saved to believe so that they may be saved from the penalty of hell. We should remind those who are saved that there can be victory over the power of sin in their lives. And we should encourage both to seek after the glory of reigning in the kingdom to come—through an obedient walk with the Lord.

There are three aspects of our flesh that resist God the most: the wisdom of the flesh, the strength of the flesh, and the vainglory of the flesh. If these have not been crucified, we will not be able to do much work for the Lord.

The qualification for doing God's work does not lie in zeal, seminary study, or the love of souls; it rests on a person's being totally apprehended by God. He needs men and women who themselves have experienced the death of the Cross.

Today, what God is looking for is people who have no confidence in themselves. They are people who have no self-reliance, or self-will, and therefore can wholly trust in Him (Phil. 3:3).

God can only use people according to the measure that they are not trusting in themselves.

God will use only the might and power of the Holy Spirit to accomplish His work. And this might and power is manifested only through the foolish and the weak (1 Cor. 1:27–28; 15:42–43).

So much damage is done to God's work by those who volunteer. These are people who are not sent by Him. Yet they go without knowing that God does not approve of people who go to work for Him without being sent. He is not pleased with men's presumptuous actions, for the sin of presumption is the same as the sin of rebellion (Ps. 19:13; Deut. 1:43).

To do anything without being sent or ordered is like gold plating or like building a house on the sand. It may glitter for a while, and it may stand temporarily, but it will be destroyed at the judgment seat of Christ.

To preach the Cross without having the experience of the Cross and the spirit of the Cross, as well as the life of the Cross, is to preach the Cross without adhering to the principle of the Cross.

So many in the church today know only how to propagate knowledge and doctrine; they are not able to supply divine life.

The greatest problem of a spiritually poor man is that he does not easily recognize his poverty. One who has nothing at all will readily confess his nothingness; thus, God can easily be found by this man. But he who is spiritually poor has difficulty in meeting Him, because spiritual poverty is closely related to blindness. He who is spiritually poor is unable to see into spiritual things, because while he thinks he can see, in reality he is blind (1 Cor. 2:14).

An abundant life is a mature life. It is not a matter of merely having or not having; it is primarily a matter of what we have and how much of it we have. Abundance is when one is brought by God into a divine seeing of reality, thus entering into the realm of the spiritual in experience.

Strangely, when we receive enlightenment from God, we actually increase; and yet, we do not feel that way. From our point of view, we feel as if we have decreased, not increased.

What is experiencing the abundance of God like? Each time He gives more, we feel as if it is the very first time we have received anything. Although this seems strange, it is true.

What hinders a believer's spiritual progress most in his life and work is his flesh. Either he is unaware of God's calling on him to deny his entire flesh, or he has not overcome the strength of his flesh.

The highest expression of spiritual life is the denying of the flesh. Those who have not started out from Gilgal (the denying of the flesh) have never really commenced their spiritual journey. (See Joshua 5:2–9.)

Many people know only the battle between the spirit and the flesh; they do not perceive the spiritual conflict that rages between believers and evil spirits. This battle is joined by only mature believers.

Twenty-Eight

The Character of God's Workman

Suppose you encounter a person who is deceitful, sinful, and corrupted. As a Christian, what should your attitude be toward him? Before answering, consider this: remember the days before you received God's grace. Apart from God's grace, were you better than he is? Apart from God's grace, were you stronger than he is? Apart from God's grace, were you purer than he is? Apart from God's grace, were you holier than he is? When we look at ourselves apart from the grace we have received, we are no different. The only thing that makes us different is the grace we have already received from God.

What is having a mind to suffer? It speaks of my readiness before God to suffer; I am willing to go through trial, and I choose the path of hardship. It is up to the Lord whether or not to put suffering in my path; but whether or not it ever comes, on my part, I am always prepared for it.

The most effective way of serving the Lord is being willing to serve even to the point of death. The more you stand on this ground, the less the Enemy will have his way with you. Alas, how many people love their own selves! The failure of God's workmen can be plainly perceived right here: they love their lives too much.

Only with a measureless mind to suffer is there an unlimited scope of blessing.

Running a race is not a daily affair; training is. One needs to be trained to such an extent that his body is no longer rebellious, but responsive (1 Cor. 9:27). Then, he is truly a ready servant for the Lord.

People who are greatly used by God are people who not only are under His control, but also have self-control. If we do not have control over our earthly bodies, we will certainly fall when a special demand comes upon us.

What happens when people submit to the work of the Lord in reshaping their lives? This is what happens: the lazy become diligent, the talkative become quiet, the selfish become selfless, and the prideful become humble. Those fearful of suffering develop a mind to suffer, and the uncontrolled become disciplined. The weak, shaky, and vacillating become strong, steadfast, and immovable. And those who previously were ever busy in the ways of this world are caught up with the ways of the world to come.

God is unable to use people who think they know everything. They are not open to the tender and gentle leadings of the Spirit, because their fleshly selves have never been broken. They are also unable to detect that even before the hand of the Lord has moved, His eye has already moved (Ps. 32:8). How helpless are these know-it-alls!

Any individual who is seeking the Lord's will must leave out himself. Whoever does the Lord's will must put his self away.

The more people listen to you, the greater your responsibility becomes. Yet how great a responsibility it is when we speak wrongly and people listen! For this reason, we should learn to be careful both before the Lord and other people.

One characteristic of a man who truly knows God is this: he has no thought of forcing people either to listen to him or to follow him.

A know-it-all is a person who loves to control people. He delights in being opinionated and takes pleasure in giving orders. He knows what to do in each situation and circumstance and cannot tolerate differences. He tends to take things into his own hands and set himself up as the leader. He makes decisions for others and is always meddling in the affairs of other men—even in the smallest matters—because he likes to control everything. He is the busiest person in the world because he feels compelled to look after everything. In all matters—whether large or small—he has his own idea, his own opinion, and his own way. Hence, he is not able to walk the straight path of God.

How very different is the way in which Christians manage money from the way the world manages money! The world increases money by saving up, while a Christian increases money by giving out. To receive more, you must give more; the more you give, the more you will receive. Though we may look poor, we are not, and we make many rich. This is a spiritual principle that can be found throughout God's Word.

Twenty-Nine

Christ: The Sum of All Spiritual Things

Though there is no deliverance among those who know just a method, there is total deliverance for those who know the Lord.

Whatever is not Christ living in us is a dead work. Even every spiritual thing is dead outside of Christ.

Work is not the life of Christ, for life is effortless. Christ is life.

If Christ is not our life, we have to do the work; but if Christ has become our life, we do not need to struggle.

Aside from Christ there is no way, no truth, and no life, for He is the sum of all these spiritual things (John 14:6).

The resurrection of Lazarus is really not a tremendous phenomenon when compared with knowing the Lord Jesus as resurrection, which is a matter of great significance. Lots of people can believe the Lord Jesus as the life-giver, but to believe Him as life itself is quite another matter.

Christ is both the Lord of resurrection and the resurrection itself.

Many Christians regard good feelings as life. Other Christians reckon noble thoughts as life. But those who have learned and are experienced in spiritual matters will inform us that life is deeper than feelings or thoughts. Only Christ is life—and this life is deeper than emotions and more profound than thoughts.

That which has encountered death and survived is called resurrection; it is that which has outlived death. And there has been only One who has gone into death and come out of it.

A life that bears the marks of death, and yet is alive, is resurrection life. The things we bear in our lives that do not carry the imprint of death cannot, therefore, be designated as things pertaining to resurrection.

Things that issue out of ourselves are unable to rise again once they have gone through the Cross, for they are lost in death.

Whatever is of Adam cannot live after going into death, but the life of our Lord is more than able to pass through death and come out again.

People often serve God with their natural lives instead of His resurrection life. Many have a zeal, but few have a resurrection zeal.

Whatever enters the grave and remains there is a dead thing, but whatever comes out on the other side of the grave, bearing the marks of the Cross, is resurrection.

We need to humbly ask the Lord to be merciful to us, so that the natural in us would be gradually decreased while His resurrected life would be increasingly manifested.

Christ has not given us a righteousness; He is our righteousness. Christ has not granted us a thing called power to make us sanctified and holy; He is our holiness. Christ has not offered us a redemption; He is our redemption. Christ has not opened up a new way for us; Christ is the way. Christ has not given us a new truth; He is the truth. Christ has not conferred on us a thing called life; He is our life. Christ is the sum of all spiritual things!

If we erroneously differentiate between what the Lord Jesus gives and what He is, between the gift and the Giver, our spiritual life and growth will be greatly inhibited. For the gift and the Giver are one and the same.

Whenever we really touch life, we immediately obtain satisfaction.

In spiritual work, each time we labor we should feel full. If we hunger, something is wrong, for only the labors we accomplish outside of God's will cause us to become hungry. Therefore, in order to be satisfied, we must be doing His will.

In spiritual experience, it is not the leisurely who can eat; on the contrary, those who eat more are those who are busily occupied. If we are walking in the will of God, the busier we are, the more we eat. Furthermore, we will not be exhausted or feel empty through much toil.

Oftentimes we do what we think is good and spiritual without knowing the Lord's mind; consequently, we feel empty afterwards. Only after having been obedient to the Lord's will do we have that sense of satisfaction or fullness.

Real light is not mere knowledge; it is none other than the Lord Himself.

If we have really seen light, we will fall to the ground (Acts 22:6–7). For light not only enlightens, it also slays.

Those who are self-righteous and self-conceited have never known light; all they possess are doctrines and knowledge. Had they seen the true light, they would have confessed, "O Lord, what do I know? I know absolutely nothing!" For the greater the revelation, the deeper the blindness; the stronger the light, the severer the stroke. When Paul saw the light, he was struck to the ground, and for three days he could see nothing with his eyes.

What is God's purpose? That Christ would have first place or preeminence in every area of our lives (Col. 1:18).

Many people put *their* hope in the Lord Jesus Christ; but the Word says that *He* is our hope (1 Tim. 1:1).

A colossal problem exists among God's children today. The Christianity they know is quite fragmentary. You obtain a little grace, I receive a little gift, and he speaks a little in tongues. This man experiences some change in his conduct; that man possesses some measure of His love. This one has some patience; that one some humility. This is what is commonly known as Christianity.

But is this Christianity? It is not! For Christianity is not a little of something. Furthermore, Christianity is not a lot. Christianity is none other than Christ Himself!

God has not granted us humility and patience and gentleness. He grants the entire Christ to us. It is Christ living in us and through us who becomes our humility, patience, and gentleness. It is Christ, the living Lord. This is truly Christianity!

So many of God's children live their lives in defeat. This is due to the fact that what they get before God is a gift—instead of Christ. Though they have received many fragmentary items from God, they have not obtained the Christ of God. They possess objects and things, but not the Person.

Before we were saved, worldly objects and affairs usurped the place of Christ in our lives. Then, after we were saved, spiritual objects and affairs began to occupy what should have been Christ's place. But God's purpose is to lead us to see the place that Christ should have in our lives—that "Christ is our world," and this is His proper place.

Do you know the Lord Jesus as your Savior, or your salvation? Your Redeemer, or your redemption? Your Liberator, or your liberation? Your Sanctifier, or your sanctification? Your Justifier, or your justification? To know Him as your "er" is primary knowledge; to know Him as your "tion" is a further and deeper knowledge.

What is the law of life? It is none other than Christ becoming our whole life.

Man's concept regarding his needs is always a matter of lack or want; consequently, he usually asks God for a particular supply. How sad that we are usually more concerned with looking around us to find the supply, rather than having our eyes looking up to heaven to our Standard, who is the supply.

Many of God's people are seeking something—such as love, patience, or humility—that seems to be everywhere else except in their own lives. They look for it as a thing existing on earth, instead of looking to Christ alone. Therein lies the basic difference between real and faulty Christianity.

When we were first saved, we were shown that what we needed was Christ, not works; we were saved through Christ, and not by our own efforts. However, in the way that many matters were eliminated from our lives when we first believed, there are also many more matters that must be done away with as we continue on in sanctification. The difference is that what was destroyed when we first got saved were our sins, while what is being demolished now are so-called spiritual things. At first, it was our pride, jealously, vainglory, ill temper, and other sins that were done away with; today it is our patience, humility, and self-styled holiness that must also be destroyed in order that we may understand that Christ is our life and our all.

Christianity is Christ! And the life of a Christian is also Christ!

There are two kinds of life that exist among the children of God. One kind is a life that is full of things, while the other kind is a life that is full of Christ.

Why do you at times respond with an amen? Because you are touched by life. A brother, as he is praying, has touched your life; therefore, you spontaneously say amen. But some other person's prayer, though it may sound earnest and appealing, produces a chilling effect within you. You long for him to cease praying, for his prayer is no different from his personality. He has something; only that something is his flesh, which has the touch of death. And it reproduces death, not only in that person, but in others as well. There is absolutely no spiritual worth in it, for it is done by man.

If we are really led forward by God, we will surely discover that He hates the labor and efforts that emanate from our flesh as much as He hates our sins.

God rejects our works just as He repudiates our sins. Actually, there is only one thing He accepts, and that is His Son Jesus Christ.

Thirty

The Finest of the Wheat
(Volume One)

What is truly the church? It is that part which is taken out of Christ, and not what is naturally made with dust. The church is the new man, built by God, with Christ as the material. Whatever is natural is outside of the church, for only what comes out of Christ is the church. Human ability, concept, power—all those things that are of man—are outside of the church. That which comes from Christ alone is the church.

There are two steps needed and required for the church to be what it should be. One is the distribution of Christ; the other is the destruction of individualism. The distribution of Christ happens at the time of regeneration; the destruction of individualism occurs after our salvation in sanctification. As the Lord works in our lives daily, we eventually reach a point where we realize that, in order to please God, we can do nothing on the basis of our own individual selves. Then, from this point forward, we do all things according to the principle of the mutual edification of the body of Christ. Only when the church has reached this state has she attained God's purpose for her.

Christ's blood is for dealing with our sins, and the water flowing from His side is for giving His life to us.

Spiritually speaking, only what comes out of Christ can go back to Christ. What does not come out of Him can never return to Him. That is to say, only what has come from heaven will someday return to heaven.

Only what comes out of Christ is in the church and has spiritual usefulness. God never has used and never will use anything from the old creation to build the new creation. He will never use what comes out of fallen man to build what is of Him. In other words, He will never use the fleshly to produce the spiritual. The issue is totally a matter of source.

There are many times in the life of a Christian when it is extremely difficult to resist in warfare as an individual, but when the church arises, Satan is easily defeated. Only in the church are the blessings unlimited and abundant. And only those who know and experience the strength of the church as a corporate group keep on growing and find the riches of the Head as their own riches.

We should use authority in the church to serve our fellow believers, not to control them. Authority is not for control, but for supply.

Christianity is the life within you speaking to every situation in your life. It is only when the Spirit of God moves within you that you can tell what is really right and pleasing to God. You should only do what the life within you allows you to do. Hence, the issue is not a matter of right and wrong; rather, it is a matter of whether the life within you approves or disapproves.

Before God, we should learn to surpass the standard of right and wrong. Please understand, I do not wish to suggest that the standard of right and wrong is not good. It serves its purpose, and that is good. But for the Christian, that principle of living is not good enough, because true Christian living rises above the principle of right and wrong. If we live by the life of God, we will see that what He requires of us is higher than the demands of the law.

Spiritual things are discerned only in the heavenly realm, and earthly things become clear only with heavenly insight. Therefore, heaven is the only worthwhile viewing point.

In spiritual warfare, there are two essentials that must be maintained: position and insight. Without position, we cannot see the Enemy; and without spiritual insight, we cannot recognize the Enemy's schemes. Without these two essentials, we can neither engage the Enemy nor put up a good fight against him.

Thirty-One

The Finest of the Wheat
(Volume Two)

In order for any person to be greatly used by the Lord, he must be brought to the place where he sees that God has His need. Then he will understand that our lives on earth should not be centered only on our own human requirements, but on God's requirements. To win souls back to the Lord is for the benefit of men; to be used by the Lord to deal with Satan is for the advantage of God. To win souls solves man's need; dealing with Satan satisfies God's need.

God wishes to obtain a man who can rule over the earth. But if all our works are confined to preaching the Gospel and winning souls, Satan has not been dealt a fatal blow, and man has not attained God's highest purpose for him.

The first man (Adam) failed to achieve God's purpose. He not only failed to regain the earth, but, by falling into sin, he was even taken captive by Satan. Hence, from that point he was not only unable to rule but was now under the rule and power of Satan. Moreover, he became Satan's food. But what God could not obtain in the first man, He achieved in the Second Man (Christ). And all those who are wholly in Christ have regained through the victory of the Second Man what was forfeited through the defeat of the first man.

What God had long waited for and needed was a man who could satisfy His desire and defeat Satan. Of all the men in this whole world, there has been only one Man who has truly sought after God. There has been only one Man who could say, *"The prince of this world...hath nothing in me"* (John 14:30 KJV). And the Lord Jesus Christ is that Man!

Creation discloses God's eternal purpose. It tells us what God is really after. God wants to have a people who will do His work so that He might rule over the earth through them.

A mature Christian is one who has received the benefit of redemption and arrived at God's purpose of creation. Without redemption there can be no relationship with God; but having been redeemed, we need to consecrate ourselves to God so that His original purpose in creating man might be achieved.

The mission of the church is to testify to the salvation of Christ and the victory of Christ. Therefore, the task before us is threefold: to learn how to exercise spiritual authority, to overturn the authority of the Devil, and to proclaim the love and authority of God. Thus will men be benefited, Satan will suffer loss, and God's heart's desire will be satisfied.

The meaning of the Sabbath does not lie in the buying of fewer things or the walking of fewer miles; rather, it declares that God is now at rest because He has possessed what He originally conceived and looked for. It implies that the one thing that God hoped for and sought has now been obtained—and because of this there is rest.

Christianity is neither the elimination of weakness nor the power of the Lord alone. It is the Lord's power manifested in man's weakness (2 Cor. 12:9). This is what Christianity is all about.

The entire Bible, in both the Old Testament and the New Testament, emphasizes three attributes of God: holiness, righteousness, and glory. God's holiness speaks of His nature, His righteousness speaks of His way, and His glory speaks of God Himself. In other words, God's nature is holy, His working is righteous, and He Himself is beyond description.

The shedding of the Lord's blood at Calvary meant the pouring out of all the natural life. He poured out His soul even unto death (Matt. 26:38). Consequently, the shedding of blood denotes the removal of all that belongs to the natural, or soul, life.

All that pertains to our natural life is contrary to God and cannot please Him. But what is part of the natural life? It is all that comes to us by birth and all that will vanish with death. All of this belongs to the natural life.

There are just two positions maintained by those who truly love the Lord: death, in which all that stems from the old creation is forsaken; and resurrection, through which we learn to minister to God with the Christ who has been worked out in us—by standing before Him, waiting on Him, and listening to His orders.

Thirty-Two

The Glory of His Life

Forgiveness is like taking a bath; righteousness is like wearing a robe.

May God open our eyes to see that we do not rely on our conduct or work, either before we are saved or after we are saved.

It is in learning righteousness that we learn to deal with all unrighteousness.

If we notice unrighteousness in other people, we should pray for them. One problem, though, is this: when we are righteous, we tend to be fretful and angry at seeing the unrighteousness of others.

Where does God commence His work in us? His first step is not to put the life of Christ in us. Instead, He puts us in Christ. Before He can put Christ in us, He needs to put us in Christ.

God does not make the foolish wise; He makes Christ the wisdom of the foolish. This is real salvation!

The Word of God never says that we can be holy, nor that Christ gives us the strength to be holy; but it does say that Christ Himself becomes our holiness. And the same is true for all the virtues. None of the virtues of a Christian are his own work; they are the outflow of Christ within him. Formerly, I relied on myself to be a Christian, and I was wrong. Now I allow Christ to live His life through me.

All believers have the life of Christ in them, but only a few are willing to go deeper and experience the life of Jesus manifested in their mortal flesh. The difference is immense.

Everyone may be delivered from the law, but not everyone is delivered. The problem is not on God's side, but on man's side; for not all men desire such deliverance, nor are they willing to pay the price.

Let it be remembered that each time there is spiritual progress in your life, it is invariably preceded by a dissatisfaction with your current condition. All spiritual progress starts with dissatisfaction.

The starting point for each victory is at that moment in which you begin to hate your defeat. Those who wish to be delivered need to be pressed beyond their measure of tolerance. Why? Because only such people are open to the deliverance of the Lord.

Why did the apostle call for us to be dead to the law in order to be freed from it (Rom. 7:4)? Because it is only when we hate living in the defeat of our sin, to the extent that we are willing to die rather than have our sinful life extended any longer, that we are delivered from the bondage of it.

The one and only deliverance is when you see yourself as being utterly hopeless.

God crucified us in Christ because He saw we were—and still are—helpless and hopeless. The fact that God has crucified us with Christ reveals His estimation of us. (See Galatians 2:20.)

As long as we live, the law has its demand on us; but if we die, the influence of the law on us ceases, and it demands no more. Therefore, apart from death, there is no way to be liberated from the law.

There are two spiritual experiences in the world that are amazing. One is seeing what God has planned for you; namely, God has sentenced you to death. The other is seeing all that God has done for you in Christ. These two spiritual facts are exceedingly great.

The secret of victory is never looking at ourselves outside of Christ. This is what is meant by abiding in Him (John 15:1–11).

People always deem the making of a resolution to be the best thing in life, not knowing that it is like a reed that cannot withstand the Enemy nor has any use before God.

Whenever you take your existence outside of Christ, you immediately fall. You should see yourself only in Christ; for in Him you are in possession of two facts, namely, having died and having been resurrected.

Unfortunately, man will always add to himself the fruit of the Tree of the Knowledge of Good and Evil instead of the fruit of the Tree of Life.

Resurrection rids us of the imprisonment of death. The power of the Holy Spirit is the power of resurrection. Whoever encounters the Holy Spirit encounters resurrection.

We are told what kind of power it is that God works in those who believe. It is the same power that God worked in Christ when He raised Him from the dead (Eph. 1:18–20).

We must ask God to give us a spirit of wisdom and revelation so that we may experience the power of Christ's resurrection, for the church should enjoy the resurrection power of God on earth.

Thirty-Three

The Salvation of the Soul

The salvation of the soul is quite different from what we commonly know as the salvation of the spirit. The spirit is saved on the basis of faith; once we believe, it is settled forever. The soul is saved on the basis of following; it is a lifelong matter, a course to be finished. The spirit is saved because Christ lays down His life for me; the soul is saved because I deny myself and follow the Lord.

The soul is the seat of our natural desires; it enables us to feel and enjoy. The desires of this soul life demand to be satisfied. Yet if people seek satisfaction for these things in this age, they will lose satisfaction in the age to come. Whoever enjoys his soul in this age has already gained the pleasures to be derived from his body; therefore, he will lose of these pleasures in the age to come. (See Matthew 16:25–26.)

The Lord does not train us to be ascetics; He only wants to persuade us not to be *captivated* by the things of this world. If we begin to indulge in these things to excess, we have gone astray. Be it clothing, food, or shelter, we should not seek our own enjoyment.

God places the choice of heaven or hell before the sinner. And in like manner, He places before each Christian the choice of the world or His kingdom.

He who overcomes sin enters heaven; this is forgiveness! He who overcomes the world enters the kingdom; this is reward.

Receiving salvation of spirit is the beginning of our faith, and receiving salvation of soul is the end of our faith (1 Pet. 1:9).

God demonstrates through Christ that only He Himself can live up to the standard He has established. Hence, God not only appointed Christ to die at Calvary for us, but also makes Him to be our life today.

God's salvation causes the Lord Jesus to live in us as well as to die at Calvary for us. He not only pays all of our sin debt, but also lives in us so that we will never have to run into debt again. If you have received only half of this salvation, you will undoubtedly be miserable and fail to experience the full joy of salvation.

Actually, God asks you to do one thing only: give yourself over to Him from this point forward. It can be summed up in one word: surrender.

The most intimate of all our environments is our emotional being. If you are able to conquer your emotions, you will be victorious over other environments, too. Whoever cannot overcome environment has not overcome emotion. He who conquers environment has first conquered his own feelings.

Thirty-Four

The Spirit of the Gospel

The love of God is something the world has never known. That Christ died to save mankind is also beyond the reasoning of the world.

He who loves himself has used up all his feelings on himself. We should learn to reserve our feelings for the Gospel.

The most basic problem stifling Christian work lies neither in the scope of grace, which is unlimited, nor in the power of the Cross, for *"it is finished"* (John 19:30). Rather, it lies in those of us who block the flow of the Gospel.

Faith is something obtained; it is what God gives to man. It is part of the grace of God.

The Holy Spirit comes to apply the finished work of Christ to us, so that it becomes our subjective experience. In other words, the work of the Holy Spirit is to translate the objective into the subjective, to turn doctrine into life experience.

He who is wise wins souls (Prov. 11:30). It takes wisdom to win souls.

There is none in the world who is for the Lord, and only the Lord is for men. This is indeed grace. This is the Gospel!

What idol worshipers seek is blessing. They do not seek God, but that which is God's. What God looks for is us, not what is ours.

It is God who tore the veil (Mark 15:38); thus, the way to God is opened only by God.

What is the purpose of presenting the body to God? In the Old Testament, under the law, the bodies of the sacrifices were slain and laid on the altar. Today, God calls us to present our living bodies to Him as a sacrifice. This denotes our living as though we are dead. And as long as we live on the earth, we are to present ourselves as sacrifices, dead to ourselves and alive to God. This is not only acceptable to God, but due to the mercies we have received, it is also our spiritual service (Rom. 12:1–2).

Since God has already secured a place within us, He now asks us to present our outward lives to Him. Since it is by Him that we have life, should we be surprised that He expects us to live it for Him?

All objective truths are in Christ, and all that is in Christ has already been accomplished. All subjective truths are in the Holy Spirit, and all that is in the Holy Spirit waits to be fulfilled by the Holy Spirit in us—if we submit to Him.

Redemption is that which was accomplished nearly two thousand years ago. Salvation is that which is fulfilled on the day we enter into the reality of experiencing what the Lord has accomplished through belief. It continues on in our day every time we believe.

Believing does not transform God's Word into fact. Rather, believing is based on the fact of God's Word.

The Isaac in your life must literally be offered up to God before you will see the provision (the ram) God has given (Gen. 22:13).

Obedience without faith lacks power, but faith without obedience remains mere theory. No one who has ever been used by God has failed to go to the Cross and cross over the threshold of obedience.

A person who is spiritually poor before God may turn the pages of the Bible and read them, but he fails to touch what God's Word is saying. He has no contact with God and does not find life. This is why he is spiritually poor.

Christians should rise a little earlier to read the Bible. For when the sun is hot, the manna has vanished (Exod. 16:21).

Some Christians have never fed on the Word of God in the early morning hours. No wonder they are so weak!

To those who truly believe in God, wondrous works are quite common. Only those who are far away from God deem them extraordinary.

Wonders do not require our effort. Wonders spontaneously happen when the power of God is manifested in our lives.

The longer we are Christians, the simpler our lives should become. Those whose lives grow more complicated are being sidetracked. The closer we come to God, the simpler our lives become.

Thirty-Five

Song of Songs

We already possess every benefit of the resurrection life of Christ. However, what issues from Adam hinders the enjoyment and expression of Christ. Therefore, the important question is not how much we possess of Christ, but rather, how much we have lost of Adam.

The first step in the Christian experience is knowing the Lord on the cross. The second step in advancing spiritual experience is possessing Christ as an indwelling reality.

The more one abides in the light, the more one recognizes darkness. The more perfect one is, the more conscious one becomes of imperfections. Likewise, the more mature a believer becomes, the more he will feel his immaturity.

One is always reluctant to leave the present ground of attainment to reach out to achieve a higher spiritual plateau.

All of our spiritual experiences and exercises are the outcome of being drawn by Christ. No deliverance from any state of complacency is possible except by first beholding a new revelation of, and entreaty by, the Lord Jesus Christ Himself.

Thirty-Six

The Mystery of Creation

Through the death of the Lord Jesus, we are delivered from all that belongs to Adam—the natural. By His resurrection we can enter into all that belongs to Christ—the supernatural.

The redemptive plan of God is not meant to repair or mend the old; it is to re-create us. He discards the old.

The experience of resurrection (the third day's work) comes after that of the co-death (the second day's work), which is after that of regeneration (the first day's work).

Regeneration gives us life; resurrection gives us life more abundantly. Were a believer to stop at regeneration, he would not be able to overcome sin. Were he to remain at the stage of co-death, he would have no power to practice righteousness. Therefore, we need to advance in our experiences of Christ until we manifest His resurrection power in our lives. This is the attainment of the full provision God has made for us.

God wants us to be the body for His Son—which is to say, He wants us to experience all that the Head has accomplished for us, His body. Thus we will be delivered from the old creation and become the new creation ordained by God.

God never asks for our ability; He asks only for our inability. He does not require power from us, but looks for our weakness. His demand of us is not to be full, but empty. Furthermore, He does not accept our resistance, but instead waits for our submission (1 Cor. 1:27–29).

Fruit-bearing is not the result of keeping oneself intact; it is the result of having oneself broken, made humble and weak, and casting oneself helplessly and hopelessly upon God.

Unless we hate our soul life, with its natural ability, wisdom, and virtue, we will not be able to bear much fruit. It is only after we cast aside the natural strength that comes from our flesh and accept the hand of God with a broken heart that we are able to bear much fruit.

Only when we are weak in ourselves, empty and fully yielding as the clay to the potter's hand, can Christ begin to live out His life in us. And then, His power begins to manifest itself through us.

If we are truly raised with Christ and joined to His resurrection life, we will naturally bear fruit on earth, and our spiritual life will ascend to heaven.

Formerly—in death and resurrection—we merely overcame the flesh, sin, and the world; now—in ascension—we are to experience the conflict with and the victory over all the powers, dominions, rulers, and authority of darkness.

New believers are normally vague about spiritual warfare and lack clear insight as to the schemes, assaults, temptations, and counterfeits of the Devil. It is only upon their entering into the experience of their ascended position with Christ in heaven that they immediately begin to sense the reality of the powers of darkness around them and begin to battle with them, overcoming them *"by the blood of the Lamb and by the word of their testimony"* (Rev. 12:11).

It is due to their maintaining a ruling position that ascended believers frequently have the experience of bruising Satan under their feet (Rom. 16:20).

To be saved merely requires a person to believe in the Lord Jesus, but to reign with Christ demands faithfulness, suffering, and victory. The Cross is the way to the crown; suffering is the condition for glory.

Only those who are willing, for the Lord's sake, to suffer loss in this world, will gain in the age to come.

The millennial dominion of which the Bible speaks does not begin in the future. Actually, we can reign in life now (Rom. 5:17), even though the full realization and physical manifestation of it is in the future. We show our worthiness to be kings, ruling with Him in His day, by how well we have learned to conquer evil spirits and stop their works in our day.

One of the strange phenomena of sinful man is that he assumes that his own deeds are satisfying to God and that the life of the Lord Jesus is in no way superior to his own!

The Christ who only lives drives men away from God, but the Christ who is also torn and who dies brings all who would follow Him into the Holiest of All.

The very purpose of resurrection is to bear fruit. This is the natural result of resurrection. (See Numbers 17:8.)

Without death, there is no resurrection; without resurrection, there is no fruit. Bearing fruit unto God can come only through dying and being raised with the Lord Jesus.

Since ascension is based on death and resurrection, it signifies the fact that Christ has overcome all that belongs to the satanic kingdom. Therefore, the ascension of Christ concludes His earthly work.

According to human nature, no one likes grace. Men would rather reckon themselves good and able—that they have no sin and that they may be saved by their good works. God must therefore cause men to truly know themselves before they will confess how utterly helpless they really are.

It took more than fifteen hundred years under the dispensation of law to prove to the world that there is no one who can keep God's law and do good (Ps. 14:3).

Thirty-Seven

The Latent Power of the Soul

In our day, the work of the Devil is to stir up man's soul and to release the latent power within it as a deception for spiritual power.

One difference between Christianity and other religions is that all our miracles are performed through the Holy Spirit; whereas other belief systems allow Satan to make use of man's soul force to manifest his strength.

Satan's intention is to carry through with what he began in the Garden of Eden. Although he initiated the work of attempting to control man's soul at that time, he did not fully succeed. Why? Because after the Fall, man's whole being, including the power in his soul, came under the control of man's own flesh. In our day, Satan is preparing to complete his previously unfinished work. Once he has fully deceived mankind, he intends to release all the latent powers of men. This will be accomplished in that day when men will have wholly given themselves over to him and worship him.

All the works of the Holy Spirit are done through man's spirit, while the works of the Enemy are all done through man's soul.

What is the highest attainment in Christianity? That of complete union with God and total loss of self.

There are many defects in the church today. Many believers are interested in nothing more than expounding the Scriptures. Their knowledge is excellent, yet they neither care for, nor seek, the growth of the spiritual life that is within them.

Most people look to the circumstances around them and are influenced by them. But if we are mature in our spiritual life and are yielding to the Holy Spirit, through Him we will have the ability to be victorious over the forces that are directing those circumstances.

Whatever is done in the spirit, the soul can duplicate. And whatever is copied by the soul serves no other purpose than to counterfeit the spirit.

God works with His own strength; consequently, we must ask Him to bind our soul life.

The work of the Holy Spirit is special; as a result, He never tolerates the meddling of man's hand in His work.

The Lord Jesus was perfect, yet His whole life was one that depended helplessly, and hopelessly, on God (John 5:19). If He has shown us the way, should we not follow?

Thirty-Eight

The Body of Christ: A Reality

The most distinctive expression of life is its consciousness. If there is no consciousness, there is probably no life.

All who know the life of the body of Christ will have a consciousness of the body of Christ.

What is special in those who have God's life is that when they tell a lie outwardly, they feel bad inwardly—not because they know doctrinally that lying is wrong, but because they feel uncomfortable inwardly if they do lie. This is what being a Christian really signifies.

A Christian should not act according to what he hears from people without; rather, he should be motivated by what he is told from within.

If the love of God is present in a person, the love of believers is there. If God's love is absent, brotherly love is absent, also.

One who has "seen" the body of Christ and who thus possesses a consciousness of the body feels unbearable inside when he does anything to cause division or separation of God's children.

If you have genuinely experienced the body of Christ, you will be conscious of something wrong whenever you show your individualism.

Since the body is one, it makes no difference whether the work is done by you or by others, for the body recognizes the functions of all its members.

Fellowship is not an external exercise in social intercourse; it is a spontaneous demand of the body.

If you really see the body of Christ, you are conscious of the loveliness of God's children, the error of division, the need for fellowship, and the responsibility you have as a member of the body of Christ. All these facets of awareness occur because of body consciousness.

If our eyes have been opened by the Lord to recognize the body, we will also recognize authority. One who knows the body is able to discern—even when only a few people are gathered together—who among them has authority.

If we have genuinely been dealt with by the Lord—if our flesh has had such dealings as to have had the backbone of the natural life broken—we can do no less than submit ourselves to the authority that God has placed in the body of Christ.

If we wish to live out the life of the body of Christ, we must cover our own heads. That is to say, we must not have a personal opinion, an egotistic will, or a selfish thought.

If you maintain a good relationship with the Head, you will have a good relationship with the body. You will not be like Absalom, who separated the people from their head, David (2 Sam. 15:1–14).

The antithesis of the body is the individual. To enter into the reality of the body, one must be delivered from individualism.

Whether God puts me first or last does not matter; both are equally acceptable to me. Only those who do not see, know, and experience the body of Christ entertain feelings of pride and jealousy.

The defeat of even one member of the body touches the whole church.

We should not spend too much time in examining, analyzing, and researching a doctrine. Why? Because doctrines are like reeds that will not support you when encountering real life difficulties. Only God can carry you through these, not doctrine.

When the eyes of a seeing member truly see, the entire body is able to see. In other words, that member of the body of Christ who has insight into spiritual things becomes the eyes of the body, so as to supply sight to the body.

One who has no life brings death to a meeting, even if that one only says amen. But one who has life is able to supply that life to the meeting, even if that one only says amen.

To one who lives for the Lord and is delivered from self, the most important part of his external life is that he might manifest his function in the church.

The life and power of Christ find their richest manifestation through the body. For this reason, Satan takes great pains to try to bring about the "disintegration" of the body of Christ.

Satan uses our corrupted flesh, our stubborn selves, and the world that we covet to carry out his plan of destruction. If these elements are permitted to remain in our lives, we give Satan the tools he needs to engage in his work of disintegration.

We have only one need: to turn inwardly to God and let Him cleanse and purify us by the filtering of the Cross and the Holy Spirit, so that we may be cleansed from all the impurities that Satan has mixed into us.

The vessel that God seeks is the body, not the individual.

Whichever part of the body is disobedient, that part experiences paralysis.

All who are full of life have been obedient to authority.

Thirty-Nine

Spiritual Reality or Obsession

Only what is in the Holy Spirit is real spiritually, because all spiritual things are nurtured by the Spirit. Once something is outside the Spirit, it turns into letters, forms, and doctrine, which are dead. Spiritual things are real, living, and full of life only when they are in the Holy Spirit.

Just as no one can ever perceive spiritual things with his eyes fixed on the material world, similarly, no one can ever think through to the spiritual realm with his brain.

A wonderful thing happens after you touch reality. However, whenever you encounter someone who has not touched or entered into reality, you immediately sense it.

There is something that the Bible calls "truth." It is nothing other than reality. In relating to this truth—this reality—one is delivered from doctrines, letters, human thoughts, and human ways.

We must worship God in spirit and truth (John 4:24). What is of the spirit is real, and what is not of the spirit is not real. When the spirit contacts God, there is truth, and when it does not, there is no truth.

When a person contacts the reality of the Holy Spirit, he touches life. If what he contacts is merely doctrine, he will not receive life.

Unless there is revelation, men cannot know who the Lord is, for it is only by revelation that a person can discern Christ. We need to remember that Christ is not known by our outward senses —such as optical, auditory, and tactile. Knowing Christ is the work of the Holy Spirit. Without the Holy Spirit, no one can perceive the reality of Christ.

Many Christians are discouraged because their faith does not seem to work. They complain that they have heard the Word for many years, but all of what they know is still ineffective. Why? Because touching Christ with the hand of the flesh will never be effective.

Whether faith is operative or not depends on whether it has touched reality.

We should understand that Christ in the flesh is touchable, visible, and audible to the hands, eyes, and ears of the flesh. But Christ in the Holy Spirit can only be reached when we are in the Holy Spirit.

We must learn to live before God according to what we truly are. Thus, we should ask Him to cause us to contact that which is spiritually real.

The power of discerning comes out of what one has already seen. If we have touched the spiritual reality of a certain matter, no one can ever deceive us in that particular matter. Similarly, he who has touched the spiritual reality of a certain matter will naturally detect a counterfeit as soon as it appears, while others will be deceived.

The self-deceived are prone to be deceived by others. If we do not see something in ourselves, how can we expect to see it in others?

Spiritual discernment comes only after we ourselves have contacted reality. One who has not touched reality deceives two persons: himself, and the one who is spiritually in the same category. Yet he cannot deceive those who know what is of the Holy Spirit— those who are living in and by the Holy Spirit.

Sin is easily recognized, but the "good" that proceeds from self is not so easily detected.

When we encounter reality, the result is life; all other encounters result in death.

Preaching without reality is empty and useless, because it cannot supply the body of Christ. It is only after the dying of Jesus has been worked into us that the life of Jesus will begin to appear in others.

If we have touched reality, we will effortlessly supply it to other people, for it is the reality of God we have personally touched that becomes the supply for the church.

Revelation is the foundation of all spiritual progress. But while revelation is the foundation, discipline is the construction.

Of all the works of the Holy Spirit, two are of prime importance, namely, the revelation of the Spirit and the discipline of the Spirit. The first enables us to know and see a spiritual reality, while the second guides us into the experience of that spiritual reality.

Day after day, the Holy Spirit seeks opportunities to guide us into spiritual reality. If we refuse to accept these disciplines, we deny Him the opportunity to lead us into that reality. All too frequently, when difficulty arises, people choose the easy way out, or they simply go around it. Thus the difficulty may be avoided, but the opportunity for the Holy Spirit to guide them into spiritual reality is lost. The Spirit of the Lord is not given place to impart life and reality. Hence, by evading these disciplines of the Spirit, many Christians do not enter into spiritual reality. The result is that the body, as a whole, remains sick and weak.

One who deceives other people is a liar, and one who deceives himself is obsessed. The term *obsession* means self-deception. Since obsession is a matter of the heart, many who are proud are obsessed.

175

A liar is one who on the outside has a hard shell but is withered up within. The more confident he is outwardly, the more empty he becomes inwardly. However, an obsessed, or self-deceived, person is confident on both the outside and the inside, and is also hard on both the outside and the inside.

What a Christian ought to be most afraid of is having sin in his life and not seeing that sin. Having sin is a matter of defilement, but not seeing sin is a matter of darkness. Defilement is dangerous enough, but adding darkness to defilement is extremely dangerous.

For every obsession, or self-deception, there is a cause. One cause is that people love darkness rather than light (John 3:19). Darkness is a main reason for obsession.

A person who knows the light of God is able, as soon as he meets you, to discern your true character and to point out your faults. It is not that he is trying to pick on you; rather, his discernment is entirely due to the sharpness of his inward eye.

Knowing our faults through doctrine or teaching is superficial; perceiving our faults in the light of God's Spirit is the only thorough path.

Forty

Aids to "Revelation"

Salvation is that which is given freely; it cannot be earned (Rom. 6:23). Reward, though, is a different matter. It is not something freely received; it must be obtained through good works. It is given according to the works of each saint (1 Cor. 3:8, 14).

According to the Bible, the goal that is set before us is twofold: when we are yet sinners, the goal is salvation; after we are saved and become believers, the goal is reward. Salvation is provided for sinners; reward is provided for believers.

After a person is saved, he is placed by God on the racecourse of life so that he may run. And if he wins, he will be rewarded. But if he loses, there is no reward. Yet he cannot lose eternal life, even though he might not win the race (1 Cor. 3:14–15). Salvation was the gift that qualified him to run the race with the hope that, by winning, a reward would be added over and above the gift.

Salvation is most easy to come by, for the Lord Jesus has already accomplished everything for us. Reward is somewhat harder to obtain, because it depends on the works that we, by our initiative, accomplish through Christ.

As a sinner cannot be saved by good works (Eph. 2:8–9), so a saint cannot be rewarded by only believing (Matt. 16:27). Salvation is based on faith; reward is based on works. Without faith there is no salvation, and without works there is no reward, though both are based on faith.

What is salvation? It is not perishing but having eternal life (John 3:16). Yet this does not decide our positions in glory, since these are in fact determined by rewards. (See, for example, Matthew 10:40–42.) What is reward? Reward is to reign with Christ in the millennial kingdom (Rev. 20:4–6). Every believer has eternal life, but not every believer will be rewarded with the right to reign with Christ.

Salvation shows the grace of God because He does not recompense us according to our sins, but rather, saves all who believe in the Lord Jesus (2 Tim. 1:9). Reward, on the other hand, expresses the righteousness of God, because He recompenses the saints according to their good works. Saving sinners is His act of grace; rewarding saints is His act of righteousness. Whoever serves Him faithfully will receive a reward.

Revelation, the last book in the Bible, touches very little on the matter of the salvation of believers, but rather, strongly focuses on the question of their reward.

One event to come before the final days are upon us is the rapture of the overcoming believers. All who have the Cross worked deeply into their lives will be raptured. But those who are saved and yet mix with the world and compromise with sins will remain on the earth and pass through the Great Tribulation. Only the victorious and watchful saints will be ready to be received when He comes.

Forty-One

God's Work

Though we cannot do God's work, since it is absolutely and wholly His, we can and are invited to be coworkers through His Spirit. This is God's purpose in saving us, that we might be co-laborers with Him.

Who is a coworker of God? One who does what God has appointed him to do in His eternal purpose, and that alone does he do.

How will I know if I am working together with God? This is easily answered. Are you satisfied with what you are doing? If you do not satisfy God's heart, you will not be satisfied yourself.

At heaven's entrance stands the Cross. All that gets in is Christ, and nothing of us (the flesh) ever gains entrance. In other words, whatever in us is the unmixed life of Christ is all that God will ever recognize or have anything to do with.

God's appointed task for the church is *"the perfecting of the saints"* (Eph. 4:12 KJV). The members of the body are for the body, and the gifts to the church, which are given to the members of the body, are for the body. Both are for the purpose of building up the body.

The goal of the body is to attain the unity of faith (Eph. 4:13). How sad that as the years go by, we see more and more divisions and sects among those who are called to unity!

Body life is not something that we can study. It is a most natural and spontaneous thing. It is the expression of the life of Christ as our Head, living through us, His body.

The eternal purpose of God can never be understood or grasped by the mind. It has to come by revelation. All spiritual work comes out of revelation, and apart from revelation there is no spiritual work.

If what we have laid hold of is merely doctrine or teaching, it will leave us after a while. But if what we have found is light, or revelation, it is life. We will not be able to get away from it.

If we have truly seen anything by revelation, what we have seen we have seen; it will never leave us. And we will always see.

Every spiritual thing we possess comes by revelation, and it comes in this succession: (1) light, (2) revelation, (3) life—that is, God's life, and (4) His riches (all that He is).

To be a coworker with God, we must have revelation; otherwise, we are not working toward His eternal purpose. Furthermore, if we have not seen the eternal purpose of God, we will never see the particulars of the work God has for us to do.

Why must there be revelation? Because this light of God kills all that is not of Him—all that is out of man.

If our work were only to save people, man would appear to play quite an important role in its achievement. But if our work has as its purpose to build up the body, man must be completely ruled out; for the body is Christ—it is all for Christ—therefore, nothing of man can enter.

What really edifies and helps the body the most is not the gifts. Nor is it the utterances of those who have the gifts God has given. What really edifies and helps the body the most is the life that exists within those we contact who deeply know the Cross—those who know the Cross within and bear it daily.

A church that tries to build itself up by the gifts will always end up being a carnal church, since the gifts are for the building up of the church in the nursery stage. Why is this? Because the gifts do not alter the inner man. Only the Cross does this!

Unfortunately, in the church today the focus of attention is either on what a person says or what a person does. Little emphasis is put on what a person is.

The help you have to offer others will always be in proportion to the price that you yourself have paid. The higher the price, the more you have to offer; the lower the price, the less you have to offer.

There are two kinds of gifts that God has given to the church: one is the gift of things—like miracles, healings, tongues, etc.; the other is the gift of people to minister—such as prophets, teachers, pastors, and evangelists. The former do not give us more of Christ within; they simply substantiate God's Word. The latter have to do with the ministry of God's Word; they give us more of Christ's life within by building up the inner spiritual life of the church.

There is a gift of prophecy that may come through by way of tongues or supernatural utterances under the outpoured spirit, but this is only God's temporary way when there are none of spiritual depth, history, and maturity whom He can use as intelligent vessels for the upbuilding of the church.

Suffering is the basis of ministry. And for the life of Christ to be manifested in us, there must be the marks of the Cross on us. It is only when death has been worked into us that His life can flow out of us and into others.

What is the reason for such appalling shallowness and poverty in ministry these days? It is that ministers have experienced so little themselves. How few and rare are those who are truly rich spiritually.

You cannot possibly take anything of the old creation into the tabernacle (the ministry of the Lord)—not your old mind, your old brilliancy, your old cleverness, your old eloquence, or your old strength. Only what has passed through death is useful to God. You must first lay your dead rod before Him and allow it to blossom before you can be of use to God in service (Num. 17:1–8).

Resurrection has only one meaning: that a person has been through death and has received new life.

Working for God and serving God are two different things. And only service to God is acceptable to Him.

He who wishes to enter the ministry has only to lay his dead rod before the Lord for Him to put His life into it (Num. 17:1–8). Then he must wait for it to blossom. When there is no life left in it to extinguish—when it is dead—it will blossom.

What is the iniquity of the sanctuary life (Num. 18:1)? It is the bringing into the service of the Lord something other than resurrection.

Trusting in anything of the old creation or bringing anything of the old creation into the work of the Lord constitutes the iniquity of the sanctuary.

One can only serve God with that which is of God. Nothing but what comes forth from God can be used in His service.

Forty-Two

God's Plan and the Overcomers

The reason we do not have power is that we are not weak enough. The power of Christ is perfected only in weakness (2 Cor. 12:9). It is not Christ making me powerful that is the secret to the victorious life; it is Christ being power unto my weakness.

As long as we still have life in ourselves, we are not able to accept the victory of Christ. Though Christ may be dwelling in us, He has not been given the place of rule in us. We must come to the end of any life in ourselves, for man's extremity is God's opportunity.

Unless a person comes to see the utter weakness of self, that person will never accept the Cross and completely surrender all the managing power he has over to the Lord.

As long as the children of Israel maintained the proper relationship with the tabernacle, they were victorious, and no other nation could overcome them. But when problems existed with this relationship, they were taken into captivity. Even though, at times, they had powerful kings and great wisdom, all that mattered was whether or not they had offended the ark of the tabernacle. Furthermore, the same is true for us as God's people today. Unless we give Christ the highest place, we will not be able to overcome. It is only when we give Him preeminence that *"we are more than conquerors through Him"* (Rom. 8:37).

Only those who let Christ have preeminence in all things can enter the Holiest of All.

The increase of our knowledge of the Holy Scriptures is not spiritual growth. Only the increase of Christ in us is spiritual growth.

Revelation is what God gives us—an objective giving. Light is what God makes us see in revelation—a subjective seeing. Spiritual vision includes both light and revelation.

To have power, one needs to allow Christ to sit on the throne of his life. As Christ increases in that person, he will have power.

God often deals with us as He dealt with the children of Israel in the wilderness, by depriving us of earthly supplies of food and clothing so that we might recognize the abundance of God.

There are many who work for God but are not serving Him, because working for God and serving Him are vastly different. How few there are who are serving Him!

The measure of success in our work is determined by the measure of Christ in our work.

We are the bread in the Lord's hands. After people have eaten, they thank the One who gives the bread, not the bread itself.

The centrality of God is Christ. He is the center of God's purpose and plan. He is the center of all things. Therefore, our central message ought always to be Christ.

God leaves the church on earth not only to preach the Gospel to save sinners, but also to demonstrate the victory of Christ on the cross. And He permits Satan to remain on earth for the sake of creating opportunities for us to prove the victory of His Son.

There are three principal points to be found in the New Testament: (1) the Cross, (2) the church, and (3) the kingdom. The Cross of Christ accomplished redemption and won the victory. The church is responsible for maintaining and expressing the victory of the Cross on earth. And the kingdom will reveal the execution of that authority and power.

Just as formerly we were all an extension of Adam through the old nature, so now we are to be an extension of Jesus Christ through the new nature.

Through Scripture, we see that the flesh is overcome by walking after the Holy Spirit (Gal. 5:17–18); the world is overcome by loving the Father (1 John 2:15); and Satan is overcome by believing in Christ (1 John 3:8–9).

The reason for the church to remain on earth is to maintain and demonstrate the victory of the Cross of Christ by binding Satan in every place.

The life principle of a disciple of Christ should be this: as death is worked into me, life is worked into others (2 Cor. 4:12).

Today, the church is unable to cross over to the mainland for victory because there is a lack of priests standing in the bottom of the river Jordan (death). (See Joshua 3:14–17.)

God's overcomers must, on the one hand, be faithful in denying their own selves, the world, and Satan; on the other hand, they must know how to exercise the authority of Christ.

Ordinary or petitioning prayer is praying from earth to heaven. Commanding or authoritative prayer is praying from heaven to earth.

Satan wants us to believe that we are weak. We should confirm this to him with rejoicing. For when we are weak, Christ is strong through us. His strength is made perfect through our weakness (2 Cor. 12:9).

Forty-Three

The Spirit of Wisdom and Revelation

In eternity past, God had a desire; but in eternity to come, He will have a possession.

The Gospel of grace and the Gospel of the kingdom are not two Gospels, but one Gospel looked at from two different angles. Perceived from man's perspective, it is the Gospel of grace; perceived from God's perspective, it is the Gospel of the kingdom.

A person has made no spiritual progress in his life if what he saw of the treasure of God's goodness to him on the day of his new birth and what he sees now are exactly the same.

Whether we are strong or weak depends on whether we see more or less. Those who see become strong, and those who do not see become weak. The key, therefore, is seeing, for it is only in seeing that we can come into experience.

How exceedingly great is God's power? To the extent that His power worked in Christ, to that extent will His power work in the church. If the power manifested in us is less than the power that was manifested in Christ, we should acknowledge there are many things that we have not seen and understood.

What God longs for us to understand is that we do not need to obtain more of Him. What we need is to comprehend and experience the fullness of how glorious, rich, and great is that which we have already obtained from Him.

Today the problem is not, "Will God work?" but "Do we see what God has already worked?" The difference between the two is vast. Once we understand this, all that remains is to take hold of His finished work.

Many expect to be delivered in some future day from the weakness and failure they have in their lives. How unfortunate! If only they would let God open their eyes. It is revelation that unveils for us what the Lord has already done, not what He is going to do.

The Bible tells us that we do not need greater power, but rather, a *"spirit of wisdom and revelation"* (Eph. 1:17) so that we might realize the *"exceeding greatness of His power"* (v. 19) that is already in us.

It is the spirit of revelation that makes us see, and the spirit of wisdom that gives us an understanding of what we see. In other words, while it is revelation that gives us vision, it is wisdom that brings this vision into focus.

In knowing the Lord, what we see and hear and touch is not enough, for He is far greater than that. Only those who are open to and have received revelation from God know Him as the Son of God.

There is a knowing of the Lord Jesus that comes from human instruction, but as far as the Lord is concerned, such knowledge is accounted as null and void. Only knowledge given from the Father concerning the Lord Jesus is a true knowledge of Him. Why? Because no man can come to the Father but by the Son (John 14:6), and no man can know the Son apart from having revelation of Him from the Father (John 6:44).

A great problem exists in the church today. It stems from those whose knowledge of Christ comes only from instruction. Furthermore, as this knowledge of Him is a product of man's own cleverness and wisdom, it is not a rock that can stand firm. How do we know this? Because it easily falls down when it is pushed.

What is mere doctrine? It is that which is taught by flesh and blood without any light from God or direct communication with

Him. That which is mere doctrine is void of revelation and is spiritually worthless.

It is not the doctrine of Christ that saves; rather, it is the Christ whom God has revealed that saves.

If the church lacks revelation from God, then all she has will become tradition. She is then bound to fail.

Much of the weakness, failure, and barrenness that exist in the church today can be attributed to the emphasis that is placed on doctrine as opposed to revelation. If a person hears only doctrine and receives no light, that which has been obtained is not the living Christ.

Because we, as believers, have been given rights so that we might taste beforehand the power of His future kingdom, each day of our lives we can move into the experience of that kingdom to come. How sad there are so few who take advantage of it!

If we ever expect to experience the fullness of what God has given us in Christ, we must ask Him to deliver us from our own thoughts and cleverness; from the limitations of our earthly concept of time that is bound by past, present, and future; and from all the dead knowledge we have that is outside of the Holy Spirit. When this occurs, one begins to see not only all that God has done for us in Christ, but also that it is now, and it is living.

Only as we allow the light of God to come into our lives and shine upon us are we able to see our true condition and all the darkness that is within us. As this occurs, and we come face to face with the glory, holiness, and judgment of the Lord, we cannot help but deeply abhor ourselves.

It is only inasmuch as we have been united with Him in the likeness of His death that we are united with Him in the likeness of His resurrection (Rom. 6:5).

Christ is the source of life. His life is the uncreated life. He is the life (John 11:25).

Because resurrection life is the life that has endured death and has risen up again, any church or individual knowing what resurrection is will withstand any trial or tribulation.

What God sets forth in the Bible are, in this order, the kingdom of God, the house of God, and the family of God. How very tragic it is that today so many people know nothing about any of these! What is the kingdom of heaven? It is the spiritual realm of God on earth; the kingdom of heaven demonstrates the sovereignty and rule of God. What is the house of God? It is what demonstrates God's character, and how glorious, loving, and righteous it is. What is the family of God? It is what manifests the love of God and the relationship between Him and us.

When we become the children of God, we are given certain rights or authorities (John 1:12). To be saved means not only that we have entered the church, but also that we have rights to enter the kingdom. One problem today though is this: many magnify the church beyond measure, as though once entering the church one gets everything. They forget about entering the kingdom of God.

The current pitiable condition of the church is actually all of our own making. We make self the center of everything and take the Lord merely as a helper to us. As a result, there is little of the reality of the kingdom manifest in our lives. How do we know this? Because those who grasp hold of even a little of the kingdom have lives that are transformed. They are not the same as they were before.

Salvation is nothing less than to be put under the yoke of the Holy Spirit.

Being saved is not just for personal enjoyment and is certainly not for the opportunity of doing whatever we wish to do. On the contrary, it is to bring the Lord's people—with every thought they think, every word they speak, and every deed they do—into subjection to the sovereignty of God. This is the experience of the kingdom.

The Gospel of grace deals principally with blessing, while the Gospel of the kingdom is especially directed against the demonic oppression of Satan.

189

If Christians view the saving of souls as their greatest responsibility on earth, they have failed to accomplish the highest will of God. They ought to realize that there exists an even greater responsibility than that of the saving of souls. Christians are to bring this age to an end by bringing in the kingdom of God.

Wherever God's children rise up to bear a "living testimony" to the kingdom of the heavens, God will rise up to show Himself strong on their behalf (2 Chron. 16:9). Only a faithful testimony enables the Lord to rise up and work.

Forty-Four

The Spirit of Judgment

Whereas the work of creation did not ensure that sin would never enter again, God's final act of judgment will guarantee that sin will be forever gone.

The error within each of us is not corrected by argument, but by judgment. Under judgment, sin is withered within us.

When sin comes in, God uses judgment to solve it. Anything less than judgment cannot resolve the problem.

The Cross not only solves the problem of sin, but also overcomes the power of sin, Satan, and his world.

There is a vast difference between teaching and revelation. Teaching shows someone what he must do after hearing; whereas revelation is seeing the thing as having already been done. When light comes in, the problem is resolved.

If there are things weighing upon you, you should ask God to enlighten you with His strong light; then what bothers you can be removed. You should allow yourself to be judged by His light today, so that you will not be judged by it later at the judgment seat.

Only God's children have the privilege of enjoying God's continual judgment. What a privilege that *"we are chastened by the Lord, that we may not be condemned with the world"* (1 Cor. 11:32). That we are judged is really grace and enjoyment.

One day God will totally destroy the power of sin, but today He wishes to have it first destroyed in His children.

Today God's children do not lack power; they lack enlighten-ment. When God enlightens you and shows you the sinfulness of your sin, that sin leaves you.

If we reject light, we must incur chastening. When we accept the judgment of light in a certain matter, we are spared; whereas those who reject light must be disciplined.

Many of God's children, even after repeated discipline, either fail to see the light or reject it. This is the reason that numerous chastenings fall short of their intended purpose. People are not willing to see the crookedness and unrighteousness in their lives.

When people want to draw close to God, they are chastened, and when they are far away from Him, they enjoy the world's pros-perity. Why is this? Because the closer we wish to come to God, the more discipline we must receive (Heb. 12:6).

We should be sorry when God allows us to go free without dis-cipline. Why? Because there is nothing worse for a believer than being given up on by God. To be chastened is to be as a son; not to be chastened is to be as an illegitimate child (Heb. 12:8). If someone is never chastened, I would be fearful for him. For chastening serves as God's warning.

Judgment is a fundamental enlightening. Once he has been struck down with judgment, a person will immediately see with the least amount of light. This enables one to properly discern and judge not only his own life, but also the lives of others, and to learn from them. As this occurs, spiritual advance will undoubtedly be quite noticeable. Thus, according to the light of His judgment, one is brought to life (Ps. 119:156).

In the outer court, the light is natural. In the Holy Place, there is artificial or man-made light. But in the Holiest of All, there is neither natural light nor artificial light; there is only the light of the glory of God. Therefore, only in the Holiest of All can one see according to God's light.

The church is now the judgment of God. In other words, she is to exercise the judgment of God in her affairs. However, while the

Protestants are afraid to use the word *judgment,* the Catholics exploit it. Yet we ourselves should look for spiritual reality.

According to the Bible, judgment is in the church, but the church cannot judge until light shines on her. Hence, she is not to be authoritative, but mournful. She must judge herself first; she herself must repent if she is to be capable and worthy of properly exercising the discipline of God on others.

Love is God's positive strength, patience is God's waiting strength, and anger is God's destroying strength.

It is more difficult to reprove than to comfort.

To reprove and to scold are quite different. A weak person may scold, but he cannot reprove. Only those who have received discipline from the Holy Spirit have the ability to reprove.

God uses judgment to maintain His glory and to eradicate sin and everything else that is contrary to Him.

Believers are heavenly citizens whose task is to touch the world with the Gospel. As such, while on earth, we must indeed be law-abiding, but we should not perceive ourselves as citizens having public rights in the world. Instead, we should be very hesitant to lay claim to earthly rights, since the claims of our heavenly citizenship take priority over them.

It is impossible to preserve the characteristics of a Christian by assuming public office. Why? Because the world requires the ministering of justice from a public servant; whereas the ministry of love and grace is what God requires of a Christian.

The Bible has teachings for us on how to be masters and servants. But we should take note: it has no teaching on how to be public officials.

Obedience is a matter of action; whereas submission is one of attitude. God alone deserves unlimited obedience; all who exceed the measure of authority that God has given are not worthy of obedience. Therefore, the obedience a Christian renders to his country, or to any authority other than God, is a submissive one and is not absolute.

Some believers are set on improving the world, but unfortunately, they end up being defiled by it instead. Why is this? Because we are called only to rescue people out of the world, not to change the world itself. The world already stands condemned before God.

Sinners do not care how they are saved, as long as they are saved. But since God is righteous, He must maintain His righteous nature. Therefore, the path He uses to save us cannot fall short of His glory and righteousness.

God's love leads us to the Cross, but the Cross leads us to righteousness. God's love caused Him to give us His Son; God's righteousness enables us to approach God through His Son. Before the Cross, it is a matter of God's love; after the Cross, it is a matter of God's righteousness.

That the righteousness of the Lord Jesus saves us is not taught in the New Testament. What the Bible does say is that the righteousness of God saves us. The righteousness of the Lord Jesus belongs to Him alone, and it gives Him a place before God. However, the Lord Jesus Himself *is* our robe of righteousness. We can approach God only because we are in Christ, not because we are righteous.

It is the blood of Christ that deals with my sins, and the Cross that deals with me as a sinner. There is no Cross in the former and no blood in the latter.

In the Bible, there are two kinds of light spoken of: one is holiness, and the other is the Gospel. If we walk in the light of the Gospel, God will reveal the light of His holiness to us from behind the veil. This is walking in the light of fellowship (1 John 1:7).

The problem of sin is not an external one, but an internal one. In the beginning of our Christian walk, we tend to think that though our deeds are sinful, our hearts are good. But as we come into a deeper knowledge of the Lord, we begin to see that though our deeds may be good, our hearts are sinful.

The two most important things for a believer to become aware of after he is born again are these: what he has gained in regeneration and how much is left of his natural endowment.

Although the Bible never teaches us to crucify ourselves for the sake of sin, it does tell us to bear the Cross for the sake of self. This is because the way in which the Lord deals with self is different from the way in which He deals with our sins.

A believer can overcome sin completely in a matter of a second, but he needs to deny self all of his life. Overcoming sin is an accomplished fact; overcoming self is a lifelong, daily affair.

The blood of Christ deals with sin; the Holy Spirit through the Cross deals with self.

What is pitiable is that so many Christian workers do not present God's full salvation to the sinner. Thus, what is believed and received is only half of complete salvation. If a person believes and receives the full salvation of God at the moment of regeneration, he will experience in his Christian life fewer defeats in fighting against sin and more victories over his battle with self. Unfortunately, however, such believers are rare.

The flesh makes self the center of all things, while the spirit centers all life on Christ. Such is the battle that rages in all believers until victory is gained over self.

God's purpose is not to reform the flesh, but to destroy its vital center. In giving His life to man at the time of regeneration, God intends for us to use His life to destroy the self of the flesh.

To be carnal is to be under the control of the flesh, and to be spiritual is to be under the control of God's Spirit.

Man fails to obtain the full salvation of God, which is victory over sin and self, not because he does not know it is available, but because he himself does not determine to have it.

All who attempt to overcome sin by their will are wretched Christians. Why? Because any victory obtained in this manner does not originate with the Lord. Furthermore, since it is not a change of nature, it is only temporary.

When God gives us new life, He also gives us *"the law of the Spirit of life"* (Rom. 8:2). This law allows for a believer to effortlessly do good if he is following after the nature of the new life that he has received.

A bird would say it is very easy to fly but very difficult to swim. A Christian should be able to say it is very easy to overcome but very hard to sin. Amen!

Faith is composed of two basic principles: (1) to cease from man's own work and (2) to wait for God to work.

As our faith at the time of regeneration was given to us by God, so our faith for daily living must also be given by Him. Hence, all faith is given by God, and we must always be dependent on Him for the supply of it.

God does not give us faith so that we might fulfill our own desires, for our proper place is death. According to God's will, a believer lives on earth for the Lord's will and glory alone. Though God desires to use us as His vessels, this calls for us to die to self.

As soon as God grants faith, the believer instantly exhibits the work of faith, which is rest without worrying. Whatever is humanly manufactured is not faith and therefore does not give rest.

There are two reasons for a believer's lack of spiritual growth: the first is not knowing one's self; the other is not knowing the riches of the Lord.

The first step in the operations of the Holy Spirit upon us is to create in us a longing that causes us to be dissatisfied with our current situation or life. Why is this? Because the Holy Spirit must start with the work of emptying before He can move on to the work of filling.

For the purpose of emptying us, the Holy Spirit allows us to meet with difficulties that we cannot overcome by self. This teaches us to rely on Him. You see, God must hollow us out before He can fill us.

God so orders our environment that He might lead us into a deeper knowledge of Himself, as well as a deeper knowledge of ourselves and our emptiness. He even lets us fail at times, so that we may know our emptiness and uselessness.

While it is we who are responsible for submitting to the work of God's Spirit for our being emptied, the Holy Spirit is responsible for our filling.

In God's work, He looks for men to work with Him. God gives you wealth in order that you may supply the need of His work. If you fail in this regard, He will be forced to raise up others.

As Adam was not made for Eve, but Eve for Adam, so the one great purpose of a believer on earth is to live for Christ.

Forty-Five

The Testimony of God

The testimony of God is God speaking for Himself. If He fails to speak, there is no testimony. Hence, to testify for God requires of man that he touch God Himself so as to be able to speak the words that God wishes him to say. Man should speak only after God is known, seen, and revealed to him.

A testimony may become a doctrine, but a doctrine may never become a testimony. Why? Because testimony is a matter of touching the Lord.

Resurrection is the one and only condition for the service of God today.

God's chastening of His own people is for the purpose of vindicating Himself. He must defend His holiness. If His people are unable to maintain a proper testimony, it means that God must come forth to defend it.

When God chastens us, He, in effect, vindicates Himself. The more we submit ourselves under God's disciplinary hand, the more He is vindicated, and therefore the quicker the discipline will pass.

One problem among believers is that we are usually more concerned with whether or not we have left the world, instead of being concerned with how much of the world still remains in us.

Make no mistake; the deepest, sharpest, and most subtle of the Devil's devices is to attack the person of Christ.

Who Jesus is—this is the foundation of the testimony. All false teachings and destructive doctrines assault this central theme either directly or indirectly: they attack the person of Christ.

Today, the testimony of Jesus Christ is deposited in a vessel that is called the church—the body of Christ. It is deposited in the following fashion: first, this testimony is the sum of all the revealed truth; and second, this testimony is the power of the truth as incorporated in the vessel.

As of the moment we are saved, God sees us as perfect and complete in Christ (Col. 1:28). However, it now becomes the work of the Holy Spirit to impart Christ's perfection into our experience. And through our faith and obedience to the Spirit's leading, His task is accomplished. In this way, God's seeing and our experience become united in reality.

We must see that the Lord Jesus not only died "for us," but also died "as us."

It is only on resurrection ground that judgment is over, and on this ground alone there is found no more condemnation.

In the Old Testament, all the grace of God flowed from the ark; likewise, during the new covenant period, it is all given to us through Christ.

Perhaps some will ask why we do not see God's judgment in the church, especially when so many are substituting God's will with fleshly means. This might be due to the fact that the time has not yet come to judge the situation. Or, it could be that the ark (God's presence) has already departed from the midst (Ps. 78:60–61). However, in either case, we should not be tempted to mock the Lord because of His patience and forbearance.

The most important element in spiritual work is knowing that everything must be done according to the pattern shown on the mount (Heb. 8:5)—in other words, according to the counsel of God. In building the tabernacle, nothing was left to man's own personal discretion. In like manner, God has His foreordained plan as to the work of the building of His church. And any substitution or variation, though accomplished with the best of intentions, will be rejected.

The glory of a servant of Christ does not lie in His ingenuity in doing God's work, but rather, in his careful execution of what he understands to be the will of God. To know the Lord's counsel and to execute it accordingly is to the glory of a faithful servant of Christ.

God has not given His servants any ground for personal opinion-making.

The greatest blessing to a servant of Christ is to arrive at the mountain of God's direction, knowing the work that is appointed to him and being acquainted with the foreordained pattern of that work.

There are two kinds of sin before God: the sin of rebellion—not doing what one has been told; and the sin of presumption—doing what one has not been ordered to do (Ps. 19:13).

Rebellion is failing to do what God has charged you to do. Presumption is doing what God has not commanded at all.

What should matter to a servant of Christ is not only knowing what God wants Him to do, but also knowing the time He wants it to be done and using the means He has provided for it to be accomplished.

Concerning the Lord's work, there are probably more volunteers than those who have been chosen by Him. There are many who can say, "I come," but cannot say, "I am sent." Many say, *"Here am I; send me"* (Isa. 6:8 KJV), but few are willing to wait for the word *"Go"* (v. 9). Because of this, a great deal of so-called divine work is full of death.

All of the service offered to God can be traced to either of two sources: one proceeds from God; the other proceeds from man.

While one is desired by God, the other is what man thinks God may desire.

Those who know the Lord only superficially assume they can do anything not prohibited in the Bible. But those who know Him more intimately understand that they would be committing a sin of presumption if they attempted to do what God has not commanded to be done, even though the Scriptures have not forbidden it.

Whatever comes out of the natural life cannot please God, regardless of how pure the motive, how good the aim, or how appealing the result. If it fails to issue out of His will, it will not gain His approval.

Frequently, God's people are mistaken by thinking that He requires only service from us and leaves the way of service to our discretion. How sad!

The Lord desires His people to obey His commands more than to help in His work. The Lord does not need any man to uphold His glory, but He is looking for people who will uphold a proper testimony before man.

Unless our wisdom is judged and our thoughts are delivered to death, we cannot perform divine work.

After having been dealt with by Him and having learned obedience and fellowship, we then have the privilege of being a vessel fit for His use. But first we must receive His dealings.

God places two considerations before men. First, He presents eternal life to sinners; second, He presents the kingdom to those who already have eternal life.

For a Christian, having eternal life is already a settled matter, but having the kingdom depends on how well one runs the race to gain the prize (Phil. 3:14).

The writer of Hebrews likened what lies before us to running in a race and even mentioned two things that can hinder our progress:

"sin" and *"every weight"* (Heb. 12:1). Sin hinders our spiritual progress the most. It disqualifies people from running the race. Sin is trespassing the rules, and he who trespasses the rules is not allowed to run the race. He is ordered to the sidelines. Not laying aside every weight, though it will not keep us from running, will certainly hinder us from running fast.

He who has lost the privilege of running in the race loses the prize of entering the kingdom and reigning with Christ.

Why do we run the race *"with patience"* (Heb. 12:1 KJV)? Because the reward is not given at the start, nor in the middle, but only at the very end of the course.

Jesus is said to be *"the author and finisher of our faith"* (Heb. 12:2). Thus, since our faith originates and concludes in Him, we must look to the Lord alone. Then His holiness, His victory, and His righteousness will continually be manifested in our lives.

Whenever God allows a cross to fall on us, He has a particular reason. Each cross has its spiritual mission; that is to say, it is sent to accomplish something special in our lives. If, in this matter, we endure according to God's will, our natural lives will be further dealt with, and we will have a greater capacity for being filled with the resurrection life of the Son.

So many Christians only sail with the wind. It makes me wonder whether they are on the way that is appointed by the Lord.

To love the world requires no effort; to follow the world demands no strength. It is only when one is walking faithfully with God that he will feel the blowing of an adverse wind.

Forty-Six

Spiritual Knowledge

Christians should have two kinds of knowledge: one of the Scriptures and one of the power of God (Matt. 22:29).

Generally speaking, there are two classes of people among those who sincerely seek after the Lord. One knows the Bible but knows little of God's power; the other knows God's power but knows little of the Bible.

At Christ's birth, those who sought Him earnestly (the Magi) had little knowledge of the Scriptures; whereas those having great knowledge of the Scriptures (the scribes and chief priests) did not seek Him. By this we can see that having scriptural knowledge does not necessarily mean one knows God.

One principle of Scripture is certain: if you wish to know God, you must learn to have transactions with Him; and if you refuse to accept these dealings from God, you will never make any substantial spiritual progress.

Many believers pay little attention to the Bible. How sad that many, in their entire lives, do not even master one book! But sadder still is the fact that many never know God in a real way. We should all have repeated dealings with God and pray until we get His answer. Why? Because we learn our lessons through these repeated transactions and, by them, come to a true knowledge of God.

The difference between sermonizing and testifying is that sermonizing cannot help others as much as testifying does. As you testify, you are describing the actual situation—as though you are holding out the very thing you are talking about. Though you may not speak well, you cannot speak wrong, because you are depicting something that is real to you, an actual scene that is both visible and touchable.

If you learn the ways of God accurately, you can ascertain whether or not God will answer certain prayers. Then, when you pray with people, you will know whose prayer will be answered and whose will not. This does not mean that you have become a prophet; it simply indicates a discernment, on your part, of the spiritual condition of the persons praying. By this you are able to learn the results of their prayers.

Each and every time we seek God's will, our self must be dealt with by Him. If we do not lay our self aside and forsake everything, He will not reveal His will to us in the matter.

The error with people today lies in their mistaking the knowledge of the Bible to be spiritual knowledge, and not understanding that true spiritual knowledge is learned from God. If anyone desires to learn from God, he has to deal with Him, as well as be dealt with by Him.

There has never been a Christian who ever made progress in his spiritual life without first knowing himself.

An essential part of the Christian's spiritual life is to judge himself, reckoning his flesh to be undependable and useless. Only after this has been done can he wholly trust in God by walking in the Spirit and not in the flesh.

Only those enlightened by God know how to judge their own flesh. And only those who judge their own flesh are able to be used by God.

Those who do not know themselves cannot be filled with the Holy Spirit, since in their hearts they are neither hungry nor thirsty.

If we really want to examine ourselves, we should first ask ourselves whether we are trustworthy. Why? Because according to

God, our self is so corrupted that He deems it to be no good. And if this is true, how can we then employ it for the purpose of self-examination?

Whenever we turn to look at ourselves, we are immobilized and cannot advance; but if we look at the light of God, we will unconsciously move ahead.

The way to victory lies not in analyzing ourselves incessantly, but in looking to Jesus; not in recalling an evil thought, but in remembering the good thought; not in getting rid of what is ours, but in letting Christ so fill us that we forget all that is ours. The moment we recall ourselves, we cease to move ahead.

Paul learned that it is only when the light of the Lord shines that one is able to discern what is right and wrong.

When God's light shines on us, not only does our evil look bad, but even our good seems to look bad.

Only after one has been enlightened by God will he fully sense the sinfulness of sin. We who work for God should not use our arguments to convince people of their sin; instead, we should ask the Holy Spirit to convict them. The light of God alone can cause people to see their real condition as God sees it.

Only as we are enlightened by His light do we immediately recognize the total depravity of ourselves.

A shallow Christian may at times know a particular fault when he is under God's special and occasional illumination, but a deep Christian is continually under God's enlightenment and truly knows himself, not in part, but in whole (1 Cor. 13:12).

When God's light comes, not only is our good manifested as being no good, but our bad side—that which we usually acknowledge as such—becomes exceedingly ugly.

Self-knowledge obtained by self-analysis merely represents what you think of yourself. A knowledge of self received through God's light reveals what God thinks of you.

A Christian is a light (Matt. 5:14). And as he lives in God's light, he is much feared by others, for in seeing him they feel condemned.

When you draw near to a person who lives close to God, you feel His presence. The person does not make you feel how gentle and humble he is; he makes you sense God.

The closer one lives to God, the more he knows his own weakness. He who receives more of God's light invariably sees more of his own corruption.

George Whitefield once said, "I am forced to confess that even my repentance needs to be repented of; even my tears need to be washed in the precious blood of my Redeemer. Our best works are but the most refined sins."

The depth of our consciousness of sin is determined by the degree of God's light we receive. Many of the things we thought were not sinful at the commencement of our Christian life, we find are in fact sinful as we grow in grace. What was deemed to be right in the past is now understood to be wrong because we have received more light from God.

The light of God we receive for work today is the very light God will use to judge us at the judgment seat of Christ. What God's light has condemned now as not being in accordance with His will, His light will condemn in the future; what God's light has approved of now will be approved of in the future. Therefore, we should ask for His light to examine us now, so that we can please God and be rewarded at the judgment seat of Christ.

A great number of believers desire to know God's will. They even ask Him for it, yet they do not receive any insight as to what His will is. This is for no other reason than that there is a wicked way in their hearts, and since they lack self-knowledge, they do not see it. If they ask God to enlighten them so that they may know themselves and have all obstacles removed, God will surely lead them.

All who turn to look at themselves will either become immobilized or turn backwards. This is especially true in spiritual progress.

A believer's mind is sick if he is unable to think, and his mind is equally sick if he always thinks. The minds of some are so dull through bondage that they cannot think of anything, while the minds of others are so active that they cannot call a halt to their incessant thinking.

Many cannot accept God's Word because their inside is already filled to capacity. Hence, if what is already within them is not cleared out, they will never be able to understand the Word of God.

Our old man not only needs to be crucified, but it also needs to be put away. That our old man has been crucified is something to believe; it is a matter of faith. Putting away, on the other hand, is a matter of the will. For us to put away something requires us to exercise the will (Eph. 4:22).

God is known in three different aspects: glory, holiness, and righteousness. Glory points to God Himself, holiness refers to God's nature, and righteousness indicates His way of doing things.

All who do not know what sin is do not know what holiness is, for holiness is the knowledge of sin.

Forty-Seven

Ye Search the Scriptures

The Scriptures cannot be mastered through cleverness, research, or natural talent, because the Word of God is spirit (John 6:63).

"It is the Spirit who gives life; the flesh profits nothing. The words that I speak to you are spirit" (John 6:63). To His believing disciples, the words of the Lord were spirit and life; but to the unbelieving Jews, they became flesh and dead letters.

What are words according to the wisdom of man? The things that the eye sees, the ear hears, and the heart contemplates—these are man's words. But revelation comes from the Holy Spirit, for He alone knows the things of God. (See 1 Corinthians 2.)

A spiritual man is the type of person who not only has the Spirit of God within, but also lives under the Spirit's power and walks according to the Spirit's principle. Only this type of person is able to judge all things (1 Cor. 2:15).

Light has a precise law. It enlightens all who are open to it. And the measure of one's openness determines the amount of illumination one has.

Sooner or later, he who serves two masters will encounter this dilemma: he will eventually come to love one and hate the other. Thus, if a person does not consecrate himself fully to the Lord, he will eventually serve mammon (riches) wholly (Matt. 6:24).

Whenever we are careless and allow, in however small a way, for our own selfish gain, the light we have from God becomes veiled.

How can our eyes be single (Matt. 6:22 KJV)? When one has put all his treasure in the Lord's care, his heart will just naturally gravitate to the Lord. By sending his treasure to heaven, the believer has sent his heart as well. Thus his eyes will be single.

What is meant by having our whole body full of light (Matt. 6:22)? It means having sufficient light to teach our feet to walk, our hands to work, and our minds to think. In other words, it is having light in every part.

Only one kind of person is unclear about the path before him: one whose eyes are not single. If one truly wishes to walk in the way of the Lord, he will see the path clearly marked out ahead of him.

The measure of our obedience before God determines the amount of light we receive. If we obey God persistently, we will see continuously. Without consecration, there will be no seeing; without consistent obedience, there will be no increase of light.

A willingness to do God's will is the condition of knowing His teaching (John 7:17). Obedience is the condition of knowing God's will.

Spiritual eye-salve is purchased with a price; it is not freely given (Rev. 3:18). All seeing is costly; it is not granted cheaply.

The Bible is a book that exposes its readers. To ascertain a person's true character and habit, you need only ask him to read a chapter and then tell you what he got out of it.

There are three things that God desires us to penetrate in our study of His Word. First, the Holy Spirit desires us to enter into His thought. Second, the Holy Spirit inserts many basic facts within the Bible for us to enter into. Third, the Holy Spirit wants us to enter into the spirit of what has been written. Furthermore, it is only the instructed and disciplined who may enter.

The more instructed a person is before God, the more apologies he will make. One who has learned much is more sensitive to the feelings of others and invariably apologizes more.

The Word and the spirit are inseparable. Why? Because the ministry of the Word is a release of the spirit. Whoever rises up to be a minister of the Word must release his spirit; otherwise, he cannot be one with the Word.

What is the discipline of the Holy Spirit? It is God's Spirit arranging all our daily circumstances—through which He works—until our spirits become one with the spirit of the Bible.

Failure to touch the spirit behind a certain passage of Scripture means a failure in understanding that passage. For the substance of the Bible is the spirit.

Only a kindred spirit may touch the spirit of the Bible; an alien spirit cannot do so. Hence, at the height of the study of the Bible, the spirit of the person who studies God's Word is brought into one with the spirit of the person who has written it.

If our spirits have not been brought into oneness with the spirits of the writers of the Bible, we can at most be teachers, but we cannot at all be prophets. Why? Because the most we can touch will be teachings or doctrines, but not the spirit.

If we read this Book according to the letter, we will soon find it aged; the same will be true if we merely try to think on it. But if we read the Bible by our spirits, we will be refreshed each time we read.

Whenever a passage of Scripture appears meaningless to us, we need to realize that it is not the Bible that is meaningless; rather, it is our spirits being inadequate, since each passage of the Bible is full of spirit.

It is only after we have received much discipline that the sensitivity of our spirits becomes rich and delicate. Therefore, it is immensely important that we have abundant dealings with the Lord.

In the Bible, what is done for us is salvation, what is done in us is holiness, and what is done through us is ministry or service. If we can distinguish these three aspects clearly, we will be able to set all the teachings of the Bible in their proper order.

Forty-Eight

Spiritual Authority

Satan is not afraid of our preaching the Word of Christ, yet he is very much afraid of our being subject to the authority of Christ.

The conflict of the universe is centered on who will have the authority. And our conflict with Satan is the direct result of our attributing authority to God.

The greatest of God's demands on man is not for him to bear the cross, serve others, make offerings, or deny himself; the greatest demand on man is for him to obey.

For authority to be expressed, there must be subjection. And if there is to be subjection, self must be excluded.

As God's servants, we are not given the option of finding work to do; rather, we are to be sent to work by God. Once having understood this, we will truly experience the reality of the authority of the kingdom of the heavens.

Authority in the world will be increasingly undermined until, at length, all authority in the world will be overthrown and lawlessness will rule.

Satan laughs when a rebellious person preaches the Word, for in that person dwells the satanic principle.

Only one who is under authority can be an authority. Therefore, wherever we go, our first thought must be to find out who are those to whom God wants us to be in subjection.

When we first begin to follow the Lord, we are full of activity and quite short on obedience. Then, as we advance in spirituality, our actions gradually diminish until we are filled with obedience. Thus, as man's obedience increases, his actions decrease.

There is no authority except from God; by tracing all authorities back to their source, we invariably end up with God.

Whenever a few brothers in Christ come together, immediately a spiritual order falls into place. It is only after we have learned who we are subject to, that we naturally find our place in the body. Alas, how many Christians today do not have even the faintest idea concerning subjection!

Since the Fall, disorder has prevailed in the universe, and most are of the opinion that we, without God's help, are able to distinguish good from evil and to judge what is right and wrong. We seem to know better than God. This is the folly of the Fall. We need to be delivered from such deception, because this is nothing other than rebellion.

As faith is the principle by which we obtain life, so obedience is the principle by which that life is lived out.

In order to recover authority, obedience must first be restored. However, many have cultivated the habit of being the head without ever having known obedience.

The one who is not subject to authority will eventually be a slave to him who does obey authority (Gen. 9:20–27).

Strange fire is what originates from man (Lev. 10:1–2). It does not require knowing the will of God or obeying the authority of God. Only true service is initiated by God.

Spiritual authority is not something one attains through effort. It is given by God to whomever He chooses. How very different is spiritual authority from natural authority!

All sins release the power of death, but the sin of rebellion releases it the most. Only the obedient can shut Hades' gates and release life.

People who walk by reason and sight go the way of reason; only those who obey authority by faith can enter Canaan. None who follow reason can walk the spiritual pathway; it is above and beyond human reasoning.

Authority is not a matter of outside instruction, but of inward revelation.

Since authority cannot be established without obedience, God created two kinds of living beings for this purpose. But God was unable to establish His authority, both in the angels that rebelled and in the Adamic race that fell. Consequently, perfect accord was reached within the Godhead that authority would be established in the obedience of God's own Son.

When the Son left the glory, He did not intend to return on the basis of His divine attributes; on the contrary, He desired to be exalted as a man. Jesus was exalted by God after He was obedient. In like manner, God wants to affirm this principle of obedience in us now, so that we also will be worthy to be exalted in that coming Day.

Our usefulness is not determined by whether or not we have suffered, but rather, by how much obedience we have learned through that suffering (Heb. 5:8).

While a deficiency in sensing sin deprives one of living as a faithful Christian, a lack of ability to sense authority disqualifies one from obeying.

God Himself will not supersede delegated authority; rather, He has chosen to be restrained by the authority He has delegated.

The first phase of God's work is to make Himself Christ's Head. The second phase is to make Christ the Head of the church. And the third phase is to make the kingdom of this world the kingdom of our Lord. The first phase has already been accomplished, and the third is yet to come. Today, we are in the middle phase.

Today the problem with the church is that everyone desires to have everything in himself and refuses to accept the supply of other members. This creates poverty in the individual as well as in the church as a body. Only by accepting the functions of others—and their authority—can we receive the wealth of the whole body. As it is by submission that we come into possession of the riches God has given, so it is by our insubordination that poverty exists.

We often misunderstand authority as something that oppresses us, hurts us, and troubles us, but God does not have such a concept. He uses authority to replenish our lack. His motive in instituting authority is to bestow His riches on us and to supply the needs of the weak.

God gives us His riches indirectly by placing brothers and sisters above us in the church who are more advanced spiritually, so that we can accept their judgment as ours. This enables us to possess their wealth without personally having to go through their painful experiences. God has deposited much grace in the church. By our recognizing these authorities, these riches can be released. When this occurs, the wealth of each member becomes the wealth of all.

Those who hearken to God's direct authority but still reject delegated authority are nonetheless still under the principle of rebellion.

Each time one speaks out against another, it means a loss of power. And this loss of power is greater when disobedience is manifest in words, as opposed to having it remain hidden in the heart.

Only one who knows God truly knows himself.

Formerly, I had many arguments to support my many thoughts. But now I have no more arguments, for I have been captured. As a captive, I have no freedom, because a slave only accepts his master's thoughts and does not offer his own opinions. Consequently, it is only those who have been captured by Christ who accept God's thoughts and do not offer any counsel of their own.

Wherever there is a church on this earth that truly obeys God's authority, there is the testimony of the kingdom. And there Satan is defeated.

In the past we found freedom in living by ourselves; now we find true freedom in having our thoughts recaptured by God and brought into the obedience of Christ (2 Cor. 10:5). In losing our freedom, we gain true freedom in the Lord.

God alone should receive our unqualified obedience without measure. Any person can receive only qualified obedience. Furthermore, though we should submit to any person who has received delegated authority from God, we should disobey any order that offends Him.

Obedience is related to conduct; it is relative. Submission is related to heart attitude; it is absolute.

How can we judge whether a person is obedient to authority? (1) A person who has known authority will naturally try to find authority wherever he goes. (2) A person who has met God's authority is soft and tender. He is afraid of being wrong, and thus he is soft. (3) A person who has met authority never likes to be in authority. The truly obedient are always afraid of making an error. (4) A person who has contacted authority keeps his mouth closed. He does not speak carelessly, because inside of him there is a sense of authority.

The measure of one's knowledge of God's will is the measure of his delegated authority. No one can know how to exercise authority until his own rebellion has been dealt with. Hence, one cannot be a delegated authority until he has learned to be under authority.

All authority is established by God; therefore, no delegated authority need try to secure his authority by striving with men, for the more authority God has entrusted to us, the more liberty we grant to other people.

When the delegated authority entrusted to you is being tested, do nothing; there is no need to be in haste, to strive, or to speak for yourself. If your authority is really from God, those who oppose you will find their spiritual course blocked, and there will be no more revelation to them.

Authority and self-defense are incompatible; vindication should always come from God. Those who are disturbed and overwhelmed by words of slander prove themselves unfit to be a delegated authority.

Authority attained through fighting is not authority given by God. Since His kingdom is not of this world, His servants need not fight for the establishment of it.

If God gives revelation to a person, his authority is established. But when God's revelation is withdrawn, the man is rejected. If God is willing to give us revelation and to speak with us, if we have face-to-face communion with Him, no one can eliminate us.

Revelation is the evidence of authority. If we strive, it only proves that our authority is wholly carnal, dark, and void of heavenly vision.

A faithful servant, though personally rejected and despised by others, will bear the burdens of many. The Israelites rebelled against Moses, yet he bore their sins; they opposed and rejected him, but still he interceded for them. If we care only for our own feelings, we will not be able to bear the problems of God's children.

God has one thought: to establish His own authority. We ourselves have no authority; we are only representatives of His authority. Thus we need to learn, on the one hand, how to submit to God, and on the other, how to represent Him.

A person's authority is based on his ministry, and his ministry is, in turn, based on resurrection. If there is no resurrection, there can be no ministry; if there is no ministry, there is no authority.

No one in authority should ever permit another person's authority to be damaged in order to establish his own.

The more one knows of being an authority, the more capable he is to maintain that authority.

How do you know if you are a qualified authority? If the authority you possess cannot be offended, you are qualified to be in authority. Do not imagine that you can freely exercise authority because you have been appointed by God. Only the obedient are fit to be in authority.

Let no one defend or speak for himself. The lower one prostrates himself before God, the quicker He will vindicate on the person's behalf.

God gives authority only to those who have an awareness of their own incompetence. When we lift ourselves up, we are rejected by God. Men must fall before God; then they can be used by Him.

At the future judgment seat of Christ, even the humble will be greatly surprised. And if this is true, how much more will the horror of the proud be on that day! We must have a sense of our incompetence, because God uses only the useless.

To be in authority requires that one be able to climb high, to not fear loneliness, and to be sanctified.

Forty-Nine

The Ministry of God's Word

Briefly stated, throughout the Bible, there are three different kinds of people whom God used to preach the Word. In the Old Testament, God's Word was spread by prophets; hence, we have the ministry of the prophets. At the time of the earthly pilgrimage of our Lord Jesus, God's Word became flesh; thus, we have the ministry of the Lord Jesus. In the New Testament, God's Word was propagated by the apostles; the result is the ministry of the apostles.

The Bible is not some collection of devotional articles; it is men performing and living out the Word of God. The governing principle throughout all of the Bible is the Word becoming flesh in us. Consequently, it is extremely hard for those who do not know the true meaning of incarnation to understand what the Word of God is.

The problems of the church today rest on the shoulders of those who minister: one may speak on the Spirit, yet the people listening hear only flesh; others may speak on holiness, yet what the audience hears is only a lightness of spirit; still others may talk of the Cross, yet where are the marks of the Cross on them? So many preach on the love of the Lord, yet the impression they convey to the hearers is not of His love, but of their own disposition. There exists an abundance of preaching and very little "Word." Why? Because true ministers of the Word are so hard to find.

We are always trying to find God's Word, but God is continually looking for those whom He can use. We are seeking the Word of God, but God is looking for those who will minister His Word.

The breaking of the outward man does not at all imply that God also rejects our human elements. On the contrary, He wants to utilize our human traits. The problem is, we do not know where to start or where to end—that is, we do not know how much in our lives is to be retained and how much is to be broken by God. Only those who have been taught by Him can quickly discern if a ministry is clean or unclean.

The purity of the word released depends on the amount of discipline received before God. The more one has been broken, the purer the word will be; the less one has learned, the more corrupt its release will be.

It is not God's intent to use a donkey as a prophet; He calls man to be the prophet. Yet in terms of difficulties, it is not easy for God to speak through man. The result of this difficulty is that God will sometimes even use a donkey to speak His Word, if the prophet fails in his work (Num. 22:28).

Whether there can be ministry and more ministry in the church depends on us; the poverty and darkness of the church are due to our weak condition. May we solemnly pray, "O Lord, break us so that Your word may flow through us."

Why was the law given? *"It was added because of transgressions"* (Gal. 3:19). After man fell, he could not tell what sin was. So, although God first gave man grace and the Gospel, man was unable to receive them. The law was then added to condemn sin in order that man might be made a partaker of God's Gospel and promise.

The Bible is "God-breathed" (2 Pet. 1:21). In this way, God made it a living Book. It became a living Word, spoken by the living God. The distinctiveness of this Book is its dual feature: on the one hand, the Bible has its outer shell—the physical part of the Bible— similar to the part of man that is made of dust; on the other hand, it has its spiritual part—that which is in the Holy Spirit—what is God-breathed and God-spoken. Many ministers serve only from the physical part, but a true minister of the Word serves the church from the spiritual portion.

Ministry of the Word requires revelation from the Holy Spirit. Whenever anointing, enlightenment, and revelation are lacking, there is only an outward expounding of the Scriptures. Without the Holy Spirit's fresh anointing and revelation, even the same word will not produce the same results, and the ministry of the Word has ceased.

What is God's Word? It is when God Himself comes forth. It is Him not only speaking to you, but also speaking through you. If God is silent, there is no word to deliver. How absurd that many so-called spokesmen of God neither expect Him to speak nor antici-pate His revealing Himself while they preach! Their whole focus is on displaying the doctrine they have formulated.

Doctrine without life begins and ends with truths and teach-ings. It exists only in the realm of the letter; it cannot minister the life of the Lord Jesus to others. The Bible divorced from the person of Christ becomes nothing more than a dead book of doctrine.

God is Spirit; therefore, He must be worshiped in spirit (John 4:24). God's Word is also spirit, and it must be received in spirit. And since God's Word is spirit, it is effective in release only when the spirit of man is exercised.

The Christ we know by revelation gradually becomes the Word in us. When we progressively see the reality of Christ through the Word, we are able to supply Him to others, along with the Word. By the mercy of God, those people who receive such a word will find the Holy Spirit working in them to transform that word into Christ in them. This is called the supply of Christ—that is, Christ is supplied through the Word of the Bible; men receive Him when they receive the Word. This forms the basis for all ministry of the Word.

Outside of Christ, there is neither life nor light, neither sancti-fication nor righteousness. Once a man is brought by God into this revelation of Christ, he begins to realize there is nothing apart from Christ; Christ is everything.

We think that if only we can spend time studying the Bible, we can comprehend it—with or without prayer. This is the folly of human thought, which manifests itself through those who think they are competent to study the Bible.

What is God's order? First it is to know the Lord, then to find Him in the Book. Man's problem is that he reverses the order of Christ and the Bible. Men insist on knowing the Bible first and knowing the Lord afterwards.

Who is a minister of the Word? One who translates Christ into the Bible. He tells people of the Christ he has gotten to know, using the words of the Bible. The Holy Spirit then translates these words back into Christ in those who receive them.

The poverty of the church today is due to the poverty of the ministers. The Christ we know is not full enough; the dealings we receive are not sufficient and thorough. As a result, we have little of the supply of Christ.

A true minister does not preach about Christ; he preaches Christ. He is not delivering a message, but a Man.

Fruits are produced according to their respective realms, either the realm of doctrine or the realm of revelation. As a result, the word spoken in one realm can only produce the fruit of that realm, and never that of the other. After people have heard a speaker, their lives and their flesh will either continue to remain undisciplined by his message, or they will be changed.

Knowledge produces only knowledge, and doctrine produces only doctrine. But revelation can beget more revelation (Ps. 36:9).

Many who read the Bible today touch merely the letter of the Bible, not the living Word of God. Whenever the Spirit ceases to reveal, the Word turns into mere doctrine. When the anointing fails, there is no more seeing, and hence no more ministry.

By walking according to the Spirit, the law of the Spirit will be manifested in you. But if you walk after the flesh, the law of sin and death will be manifested. Who, then, is he who follows the Spirit? One who sets his mind on the things of the Spirit. For when one's mind is on the things of the Spirit, one walks according to the Spirit. And one who walks according to the Spirit overcomes the law of sin and death (Rom. 8:2, 5).

What are the results of the disciplines of the Holy Spirit? No discipline, no revelation; no thorn, no grace. God desires that we come to know how utterly weak we are. Why? Because as soon as weakness leaves us, power likewise departs. Where there is weakness, there is power (2 Cor. 12:9). This is a spiritual principle brought to bear by discipline.

To be perfect in the knowledge of the Lord requires many trials. And with each new dealing, each new discipline, we are awarded a new and further unveiling of knowledge. In this way, our knowledge of Christ is increased day by day, and we are able to supply the church with the Christ we know.

Each trial produces some word. As the number of trials increase, so your word is enriched, and you become wise in the way of obtaining the word.

Those who have forsaken the most have the most to give to others. If you have forsaken nothing, you have nothing to give.

Here is the underlying principle of the ministry of the Word. We are tested first in all sorts of trials, so that afterward we may supply others with what we have learned.

In the process of speaking, a minister is in need of two things: a usable feeling and a usable spirit. Why? Because it is often our feelings that determine whether the spirit is able to come forth. If our feelings are blocked, the spirit is obstructed.

Why do God's children frequently mix up spirit and feelings? Because the spirit cannot come out independently; it flows through feelings; it flows through the channel of our emotions.

If our outward man has not been broken by the hand of God, our feelings cannot be tender and delicate, for there is no wound; there has been no suffering. It is only where one finds wounds and suffering that one will also find tender feelings.

The grain must be ground and broken before the powder can be fine. Under pressure, the one grain of wheat is no longer a single grain; it has become three, five, seven, even a hundred particles. It is now truly fine. The more the wounds and the deeper the suffering, the finer the inward sense of feeling.

One who has had the Cross worked into his life has been broken by the Lord. His stubborn will is no longer stubborn; his big brain is no longer inflated.

After many dealings from the Lord, you will be able, in your feelings, to express fully and exactly what is in your heart. You will truly be glad when your heart is glad, and you will actually grieve when your heart is grieved. Whenever the Word of God comes to you, and whatever the flavor of that Word is, you will have the corresponding emotion in you. Your feelings will be able to catch up with the Word.

Why is it that the emotions of many cannot be used? Because most people's emotions are spent on themselves. Since the quality of the word in us is controlled by our emotions, the secret of sensitive feelings lies in not making ourselves the center. The finer we are ground, the more selfless we become, and the more effective our feelings become. The richer our emotions, the richer the word in us.

A man's word is measured by his brokenness before God. The more spiritual a man is, the richer his feelings. A spiritual man is rich in all kinds of feelings.

The effect of the word on people is not determined by the word itself, but by the spirit with which it is delivered. A minister is able to release his spirit or to check his spirit; he can let it explode or keep it weak.

The Lord works in our lives not just once, but many times—to build up our inner man, as well as to crush our outer man. And it is through these many dealings that our spirits grow stronger and stronger.

Each trial the Lord gives us can either break us into an unusable vessel or make us more glorious. If it does not cause us to be better, it will render us worse. Those who cannot stand the trial are unusable, and those who overcome the trial add one more victory to their lives.

The exercise of one's spirit is governed by just how much of it is usable, for we can only use the part of it that is trained. Also, this giving forth of the spirit requires one to forsake something; it goes forth at great cost, as a burden, with pain and privation. Yet each time the spirit launches out, it touches man's weakness and man's death.

There is no work that demands such a high degree of concentration as that of the release of the spirit. Your spirit must be mingled with your words, for they are sent out through the spirit, and only words pushed out by the spirit are strong. As this is done, people will see the light and touch reality.

Particularly in a strong ministry, the spirit is not merely pushed forth—it explodes. When the words are delivered, the spirit is released in such fullness that it simply explodes. Under these circumstances, you will find people prostrate before God.

Just as the body of man expresses the thoughts of a man, the body of Christ (the church) expresses the thoughts of Christ. The thoughts of the Head can only be manifested through the body. Without the body, the Head has no way to express itself.

In the Old Testament, the principle for blessing was that it came down from heaven. In our age, the blessing has come to earth, and the Holy Spirit is to lift the church up to heaven.

What is ministry? It is the impartation of spiritual riches to man. The church ought to be dispensing these gifts, because they are already in the church.

Spiritual humility comes through our being enlightened by God so that we might have a real knowledge of ourselves. Soulish self-abasement is the result of looking at man, comparing ourselves with others, and being afraid of men.

The chief matter of concern for the minister who has learned little before God is the wounding of his spirit. In other words, when one is just beginning to learn, he often wounds, or hurts, his own spirit. Thus it fails to come forth. To the more experienced, however, the main difficulty lies in the loss of contact between the word and the spirit.

If anyone is proud about preaching, there can be only one result: though he can preach well, he has no ministry of the Word. He may feel elated after his preaching, but he will never be a minister of the Word.

In the ministry of the Word, preaching just to make people understand is the lowest level. How do we know this? Because ministry, when exhibited at its highest level, causes people to see and fall.

God never reveals Himself to "the wise and intelligent," for such people are unable to receive revelation directly from Him. They are also unable to receive it from a minister of the Word. Moreover, whenever "the wise and intelligent" are found among the audience, the Word of God is either dramatically weakened or totally obstructed from being released.

The more spiritual the nature of your delivery, the more easily you will be affected by people; the less spiritual your message, the less influenced you will be. A minister of the Word dreads "the wise and intelligent."

The situation in Matthew 12 is this: after the Lord Jesus cast out demons by the power of the Holy Spirit, the Jews insisted He did so by Beelzebub, for the Jews hated the Lord without cause. They inwardly knew He cast out demons by the Holy Spirit, yet they hated Him so intensely that they blasphemed against the Holy Spirit by saying He cast out demons by Beelzebub. They harbored deep prejudice within themselves. They knew they would have to believe in the Lord if they were to acknowledge that He cast out demons by the Holy Spirit. But they had already decided not to believe, and so they preferred to reject the Lord. Consequently, they adamantly remonstrated that He cast out demons by Beelzebub. Their hearts were as hardened as flint. Toward such as these there can be no forgiveness, not in this age or in the age to come (Matt. 12:31–32). The unpardonable sin is committed when people vehemently deny the distinctive work of the Holy Spirit by speaking aloud that it is the work of Beelzebub. Among the many names of Satan, Beelzebub is the foulest, because it means "the lord of the flies."

Fifty

"Come, Lord Jesus"

The effects of the teaching of Balaam are these: (1) eating things sacrificed to idols—which is to say, to be mixed with other religions, and (2) committing fornication—which, in this particular case, means to befriend the world (Rev. 2:14).

Today, Protestantism acts as though it were a cup. As has been repeated throughout history, whenever God has moved to bless a people, the people have inevitably organized themselves so as to contain the movement. During the first generation, the cup is full, and blessings are in great supply. With the second generation, however, the cup is only half full, and the message becomes less clear. Then, by the third or fifth generation, only the cup remains—with nothing in it. The people then contend about whose cup is best, though not one has anything to drink.

There are at least four things that Judaize Christianity: an intermediate priesthood, a written code, a physical temple, and earthly promises. Those who truly know God have had the influences of Judaism completely nullified to the point that not one of these elements exists in their spiritual life.

What is blasphemy? Whatever exalts oneself and debases God is blasphemy.

Fifty-One

Interpreting Matthew

The primary purpose of the Holy Spirit coming down to earth is not for us to be filled with Him. Rather, His coming down is for the purpose of proving that Jesus is the Christ of God.

God loves mercy more than judgment. And He calls a person with such compassion "righteous."

One of the greatest signs of humility is the fear of being wrong.

We are saved to such a degree that even as God is, so will we be. Henceforth, God's security has become our security; His destiny has become our destiny; and His glory, our glory. This is salvation: God with us.

There can be no salvation without Immanuel ("God with us"). Why? Because when we are outside of Christ, God is not Immanuel to us; outside of Christ, man is God's enemy. It is only when we are in Christ that He is Immanuel. Anything more or less is not salvation.

The "kingdom of the heavens" means only one thing: the authority of the heavens is manifested on earth. This authority is not seen by our works, our suffering, or our sacrifice; this authority is seen only by our obedience.

Repentance is not the washing of hands and feet; it is burying the whole body in water. If you commence to touch the spirit of repentance in this way, the kingdom of the heavens is indeed at hand (Matt. 3:2).

Being baptized is to stand in the place of death, thus having no position before God.

Repentance is negative; faith is positive. Repentance causes me to lose myself; faith enables me to gain Christ. Repentance is the impression; faith is the expression.

The first sin of man was to do away with the need of depending on his Creator. Man's desire was to be independent, rather than to commune with God and be dependent.

Concerning God's work, man has no right to decide anything, no right to choose the way of the church or the method of the work. Furthermore, whenever our own needs become the motivation of God's work, we walk fairly close to Satan's way.

Keeping the law is like trying to kindle a fire in water or like seeking gold in sand: the more you are incapable of doing, the more you are required to do. This is the law as it was given in the Scriptures. For the law in the Scriptures was not given to us to be kept; it was given to us to be broken. It exposed the inability of our natural self to keep it and magnified our sin.

It is not a blessing for Christianity to travel the road of earthly possessions. Rather, it is a sinful thing. Take the Lord, for example: at His birth, He borrowed a manger; at His death, He was buried in another's tomb; and while living, He had no place to lay His head. Christ has shown us that Christian character is expressed through an attitude of loss toward all that the world has to offer.

Why mourn about the darkness and injustice all around us? Because we have love. Without love, there will be neither crying nor mourning. There can be no such reactions where love is absent.

Grace is freely given by God to sinners; reward, on the other hand, is for those who have already been saved by grace. (See Romans 5:2.) Eternal life is absolutely according to grace through faith, but the millennial kingdom is altogether obtained by works.

The meaning of prayer is this: God has a will; I touch the will of God, I pray, and God will answer. Real prayer actually never originates on earth; it always begins in heaven.

We see faults in others because we ourselves have faults. The more unclean we are, the more uncleanness we are able to see in others. Conversely, the holier we are, the less we will find to fault in others. Criticizing costs nothing, but restoration is priceless.

Men ought to know that life is of greater consequence than works; inner grace is far more important than outward gifts. The fruit of the Spirit is far more necessary than the gifts, and love is more significant than power.

Why does the world need so much amusement? Because its people need these stimulations to help them forget their distresses. The more unrest and unhappiness one has inside, the greater the need and desire for outside stimuli. Christians are satisfied within; therefore, they do not need these stimuli.

Who is worthy to be His disciple? Those who put Christ first. All Christians who have problems in their lives will find this common cause for them: inadequate consecration.

The highest glory lies not in what I have to give the Lord, but in His acceptance of me. That He is even willing to accept me—this is amazing grace.

Many times when we sense the need for power, what we really need is authority. And the more we know God, the more we will have of His authority to use, and the less we will have the need for power.

In the sight of God, men are not just sinners; they are also dead ones—they have thoroughly died. To look upon oneself as simply a sinner is still an overestimation of oneself. One ought also to reckon himself as one who is dead (Eph. 2:1). When we arrive at this point in our estimation of ourselves, we will not struggle any more, because if we have truly given up all hope in ourselves, we will begin to look up to God. Then His life will begin to be manifested in us.

Those who seek glory from man are not worthy to be God's servants. Yes, woe to us when the world speaks well of us (Luke 6:26)! For when our path is smooth, we should ask ourselves if the Lord has ever traveled this path.

Since salvation does not depend on our efforts, the more we try to attain it, the further we are actually removed from it. We are saved by faith, not by effort or works of righteousness (Eph. 2:8–9). But the millennial kingdom is a different matter. It is entered forcibly by those who, having become disciples of the King, do violence to their self-life (Matt. 11:12; Luke 16:16). This is the qualification to enter the millennial kingdom.

When is the Cross the heaviest? While you are bearing it. When is it no longer heavy? When you are hung on it. If it is the Cross itself that bears you, you will not feel any more heaviness. You have died, so you feel no pain. If you have truly died to self, you will feel no yoke at all. This is the yoke that is easy and the burden that is light (Matt. 11:30).

First Jesus saved us from the penalty of sin so that we would not perish. Now He saves us from the power of sin so that we may not fall. In the future He will save us from the presence of sin so that we may be wholly spiritual.

The salvation of the Lord is perfect; He is not a half-Savior. Not only does He save those who are in their sins, but He also saves them out of their sins. He delivers those who were bondslaves to sin from the power of sin. If we have not received the salvation from the power of sin, we have received only half of Jesus.

In the Old Testament, God is presented as being for His people. In the Gospels, He is presented as being with His people. In the Epistles, He is presented as being in His people. These three steps disclose the way, the end, and the means of God's dealing with man.

The Son of God condescended to be the Son of Man so that we, the children of men, might be called the children of God.

It is better to have a heart full of the compassionate love of Christ than to have a head filled with the knowledge of the letters of Scripture. How much more preferable it is to have a heart that remembers the Lord, when compared with a mouth that only verbalizes the words of Scripture!

Just as the world was at the Lord's first coming, so it will be at His second coming. How pitiful that there are many who know the Lord is coming and even study prophecy about it, yet they are not waiting expectantly for His return! How do we know this? They still live for themselves and mind the things of the earth (Col. 3:2).

Fifty-Two

The King and the Kingdom of Heaven

The failure of Adam was in his not doing what God had ordered; the victory of Christ Jesus is in His not doing what God has not ordered.

One of Satan's chief aims is to deprive God of man's worship. For this reason, God states in His Word over and over that He is a jealous God (Exod. 20:5; 34:14; Deut. 4:24; 5:9; 6:15; Josh. 24:19).

Why is it that Satan still remains on earth today? Because those who belong to Christ have yet to experience the victory of Christ.

The Old Testament principle is to first walk and to then live; the New Testament principle is to first live and to then walk. One is work; the other is grace. This is a wonderful principle of the Gospel: our forgiveness precedes our walking. (See Matthew 9:1–8.)

The Gospel of the kingdom is the Gospel of grace, with the additional element of the powers of the age to come.

What is meant by taking up the cross? It is submitting to God from the heart. In the Garden of Gethsemane, our Lord had His mind set on doing the Father's will. The result was that He went from there to take up the cross. Taking up the cross means being determined to do God's will and nothing else.

Being a perfect servant of the Lord does not depend on the result of the work, but on whether one has done the will of God.

Of the Ten Commandments, nine are moral; only one is ceremonial: the keeping of the Sabbath.

The kingdom of God is the sovereignty of God. What is the outward manifestation of that kingdom? Casting out demons is one of the most significant manifestations of the reality of the kingdom of God. Wherever His sovereignty is, demons have no power.

Upon believing, we are saved, and we become part of the church. But the kingdom of heaven is the realm in which we are called to be disciples. And God causes us to begin enjoying these privileges of the kingdom here and now, while we perform our duties and fulfill our responsibilities as His disciples.

The denying of self is the repudiating of one's own ideas. And the only condition for following the footsteps of Jesus is the denying of self. These are the footsteps of Christ, and they lead us to the kingdom. Believing puts us in the church; following the footsteps of Jesus puts us in the kingdom.

"For whoever desires to save his life will lose it, but whoever loses his life for My sake will find it" (Matt. 16:25). Saving the soul means gratifying one's own mind, will, and emotions in this age. The one who now chooses to lose the pleasure of gratifying his own mind, will, and emotions gives his life as a sacrifice to the Lord. The one who refuses to lose these pleasures in this age will lose them in the age to come; that is, he will suffer shame during the kingdom age, though he will still retain eternal life. What will it profit a man though he might gain all the world has to offer, yet in the end lose what God offers (v. 26)?

In order to know whether one will be rewarded in the future, one can examine his own deeds. If he loses his soul today, he is sure to gain it in the future; if he guards or keeps it today, he is sure to lose it in the future.

To enter the kingdom, one must become like a little child. But maintaining this position is the basis for all subsequent greatness. If, having been born again, one always keeps himself like a little child, he will be great in the kingdom of heaven (Matt. 18:2–4). Unfortunately, many forsake this condition; though they are but children, they act like grown-ups (1 Cor. 3:1).

Your position in the kingdom is exactly the opposite of your place today. Though we wish to be great and first in this world, the Lord calls us to be great and first in the age to come. How we covet the reward but are unwilling to pay the cost!

The theme of Romans is that no sinner can be justified by the works of the law, while that of Galatians is that no saved person can be sanctified by the works of the law. These two letters have sufficiently proven that neither justification nor sanctification comes by the works of the law. Accordingly, we must die to the law, so that through God's grace we can be justified and sanctified, by His grace through the Lord Jesus Christ.

Since the law was made for the flesh, anyone who tries to keep the law after he has become saved is reckoned an adulterer according to Romans 7. Our attempt at keeping the law indicates we have not died. In such a situation, how can we be married to Christ?

The indwelling Holy Spirit is received at the time of regeneration, but the filling of the Holy Spirit comes thereafter through a continual seeking. Each believer has the Holy Spirit, yet not all have the fullness of the Holy Spirit.

Most Christians imagine that receiving oil (the Holy Spirit) one time is enough. But God desires us to receive it continually. And the subsequent receiving is different from the first. The first God gives freely; thereafter, He demands a price to be paid. If anyone refuses to pay the price—denying self and seeking earnestly—that one will not receive more oil.

Having received the new covenant, most Christians know the new desires, but not the new power. Yet how disappointing it is, and even painful, to have a new desire without the power to fulfill it! This proves the need to be filled with the Holy Spirit.

The relationship we have to the Father pertains to salvation and eternity; the relationship we have to the Son pertains to overcoming and reward.

One basic difference between the old covenant and the new covenant is that the old demands work before life. This means being servants before becoming children. The new covenant, though, gives life before works—that is to say, being born again before becoming servants. Why is this? Because God does not want believers to serve Him by their flesh.

The use of the gifts without oil (the fullness of the Holy Spirit) is very dangerous. This was the problem that was manifest in the church at Corinth. Its members were full of confusion because they had an abundance of gifts and a scarcity of oil. Exercising one's gift should only be accomplished by the fullness of the Holy Spirit.

Whether a person is or is not to receive a reward at the judgment seat is not determined at that time—it is decided today. Earning is not done at some future time; it is accomplished in the here and now, through a life of faithful service to Him. Sacrifice now, receive eternally; receive now, sacrifice eternally.

The blood deals with sins; by the blood, our sins are forgiven. But the blood does not guarantee we will not sin again; for this we need the Cross. The Cross deals with the power of sin; only the Cross can deliver us so that we will not sin again. Yet for those times when we do, the blood is still there to forgive.

Fifty-Three

The Word of the Cross

Suffering is glory. Having suffered with the Lord, we will be glorified with Him. Suffering is future glory, and glory is present suffering.

This is a most valuable lesson I have learned in discussions with people: whatever matter it may be, once an opinion has been raised, do not insist any longer. If people do not listen, retreat into prayer. Bear all things for Christ's sake.

When a soldier goes out to the battlefront, he is ready to die. It is normal for a soldier to die; it is exceptional for him to live. Why, then, should the soldiers of Christ be exceptions? A soldier looks for victory, and a general is made out of wounds.

In offering to God, it is easy to offer what we are able to do. It is hard to offer the heart (that is, the desire to regain what we are sacrificing). It is relatively easy to offer up Isaac; but to offer the heart (the desire to regain Isaac) and to let God keep one's heart—that is fairly hard.

The Cross is composed of two sides, yet they are inseparable. On the one side is death; on the other side is resurrection. A natural man is not able to know death since he does not even know life. Yet how can the spiritual man know life if he does not know death?

"Death" is the believer's passive way with sin; whereas "life" is his active way with righteousness. Many believers are stuck in the "death" position; thus they are very weak and without power. In their death they fail to experience life, for without passing through death, life will not come.

The "life" side of the Cross is comprised of three aspects: (1) to be alive with the Lord, (2) to have the Lord living in me, and (3) to be living for the Lord. Only upon having accomplished these three aspects will the believer live the victorious life.

If one dies daily, he lives daily; if one dies to sin, he is alive unto the Lord (Rom. 6:11). It is upon reaching this stage of spiritual experience that a Christian's life becomes victorious. One is then prepared to do battle in spiritual warfare with Satan. Sadly, most Christians never move past the conflict in Romans 7. And since this is no more than a battling with the old man, it cannot be called spiritual warfare.

People love to talk about the Lord Jesus and His death, but they dislike talking about the Lord Jesus and the Cross.

For the sake of doing the Father's will and saving the world, Christ would not come down from the cross. For Him, the issue was clear: to save Himself, He must forsake men; but to save men, He must forsake Himself. He gave Himself up for us. Oh, how He must love you and me!

"Righteousness" deals within the bounds of the law. In it there is neither mercy nor love; whoever violates the law must be punished according to the law. "Love," on the other hand, is kind and merciful; it shows unlimited and irresistible affection toward all. According to His love, God offers grace; and according to His holiness, He provides it in a righteous way.

Regeneration is only the first stage of spiritual life. When one is regenerated, he receives life, though this life is just in its infancy. After this, co-death and co-resurrection with the Lord are to be the experience of every believer. They are the marks borne by one who is mature in the Lord. How unfortunate that so few bear them!

The moment one believes, he is born anew; being regenerated, he receives eternal life. Though this life is yet to be matured, it nonetheless is sufficient to last eternally.

God cannot ignore sin and treat it as nothing. To do this would destroy all measure of His righteousness. While the fulfillment of the law shows forth His righteousness, propitiation expresses God's love for us.

The people of the Old Testament looked forward to Christ; we look backward. If they, by faith, could accept a future Savior, why can we not, by faith, believe in a past Savior?

The cry of believers today is for greater faith. But from where does greater faith come? Faith has its source, and it is not believers; it is God. Unfortunately, the faith of believers is not in God but in their possessing greater faith.

It is because believers themselves do not depend on God, in riches or in poverty, that they are unable to see what He can do for them. If we profess faith in God, our faith should be evidenced in a practical way: by our daily walk.

Faith and rest are inseparable, and those who have believed have entered into that rest (Heb. 4:3). Hence, the first work of faith is to cease from one's own works and to rest in the love, wisdom, and power of God.

A common misconception Christians frequently embrace is in thinking that those who are sincere cannot be deceived. They think, "As long as I am sincere in my heart, I will not be misled." Who would imagine that it is these sincere souls who are the most deluded!

Satan usually beguiles believers by first suggesting to them that they will not be deceived. That is why those who believe they cannot be deceived are usually the most deceived. God does not promise to protect us unconditionally. On the contrary, it is only after we have learned to cooperate with Him that we become fully protected.

Fifty-Four

The Communion of the Holy Spirit

The primary work of the Holy Spirit is to transmit the resurrected Lord to us. He does not try to convey the Christ recorded in the Gospels as far as His outward characteristics are concerned. Instead, He transmits the resurrected Christ.

The path leading to the Lord's having His way on earth today is not found in how much our walk has changed or in how much truth we know; rather, it is a question of whether or not we are really willing to pay any cost to know resurrection, the Holy Spirit, and the church. If we are, the church will have a glorious testimony.

Only when one sees what resurrection is will one be clear about what the body is.

Where can we find the work of the Holy Spirit? The work of the Holy Spirit is found wherever the resurrection power of the Lord is at work; otherwise, it cannot be reckoned as His work.

Heavenly authority is glorious and exceedingly great, but it is being restricted by earth. Even when only two people on earth recognize what resurrection is and stand on resurrection ground, they can shake the ends of the earth. Hence, today, we do not need more of what we already have; rather, we need to see how glorious, rich, and great is that which we already have.

For the Holy Spirit to come upon you, you yourself must express your desire, and so He comes. It is not the Holy Spirit working independently; it is you who works actively, and the Spirit comes to help. In the measure of your allowance will be found the measure of His coming.

The outpouring of the Holy Spirit is the evidence of the exaltation and victory of Jesus the Nazarene. We receive the Spirit's outpouring, not to prove our faith and victory, but to prove that Jesus is Lord and Christ.

To receive the outpouring of the Holy Spirit, certain conditions must be fulfilled. First, there should be no conscious sin undealt with in the heart; second, there must be hunger in the spirit; third, there needs to be fervent prayer.

Receiving the outpouring of the Holy Spirit is like the opening of a door along a wall: after opening it, there will be constant contact with things within the spiritual realm.

Each and every time you experience the outpouring of the Holy Spirit, you must apply the test of the spirits (1 John 4:3; 1 Cor. 12:3). You must challenge the person being poured upon by asking him if Christ has come in the flesh or by asking him if Jesus is Lord.

In the assembly of the church, the outpouring of the Holy Spirit is for the building up of others, not for self-building. This is the principle laid out for us in 1 Corinthians 14.

Let us be fully aware that though we obey the Spirit who dwells in us, we ourselves govern the spirit that falls upon us. When we seek the outpouring of the Holy Spirit, we must control that which is poured out upon us. Why? Because if we are not careful and do not maintain control of the situation, Satan can easily bring in a counterfeit.

The outpouring of the Holy Spirit is expressly linked to the exaltation of the Lord Jesus, and not our prayers or good deeds.

The work of the Holy Spirit is threefold. First, He gives people life; second, He dwells in people as life; third, He falls upon people as power.

The Holy Spirit indwelling man is for life; whereas the Holy Spirit upon man is for power.

The Holy Spirit falls upon believers to clothe them with the Lord's power in being witnesses and to manifest the gifts of the Spirit. In this way, we are equipped with talent to work for God and power to accomplish His will.

The work of the Holy Spirit within man is for life and living, enabling us to bear the fruit of the Holy Spirit. The work of the Spirit upon man is for witness and service, causing us to manifest spiritual gifts.

Those people who are filled with the Holy Spirit inwardly and have the Holy Spirit fall upon them outwardly possess great power in serving the Lord.

Those who desire to enter into service for the Lord must first have the blood applied. Then, after the blood, the oil can be poured (Lev. 14:14–17). The Cross must first work upon your ear, hand, and foot before the Holy Spirit can help you walk and work. First comes the victorious life, then the outpouring of the Holy Spirit.

If a person has the proper life within and the outpouring of the Spirit without, he can be very useful to the Lord.

The outpouring of the Holy Spirit should be sought only in time of need and should not be treated as an object of amusement for our spiritual enjoyment.

Concerning the testing of the spirits, we must at all times test the spirit, whenever there is any kind of outpouring (1 John 4:1). We have to test each time. Why? Because we are no match for the Evil One in the spiritual realm. Thus, it is very important to test the spirit.

The Bible mentions two kinds of power. One is the power of the resurrection, which is inside of us; the other is the power of the Holy Spirit, which is outside of us. The latter is the power that is manifested at the Spirit's outpouring.

In helping brothers and sisters in Christ, we must be sure that we first help them experience the victorious life and then lead them to seek the outpouring of the Holy Spirit.

In the Bible, resurrection is linked with death, and filling is linked with emptying. Also, while the infilling is for only a special group of people—those who have emptied themselves—the outpouring is for all the saints.

With respect to the filling of the Holy Spirit, it is the risen Lord who infills us because of our obedience. It requires a holy life in us. But in regard to the Spirit's outpouring, the ascended Lord pours forth the Holy Spirit upon us because of our faith.

If you want to be filled with the Holy Spirit, you must empty yourself; you must be hungry and unsatisfied. Never accept what you have already received as being sufficient; never reach the point of being content with what you have received. In this way, you will always receive more and more.

If you can bear the digging up and burrowing down that the Lord does in your life, you will be used greatly by the Lord. But if you fret and have controversy with God, you at once lose your victorious life, and any outpouring of the Holy Spirit will be of no help. Let the Cross cut and pierce you deeply, for each cutting of the Cross severs something from you that you love and long for. These cuttings are the work of the Cross for an increase of the measure of His grace in you.

Unless we experience the Cross and are filled with the Holy Spirit, our testimony before men will be weak and incomplete.

If a person has a need for the outpouring of the Holy Spirit, gather a few saints, take him before the Lord, and then pray together until he receives the Spirit's outpouring.

The outpouring of the Spirit on the Day of Pentecost did not occur to prove man's goodness and sincerity but to prove to all the house of Israel that Jesus is Lord and Christ (Acts 2:36).

All we have that has not come through regeneration, we must learn to let go of. For *"that which is born of the flesh is flesh"* (John 3:6). And yet, how we so depend on our natural strength to do sacred work!

243

Most people are afraid of living by the Spirit; they prefer to live according to certain rules. Men would rather live by the law, because it causes them to know right from wrong quite easily. By the law, men can know where they should go and not go, what they ought to do and not do. But the problem with the law is this: when people conduct themselves according to the law, they have put God behind their backs.

God does not want us merely to keep the dead letter of His Word. He takes pleasure in having us continually pray before Him and quietly wait on Him to supply our every need. He does not want us to rely on any "thing," because it gives Him joy when we rely solely upon Him.

Life in the Spirit has no set of rules. It lays aside all dead precepts and seeks directly the will of God. It goes only where led and does only what it has been told to do.

Everything in the Bible is living—that is to say, living in the Holy Spirit. If we turn biblical things into rules and regulations, they become dead. In order for Bible truth to be living, it must be in the Spirit.

All that is not according to the living guidance of the Holy Spirit moment by moment is the law. Even copying yesterday's leading is walking according to the law.

In theory, the guidance of the Spirit within us should be enough to lead us. But in practice, because our understanding of His inward guidance is subject to error, we still need the Holy Bible.

It is only as we obey both the inward and the outward guidance the Lord gives us that we are truly obeying God.

If you have no anointing as you minister, the more you talk, the less strength you have; and the longer you talk, the emptier you are within. You sense an incredible dryness. On the other hand, if you have an anointing and a burden in you, the more you work, the louder the amen inside you. You feel light and easy; you know this is what God wants you to say and do.

Let us always remember that we can never sense God more than the anointing that is upon us. The measure of the anointing on us is the limit of our service to God.

God's anointing oil is for the One who fully satisfies His heart, for the Scriptures say, *"Upon man's flesh shall it* [the holy anointing oil] *not be poured"* (Exod. 30:32 KJV). Therefore, we are anointed only when we are in Christ.

When a person is anointed, the oil is poured upon the head, not the body. But after the oil is poured upon the head, it flows down until it covers the entire body (Ps. 133:2). This is the picture of Christ and the church.

We know that oil is a substance that is soft and soothing in its application. Such is the way the Holy Spirit instructs us.

During the Old Testament period, when people brought out God's Word, it became the law to them. In the New Testament era, if people bring out God's Word without at the same time having the anointing of the Holy Spirit, God's Word still becomes law.

As Christians, we should not rely on our own minds or follow our own will. Instead, we should give Christ the absolute sovereignty He deserves and let Him be Lord over them. For our natural flesh is worthy only of death—worthy of being crucified on the Cross and laid in dust and ashes.

Learning from the truth means that a person acts according to the Word and the relevant teachings of the Bible that he has learned. Learning from the discipline of the Holy Spirit means that after a person has experienced the hand of the Lord dealing with him, he is gradually broken by the Lord. When this process is complete, one is fully delivered from his early stage of insubordination, murmuring, fretting, and opinions, into a state of obedience.

To judge someone's words, as to whether they emanate from the spirit or from the mind, is the initial step in spiritual discernment. Furthermore, those who cannot distinguish between what is of the spirit and what is of the mind are unable to render spiritual judgment.

The basis of our knowledge of other people is the degree we ourselves have been judged. We will know our fellow believers to the degree that we know ourselves.

The scope of your ministry will be determined by the amount of the Spirit's discipline in your life: the more the discipline, the more the enlargement and usefulness of the vessel.

An ordinary person needs only to have his flesh dealt with. But a pretentious person must not only have his flesh dealt with; there must also be a dealing with the shell of falsehood that he has added.

For one to have the ability to judge with his spirit, his outward man must be broken. Why? Because without the breaking of the outward man, one's spirit is sealed up and unusable.

In the world, social intercourse is carried on for the sake of finding close friends. But Christian fellowship is conducted on the basis of brotherly love; we love one another.

The Bible teaches us that leprosy in its hidden stage cannot be healed; but once it has been fully exposed, it can be healed (Lev. 13:13). This is a primary principle in the cleansing of sin.

When we reach out to people, if any personal agenda or self-interest is present, we will be unable to help them solve their problems. Our motives must be purified from this weakness in order to have sufficient light to meet their needs.

Today in the church, there are few, if any, who dare to reprimand people. Why? Because our own lives are not right. So we are not found worthy to dispense reproof. As soon as we would reprove others, we, in reality, would be reproving our own selves.

Fifty-Five

Worship God

By revelations we know God; by surrender we know His ways. To worship God is to worship His ways.

The Lord Jesus came into this world to restore worship to God. Satan tries to rob God of His worship, and man is tempted to worship anything other than God Himself.

Why does Satan fear the salvation of men? Because they will then be able to worship God. Hence, he hates for men to be saved.

It is not enough to know salvation; we must put worship into everything we do. The church is the firstfruits of God's creatures (James 1:18). What the world will one day give to God, we give Him first.

What is worship? It is simply this: I recognize that He is God and that I am only a man. When I see God as Father, I am saved; when I see God as God, I am finished and done with. For when we see Him as God, we can only fall down humbly and worship Him. The whole matter rests upon our seeing.

"Our God is a consuming fire" (Heb. 12:29). Everything that can be burned He will burn. As Daniel's three companions could not be consumed in the fiery furnace (Dan. 3), so it is with all who have had drastic dealings with the Cross; all that has already passed through His judgment of fire into new life cannot be burned.

Why does God choose the foolish, the weak, and the base (1 Cor. 1:27–28)? Because their souls are not puffed up. If we live after the spirit, God gets what He wants: worship. If, however, we live after the soul, Satan gets from us what he wants, which is also worship.

Worship is giving glory to God. The worship I give God is His glory.

What is worship? I bow under the ways of God (Heb. 11:21)—that is worship!

According to God's thought, the church has been placed on a war-footing. Hence, if the church is not a militant church, it is not the church at all.

As Christians, we have three enemies: the world, the flesh, and the Devil. According to experience, the world is the first to be overcome. And it is also the lowest plane of victory. Next is the flesh. Light results in the flesh not being able to rise up as it did before, by removing its strength. Last is the Devil. Since he is a spirit, only those who have been set free from their flesh can, in their spirits, know the battle in the spirit realm. The world and the flesh first have to be dealt with in our lives before we get to the third enemy—the Devil. Those who have not been delivered from these will be unclear about Satan.

In the Bible, males between the ages of twenty and sixty were most valuable. The price of their worth was placed at fifty shekels of silver (Lev. 27:3), the highest paid of any age. Why? Because these were the fittest, the ones most able to war (Num. 1:3). In other words, God's estimation of each individual is measured by his or her ability to engage in warfare with the Enemy.

If we are ruled by self, by circumstances, by man, or by anything of the world and this earth, we are unfit for the warfare of the spiritual realm.

Even if the earth is supplying you with only a few things, take them sparingly. Otherwise, someday you might feel cast down if you cannot have them.

Two things are needed for revelation: (1) light from God and (2) opened eyes.

Spiritual progress is not a question of attaining some abstract standard or pressing through to some far-off goal. It is wholly a question of seeing God's standard. Spiritual progress comes by finding out what you really are, not by trying to be what you are not.

It is when you see you are dead that you die, and when you see you have risen that you rise. It is when you see you are holy that you become holy, and when you see yourself in Christ that you receive what He has already received.

God sees the church as utterly pure and utterly perfect (Num. 23:21). It is as we come to see this spiritual reality in heaven that we begin to live in the power of that reality on earth.

Alas! Christianity, in the experience of most Christians, is an endeavor to be what they are not and an endeavor to do what they cannot do. They are always struggling to not love the world, because at heart they really love it. And they are always trying to be humble, because at heart they are still proud.

It is through bitter experience that we learn we cannot help God. But it is also through bitter experience that we learn God can be limited by an imperfect heart. (See Mark 6:5–6.) And we do have full power to hinder Him.

As the body is for the full expression of one's personality, Christians are the means of expression for Christ. Moreover, it is through the body that His will is brought to bear on both this world and the spirit world of evil powers. That is why the lordship of Christ in our lives is so very important.

There are presently three wills at work in the universe: the divine, the satanic, and the human. God desires the human will to be put on His side, instead of Satan's side. Why? Because if man's will is not on the side of God, though He will not destroy man's will, it cannot be used for His purposes. God accepts this position of limitation so as to not interfere with the will of man.

What is the kingdom? *"Thy will be done in earth, as it* [already] *is in heaven"* (Matt. 6:10 KJV). This means there will be no human will coming out to limit Him.

The trouble with many believers is that they have only changed their subject of interest; they have not changed the source of their power and energy.

As God has done everything in regard to our salvation, He also does everything in regard to our service. Why? Because if He is to have all of the glory, He has to do all of the work. He has to rule out everything that is of man, so that He may have the glory.

Our natural life and natural energy will continue with us until our death. But there must be a fundamental breaking of that life, power, and energy—just as God touched the socket of Jacob's hip (Gen. 32:24–25). Thereafter, he continued to walk, but he also continued to limp. Every true servant of God knows the touch of that wound from which he can never recover.

Death, in principle, has to be worked out in a crisis to our natural life. It is by passing through these crises that God releases us into resurrection; and having passed through, we come out on resurrection ground.

Fifty-Six

What Shall This Man Do?

Where do you find Christ's kingdom? Wherever the sovereignty of the Lord Jesus is recognized. And likewise, wherever that sovereignty is not recognized, there His kingdom has not yet come.

"The law and the prophets were until John. Since that time the [Gospel of the] *kingdom of God has been preached"* (Luke 16:16). If there is still law, there is no kingdom. If there are still prophets, there is no kingdom. Why? Because the law and the prophets must yield to the kingdom of Jesus Christ.

The law is the written word that expresses the will of God; the prophets are living men who express that will. In Old Testament days, God usually expressed Himself to the Israelites by one of these two indirect means. But in our day, the New Testament day, God deals with us in a more intimate way, for Christianity involves our personal knowledge of God directly through His Spirit.

There are many who look to the letter of the Word even more than to Jesus Christ Himself as their final authority. But this is not true Christianity, for true Christianity is not based on information, but on personal revelation.

Information or doctrine is always external and impersonal. But Christianity is a revealed religion, and revelation is always inward, direct, and personal.

Perhaps the most difficult and painful aspect of the Cross is when it cuts through our zeal for the will of God and our love for His work. Our old self is always so willing to step in to do the will of God; but God has His time, and He accomplishes His work in His own way.

251

From our fallen perspective, we usually do not see that God has one condition, and one only, that He initially demands of us. It is not to believe, to repent, to be conscious of sin, or even to know that Christ died; the only requirement God has of us is that we approach Him with an honest heart (Ps. 51:17).

In the Gospels, the Lord Jesus is presented as the Friend of sinners, for our coming to Him was made possible by His first coming to us (1 John 4:19). Indeed, before we were willing or able to receive Him as Savior, He came to us as a friend. He first comes down from heaven to within our reach.

One does not need to study the theory of electricity and understand it thoroughly before he can turn on a light. In the same manner, regarding the salvation of a soul, one does not have to understand the plan of salvation before he approaches God. Rather, the initial step is a personal touch of God.

Often, when we present the Gospel, we try to make people understand the plan of salvation, or we try to drive people to the Lord through fear of sin and its consequences. And this is where we fail. Since we do not adequately present the Person, our hearers do not see Christ. Instead they see only "sin" or "salvation," whereas their need is to see the Lord Jesus Himself, meet Him, and touch Him.

Salvation as a personal and subjective experience rests on the Lord's resurrection rather than His death. Though the death of Christ was necessary for atonement objectively before God, the New Testament lays emphasis on our faith in resurrection. It is through His resurrection that we have the proof of His death being accepted.

The basic condition for a sinner's salvation is not belief or repentance, but simply presenting an honest heart toward God.

The main lesson of the parable of the sower is not that the man who receives the Word is a perfectly honest man in God's eyes, but that he is honest toward God (Luke 8:15). Whatever is in his heart, he is prepared to come to God frankly and openly with it.

Whether or not a person wants to be saved should not be our main concern. Even understanding the Gospel is also of secondary importance. What matters most is this: is he prepared to be honest with God about these things? If he is, God is prepared to meet him.

It is the existence of the Gospel, which makes possible that initial touch of Jesus, that saves the sinner, and not the sinner's understanding of it.

Because Jesus is the Friend of sinners, and because the Holy Spirit undertakes to do what men themselves cannot do, sinners can come to God just as they are. They do not need to change at all. Furthermore, it is not necessary for them to find in themselves the ability to do anything.

There are those who will not repent, and those who cannot believe. There are those with no desire for salvation, and those who think they are too bad to be saved. There are those who are confused and do not understand the Gospel, and those who do understand it yet will not acknowledge the claim of God upon them. I have met all six types of people, and many of them have been saved on the spot. Additionally, I have met a seventh type—those who do not believe in a God at all. And I have dared to say, even to them, that they do not need to first substitute theism for atheism. They can be saved as they are, without any belief in God at all, if they will only be honest about it. You see, it is not our responsibility to find God, but it is His pleasure to reveal Himself to us, if we sincerely ask Him to do this.

The Christian life can be a continuous miracle, as it was for Paul: a paradox in which the divine life planted within by the new birth shines forth through the mortal body of one who consciously walks after the Spirit.

Christianity is not the earthen vessel, nor is it the treasure inside, but it is the combination of the treasure within the earthen vessel. Why? So that all may know that it is not the earthen vessel but the power of God that is the exceeding greatness (2 Cor. 4:7).

A Christian is one in whose life there is an inherent, mysterious paradox—a person in whom not only seeming incompatibles coexist, but in whom also the power of God repeatedly triumphs. He is one who is afraid, yet determined; one who is encompassed by foes, yet is not bound; one who is about to be overcome, yet is not destroyed. It is plain enough that he is weak, yet he declares it is when he is weak that he is strong (2 Cor. 12:10). You can see this one bears in his body the dying of Jesus (2 Cor. 4:10), yet he regards this as the very ground for manifesting the life of Christ in and through his mortal body.

Christianity is not the removal of weakness, nor is it merely the manifestation of divine power. Rather, it is the manifestation of divine power in the presence of human weakness. God is bestowing His strength upon men, but that strength is manifested in their weakness (2 Cor. 12:9). All the treasure He gives is placed in earthen vessels.

Christianity is not a matter of faith only, but of faith triumphing in the presence of doubt.

What should the walk of faith be like in a Christian? Just when faith rises positively to lay hold of God, a question may simultaneously arise as to whether or not he might be mistaken. It is when one is the strongest in the Lord that he may be most conscious of his own inability; when one is most courageous for the Lord that he may be most aware of his fear within; and when one is most joyful that a sense of distress may be ready to come upon him. This paradox is the evidence of both the treasure and its placement in an earthen vessel—and that it is where God wants it to be.

We are apt to think that where sadness exists, joy cannot exist; where there are tears, there cannot be praise; where weakness is found, power must be lacking; where we are surrounded by foes, we must be hemmed in; and where there is doubt, there can be no faith. But God's intent is to bring us to that place where everything human fails, for this alone provides the earthen vessel through which He can manifest this divine treasure. If we allow Him, He will take us to the place where, henceforth, when we are conscious of depression, we do not give way to depression, but to the Lord;

when doubt or fear arises in our hearts, we do not yield to it, but to the Lord. Only in this way can the treasure shine forth all the more gloriously because of the earthen vessel in which it is contained.

Here is Christianity: not that we camouflage the vessel by hardening ourselves to suppress all feeling, but that we let the earthen vessel be seen with the treasure inside. It is not a case of getting through painful situations because one has become insensitive to pain, but rather, of retaining full consciousness and being carried through by Another, despite the feeling of pain.

To hold on to the plow while wiping away the tears—this is Christianity. It is the transcending of the earthen vessel by the treasure within.

The glory of Christianity is that God's treasure will be manifested in the humblest vessel of clay. Christianity is a paradox, and it is as we Christians live out our lives in this paradox that we get to know God. Indeed, the further we go on in the Christian life, the more of a paradox our lives become. For the treasure within becomes increasingly manifest, as the earthen vessel remains just an earthen vessel.

Our focus should be on the quality of the treasure within, not on the deficiencies of the vessel that contains it. It is because the marks of the Cross are present upon one's human frailty that the miracle of the precious treasure inside can shine triumphantly through it all.

The Cross of Christ is intended by God to be the end of everything in man that has come under His sentence of death. But for us, as Christians, the Cross has a further value. It is also at the Cross that the believer's natural life is broken, as Jacob's strength and independence of nature were broken at Jabbok (Gen. 32:24–25).

Between the old man and the new man towers the Cross. It is also the gateway into fellowship with one another in Christ Jesus.

Spending a lifetime among Christians with continuous exercise in theology will not build us into His church. It is an inner, not an outer, knowledge that brings this about. This is eternal life—getting to know Him in spirit, the only true God, and Him whom He sent (John 17:3). Flesh and blood cannot know him.

God's church is for use, not decoration. Order, instruction, and head knowledge may produce the appearance of life when conditions are favorable, but when the gates of hell come out against us, our true state is quickly disclosed. When this occurs, theory will not prevail against hell, which is what Jesus declares His church must do.

Nothing gives God greater satisfaction than to hear a confession of Himself. Jesus often said, "I am." (See, for example, John 8:58.) He loves to hear us say, "You are." We do it far too little. When everything goes wrong, and all is in confusion, do not pray, but confess that "Jesus is Lord"!

Consecration is the result of spiritual vision and cannot take place without it. Vision is also where God's work begins. Our work can begin at any time, but God's work through us begins only from divine vision (Gen. 18:17; 37:5; Exod. 25:9; 1 Chron. 28:19; Matt. 16:17; Eph. 3:3).

Satan does not mind when men hear about the purpose of God and understand it mentally. His great fear is when God's people receive an inward illumination concerning the purpose of God. Why? Because this is a life-changing experience.

The secret of gaining spiritual vision is having a readiness to pay the cost of attaining it. This occurs when one possesses humble openness of spirit to the searching light of God. He will guide the meek in judgment and will teach them His way (Ps. 25:9 KJV). *"The secret of the LORD is with those who fear Him, and He will show them His covenant"* (v. 14).

The outstanding feature of God's work is not a doctrine, but a life. And life comes only by revelation in the light of God. Behind doctrine there may be nothing but words, but behind revelation is God Himself.

God's main concern in our labors is not whether we do the work as much as it is what we use as materials. God looks for quality; it is weight that counts. Wood, hay, and stubble are light, inexpensive, and do not last; whereas gold, silver, and precious stones are weighty, costly, and eternal. If, in building for God, we use only the latter three, we can rest assured that in the end our labors not only will survive the fire, but will ensure a lasting reward. Alas, for those who have built with the former, nothing will remain. (See 1 Corinthians 3:12–15.)

In God's work, man in himself is of no use. Wood, hay, and stubble represent what essentially comes from man and his flesh. They imply what is common, ordinary, and easily or cheaply acquired. And, of course, they are perishable. Though grass today may clothe the earth in beauty, where is it tomorrow (Isa. 40:7–8)?

To create an earthly thing is easy for us. If we are content with an outward, technical Christian movement based on an earthly foundation, it is quite possible for us to do it ourselves. But it will not be part of the church. The church is spiritual, and her work is heavenly, not earthbound.

Just as a man's personality is expressed through his body, Christ is displayed through the church. She is the vessel in this age that contains Christ and reveals Him to the world.

Today, it is widely believed that if the people of God of different races, backgrounds, or Christian denominations are gathered on the ground of a creed or "basis of faith," this is the essence of the church. But Paul said these are the very things that do not exist in the church. In the church there is neither Greek nor Jew, male nor female, barbarian nor Scythian, bondman nor freeman (Col. 3:11; Gal. 3:28). If we understand him correctly, this means if we want to be Christians, we cannot be anything else but Christians!

Without Christ, I personally do not possess life. Furthermore, without the church, His body, I do not have the means to live out and express the life I possess as I should.

In the parable of the talents, the point of emphasis is not on the ten-talent person or the five-talent person. Rather, it is on the one-talent person. He is the one prone to burying his talent and losing the reward of doubling his talent from its use.

In our day, the church is suffering not so much from the five-talent people or from the ten-talent people; it is hampered and impoverished mainly from all of the one-talent people who have buried their talent. What a shame, for it is only by functioning with the life God has given us that we discover and experience the riches of what that life is.

The fellowship of the body is always two-way: receiving and giving. Never try to do everything, or be everything, yourself. This is a principle that should be adhered to. When we are functioning as part of the body, we will always leave room for others.

As Christians, we should place a great deal of emphasis on life, but this is not enough. We should also place emphasis on the consciousness of life. Consciousness is that inner sense that sees and understands without being told. A being without consciousness is one that exhibits very little evidence of life.

The nature of the butterfly is to always "go it alone." The nature of the bee is to always work for the whole. If we have truly touched upon life, we will be awakened to a growing and deepening sense of belonging and will no longer live a self-interested, self-sufficient Christian life. We will be like bees, not butterflies.

The oneness of the body is Christ's, not ours. It is because we are His that we are one. This is the reason that we are not told to hold fast to our fellow members, but to hold fast to the Head. This is the way to fellowship.

To quench the Spirit is to stifle the very consciousness of our life together as the heavenly Man. It is to injure our relationship to the Head, just as terribly as if a limb had been severed from the body.

What is the basis for our every act of life? It is not, "Is this good?" or "Is this bad?" Rather, it is, "Is it anointed? Is the Holy Spirit in this thing, and does He witness life?"

In the Christian experience, as one grows and matures, the spiritual things of God become less and less outward (that is, focused on gifts) and more and more inward (focused on life).

The health and growth of the body come from a ministry of Christ alone, and not merely from gifts as such. Hence, what is of importance to the body is not our gifts, but the personal knowledge of Christ that we convey by them.

It is not in searching, studying, or comparing that God gives life, but at the place of desperation in our lives. As this was true of the crisis in Abraham's life, so it is true of all his sons of faith.

How can I have a specific ministry? Not by doctrine, but by life. Our personal experiences of Christ are what constitute our ministry. And it is these trials of our faith that work the experience of Christ into us so that we can be used in ministry.

By allowing God to work through our personal trials and testings, praising Him and submitting to His will, we make it possible for Him to bring life through us to others. But only those who pay this price receive this costly ministry. For life is released only through death.

We can see two ministries by which the body is built up: gifts and life. Though in our day many minister by gifts, comparatively few minister by life.

For the edification of young churches and the winning of souls, spiritual gifts may take on a special significance, but they are not in themselves a mark of maturity. And they are certainly not something of which to boast. It is the amount of the Cross working in one's life that marks the true measure of his spiritual stature.

In the spiritual progress of His church, God makes ever greater use of life, and less use of gifts.

Satan's greatest fear, with regard to the church, is not in her resistance of sin, her resistance of the love of the world, or her resistance of any of his direct attacks, but in her resistance of his power of death. For Christ's death brought to nothing him who had the power of death—the Devil (Heb. 2:14). Hence, Satan has no power of death over us because we have already died in Christ. Satan fears the fact that we have died, for it is in death that Satan loses his hold on us. You see, death in Adam does not finish a man, but death in Christ does.

Those who have death recognize neither life nor death. But those who have life recognize it in others. Why? Because while the natural man may be equipped to discern between hot and cold, he is not equipped to discern between life and death.

Why is it that when some are present, it is easier to preach, and when others are there, it is harder? It all depends on the pouring in, or the draining away, of life. The spreading of life or death is a present fact in the home, at church, or wherever you are.

The spiritual power of our gatherings depends on whether those present are merely negative or are bringing in life. Those with life minister Christ at meetings, while with others even their amen is dead!

Because the body is one, the whole suffers even when one member suffers, and the whole is uplifted when one is uplifted (1 Cor. 12:26). Our awareness of what is happening in the body does not depend on information, but on our knowledge of the Lord by the Spirit of life.

Only let "the slaying of Jesus" work in you, and life must manifest itself in others. It cannot be otherwise. This is an abiding principle of the body: death works in us, and life in you (2 Cor. 4:12).

When a brother stands up to speak, you at once know whether he stresses doctrine or life. If all he has is doctrine, he never runs risks. He keeps carefully within the limits of his doctrinal system in order to be safe and avoid any possible misunderstanding. But one who stresses life will be far less concerned with technical correctness or with the exhaustive treatment of his subject. His emphasis is on presenting Christ.

God has made a threefold provision for our guidance in the Christian pathway: the Holy Spirit, the Word of God, and the body of Christ. And if we make use of the provision He has made, this threefold cord is not easily broken (Eccl. 4:12).

According to the Bible, it is not until God has removed a particular area of weakness or sin in one's life that one is considered worthy to judge on this matter in the lives of others.

Prayer should always be three-sided: someone prayed to, someone prayed for, and someone prayed against.

It is the church as a whole that overcomes. Spiritual warfare is the task of the church, not the individual. The individual himself cannot *"put on the whole armor of God"* (Eph. 6:11) any more than he can comprehend the love of Christ. It is as a whole—as the body—that we have complete protection. And without this protection, we can be singled out and defeated rather easily.

What Christ's accomplished work has made us is one thing, but unfortunately what we experience on earth, far too often, falls short of and appears to contradict that truth.

You advance spiritually by finding out what you really are, not by trying to become what you hope to be. It is only when you see you are dead that you die, only when you see you are risen that you rise, and only when you see you are holy that you become holy.

Most Christians will admit that to struggle and strive for heavenliness is wrong, yet they continue to struggle and strive. This is because they have been taught to regard heavenliness as something to be attained. For them, Christianity is an endeavor to be what they are not and to do what they cannot do. How sad!

Outward Christianity is in a sorry state. It manifests all the ailments and weaknesses of the world. Its work has been reduced to a little preaching and a little social service. Its impact on men is negligible. But what should cause us even greater personal distress is the tragedy that, as God's people, our conscience has been so little troubled about this fact.

The sanctuary value God placed on the individual was one-half of a silver shekel (Exod. 30:11–16). This speaks of redemption:

what God does for us. In Leviticus, though, we find different values being placed on individuals who are willing to make a vow to God, the highest of which was fifty shekels (Lev. 27:1–7). This value was placed on the fittest and most able to go to war (v. 3). Furthermore, if we understand correctly, God is still looking for these people in our day who are willing to take part in the age-long battle of the Lord (Eph. 6:12–13), dislodging His foes and preparing for the bringing in of His people to the enjoyment of their inheritance. And those who have attained the strength and maturity for the battle will find that God still places His highest value on those who are able to go to war.

Never answer Satan by boasting of your good conduct or by bemoaning your sins, but answer always and only by the blood of Christ. It is our wholly sufficient defense.

Sometimes we are perplexed as to why people are not hungry for the Word. But believe me, if we had something distinctive to give them, they would be hungry. If we, in our lives and actions and presence, are manifesting the life of Christ, others around us will soon develop a hunger and thirst for what we have.

It is by revelation alone that we behold spiritual realities, and by His loving discipline that we enter into those realities. Without revelation by the Spirit, we cannot commence the course, and without the discipline of the Spirit, we cannot complete it.

Spiritual poverty and spiritual scarcity are two of the greatest problems in the church. But poverty and scarcity are effects, not causes. And the cause of this poverty and scarcity is a lack of the Spirit's discipline in the members of the body.

If you never allow the Spirit to trouble you, you will be condemned to poverty all your life. Every day God places before us opportunities He wants to use to enlarge us. But all too often, when the difficulties arise, we avoid them; and when the trials come, we circumvent them. We seem to overlook the fact that it is only those who submit to His dealings whom He takes in hand to bring about His goal for their lives. Are you willing to say, "Lord, I will drink of the cup You have given; I will bear the cross You have for me; Your will be done in my life"?

Fifty-Seven

The Spiritual Man
(Volume One)

The Lord always gives a foretaste of the deeper life before He leads one into the experience of it. However, many mistake the foretaste for the fullness.

God's purpose for His children is that they be delivered wholly from the old creation and enter fully into the new creation.

To fail to develop the ability to distinguish between what is spirit and what is soul is fatal to spiritual maturity.

God cannot be known by our thoughts, feelings, or intentions; He can be known only directly by our spirits.

Before being born again, one's spirit is so withered and weak and so overwhelmed by the strength of the soul that it is impossible to distinguish between the two. To complicate matters, the functions of the two have become mixed. Furthermore, the spirit has lost its primary function—which is to relate to God—and is dead to Him. This is why it is essential for the believer, after regeneration, to allow the Word its work of dividing between soul and spirit (Heb. 4:12).

God's thought is for the spirit to have preeminence over the soul. But as man through the Fall has become fleshy, his spirit has sunk into servitude to the soul. Hence, man has descended not only from spirit-control to soul-control, but also from soul-control to body-control.

Before regeneration, the soul of man is in control of his spirit. In this state, while self rules his soul, his passions govern his body.

In other words, the soul has become the life of the body. At regeneration, man receives God's life into his dead spirit. This rebirth allows the Holy Spirit to rule man's spirit. And if submissive to the Spirit, this one now has the equipment necessary to regain control, not only over his soul, but also over his body.

A carnal Christian is one who has been born anew with God's life, but instead of overcoming his flesh, he is overcome by his flesh. This hinders God's salvation from being wholly manifested and prohibits one from realizing or experiencing the full potential of it in his life as a believer.

It is indeed regrettable that many workers fail to present the full-salvation Gospel to sinners. This leaves them, as it were, only half saved. In this state, though their sins are forgiven, they lack the strength to cease from further sinning.

Since we became flesh by being born of the flesh, it stands to reason that if we die to the flesh, we will be freed from it. And crucifixion is the one and only way (Gal. 2:20; Rom. 6:7).

Our union with Christ in His death signifies that it is an accomplished fact in our spirits. What a believer must do is bring this sure death out of his spirit and apply it to his members (his body of flesh) each time his lusts are aroused.

The flesh is Satan's workshop, his realm of operation. If the flesh as a whole, and not in part, is under the power of the death of our Lord, Satan is unemployed.

What is lacking most in the lives of Christians today is not a better living, but a better dying! We need to die a thorough death.

Defeat can always be attributed to one of two things: a lack of faith or a failure to obey.

A walk in the Spirit is not only not committing sin, but also not allowing self to abide. Furthermore, the Holy Spirit can manifest His power only in those who are living out their lives by Him.

The Cross never stops short of its outworking. If allowed, it will continue to operate deeper and deeper in our lives until all of the old creation in us has been completely crucified.

By continuously losing more of our soul life in death, we will continuously gain more of God's abundant life in resurrection.

The soul of man always attempts to retain its authority and move independently, while the spirit strives to master everything for the maintenance of God's authority. This is the war that is waged between the soul and the spirit of every believer (Gal. 5:16–18; Rom. 7:14–25).

Fifty-Eight

The Spiritual Man
(Volume Two)

One way to discern between the work of God and the work of Satan in one's spiritual life is this: God always works from the center outward to the circumference, while Satan works from the circumference inward to the center.

As it is the right relationship with Christ that generates a Christian, so it is a proper relationship with the Holy Spirit that breeds a spiritual man (Rom. 8:14).

It is the soulish (soul-controlled) person who gains assurance by grasping things that can be seen and felt. The opposite of sight and touch is faith. One who follows the spirit lives by faith, not sight (2 Cor. 5:7).

What is meant by being a "spiritual man"? It means being one who has placed himself under the total subjection of his spirit, one whose whole man is governed by his spirit.

Those who are spiritual perceive the reality of the spiritual foe and engage him in battle (Eph. 6:12). This warfare is not fought with weapons of the flesh, but with spiritual arms. It is a struggle between the spirit of man and that of his enemy—an engagement of spirit with spirit (2 Cor. 10:3–4).

Each stage of the believer's walk possesses its own particular hazard to the believer. Early on, in the physical stage, it is the war against sins. Next, in the soulish phase, it is the battle against his natural life. And last, on the spiritual level, it is the onslaught against the spiritual forces of darkness.

It is only when the Christian begins to mature spiritually that the spirits of darkness launch assaults against him. It is a battle of spirit against spirit. Accordingly, it is called spiritual warfare.

The Bible compares a newly born believer to a baby because the life he now possesses in his spirit is as tiny and weak as a naturally born infant. There is nothing wrong with his being a baby as long as he does not remain in this stage of life too long. He should be continually increasing in knowledge and experience through exercise, training, and growth, until he knows how to skillfully understand all his senses and exercise his faculties in a mature way (1 Pet. 2:2).

Milk is predigested food. Those who are feeding on it are far less capable of communicating with God directly and must instead rely on others to transmit God's message to them. (See 1 Corinthians 3:2.)

Heavenly light comes in through the conscience to expose fault and condemn failure whenever we think, speak, or act in a way unbecoming as saints. By submitting to its illumination and by eliminating what it exposes, we allow it to do its work; thus the conscience acts as a window that has been enlarged for more light to shine through to us in the future. Unfortunately, if we allow sins to accumulate in our lives, the opposite occurs: the size of the window diminishes, eventually allowing no light at all to penetrate.

If a child of God is faithful in dealing with his sins and faithfully follows his conscience, he will receive light increasingly from heaven so as to expose sins that were previously unnoticed. As this process takes place, the Holy Spirit enables one to understand more of God's law that is written on his heart, transforming what were previously vague ideas about holiness, righteousness, purity, and honesty into clearly understood realities (Ps. 36:9; 1 John 1:7).

A child of God is to live his life on earth exclusively by the grace of God. Grace implies that which is done solely by God as a gift to us. Therefore, men should have no part in that which God has declared is His responsibility to fulfill (Rom. 11:6).

In the matter of fellowship, God is not as concerned with how much we know of His will as He is with what our attitude toward His will is. If we truly seek to obey His desires, our fellowship with Him will remain unbroken, even though there are probably many unknown sins in us.

Nothing is more vital to the Christian life than to walk daily after the spirit. It is this that maintains the Christian in a constant spiritual state, delivers him from the power of the flesh, assists him in obeying God's will always, and shields him from the assaults of Satan.

Revelation in the spirit is the first qualification for a worker and should occupy a large place in the Christian servant's life. It is this alone that empowers one to perform spiritual service and to walk in the spirit.

Christians should be aware that not all senses emerge from the spirit. Do not forget: the body, the soul, and the spirit each has its own senses.

Only those who are blind to the concept of the church as a body draw lines of demarcation in its midst and devote themselves solely to their small circle or clique. Sadly, this manifests their weak spiritual condition. Those who are spiritual do not consider the members around them as their own, but rather as God's. They therefore embrace all whom He has chosen equally, making no worldly distinctions between them.

We should pour out all the burdens of our spirits in prayer until the burdens have all left us. The more that is poured out, the happier we will be. A common temptation, though, is to cease praying before the burden is lifted. When we begin to feel buoyant in our spirits, we assume our prayer is answered, not realizing that we are just beginning in spiritual work.

Every time we receive a burden in our spirits we should find out immediately through prayer what that burden is. If it is a call to war, to war we should go; if a call to preach the Gospel, let us preach; and if it is a call to pray, we should pray.

Christians deem their spiritual lives to be at high tide when they feel the presence of God, and at low tide when they feel low or dry. Yet these are only feelings and as such do not represent the reality of spiritual life. Those who have moved on to maturity clearly understand this and thus do not place much trust in these transient feelings.

God is interested in our spirits because it is there that His Spirit works to show us His will and give revelation. It is also there that we mature, resist the attacks of the Enemy, receive authority to overcome the forces of darkness, and secure power for service.

Only after the Cross has begun to work deeply in a believer's life does he truly come to know himself and how undependable his personal ideas, feelings, and desires really are. Those who have come this far have learned not only that they cannot trust themselves, but also that apart from being sustained by the power of God continually, they will unquestionably fail.

A lowly spirit is demonstrated by those who associate with the poor. It is this spirit alone that does not despise any who are created by God. God's presence and glory are manifested in the life of the spiritually humble.

Often the experience, growth, and progress of a Christian become such precious matters to him that he loses his lowliness. The most treacherous of all dangers for a maturing saint is to meditate on what he gains as he grows spiritually and to pay attention to what he has experienced. One who is poor in spirit always views himself as possessing nothing.

What we as Christians must have is a spirit of power toward the Enemy, a spirit of love toward men, and a spirit of self-control toward ourselves.

Only after one has learned how to walk by the spirit will he know how to live by its life in place of his soul life, use its power rather than his natural power to perform God's work, and apply its authority as he wars against the Enemy.

Only after a believer's spirit has been united to the Lord's as one, can he commence to live in the world as a pilgrim and sojourner (Heb. 11:13), experiencing the life of a heavenly citizen (Phil. 3:20).

One quality that characterizes a spiritual person is the great calm he maintains under every circumstance.

Consecration is the first step in one's spiritual walk; it leads the Christian to a sanctified position. No consecration means no spiritual life. And nothing is more paramount in one's consecration than his affection. If one's love is not yielded, there can be no consecration.

The Father demands absolute love from His children. He is unwilling to share our hearts with anyone or anything else. He looks not for our laboring for Him, but for our loving Him. Sadly, the kingdom incurs much loss because of the countless believers who give their spouses and children a higher place in their hearts than they give to Him.

How contrary the course of consecration seems to Christians, and yet how blessed for those who have experienced it! In order to substantiate, for the believer's own profit, his consecration to God, God strips him of the very thing that is dear to him and has been an obstacle between them.

How can we distinguish between love of the flesh and love of the spirit? If one's love is soulish, it does not empower him to be delivered from the world. Hence, the believer must continue to worry and struggle to break free from the world. But if one's love is spiritual, the things of the world will just fade away. One who participates in this kind of love begins to despise the things of the world.

At the beginning of the Christian life, the Lord uses many ways to attract the believer to Himself and assure the believer of His love. Later, He guides him further by withdrawing the feeling of love to lead him on into believing His heart of love. The first step of being attracted by the feeling of the Lord's love is necessary to draw the believer into a subsequent deeper walk. Unless we are drawn by Him, we are powerless to forsake all and follow Him.

To encounter a particular spiritual experience at a corresponding stage of maturity is both proper and profitable, but to yearn for these same experiences at a later stage constitutes a retreat or retardation of spiritual growth.

When a Christian remains carnal, he is ruled vigorously by his desires. Self-delight, self-glory, self-exaltation, self-love, self-pity, and self-importance all issue from man's desire to render self the center of everything.

Ambition arises through the unleashing of our natural inclinations. And from these desires, pride springs forth. All boastings flow from man's desires.

Haste is a symptom of the desires of one who neither knows how to wait on the Lord nor is familiar with the leading of the Holy Spirit. Furthermore, God never performs anything hurriedly; consequently, He will not entrust His power to the impatient. Haste is clearly the work of the flesh.

God desires to have a people dwelling exclusively in spirit, willing to offer their soul lives completely to death. If we bear the crosses God places before us in practical matters, we will shortly see our self-life crucified bit by bit on the crosses we bear. Every time we silently accept what goes against our natural disposition, we receive another nail that pins more of the soul life firmly to the Cross.

The Cross produces fruit, and each crucifixion brings to us the fruit of God's life. As we become willing to accept the crosses God has given us to bear, we will find that we are living out a pure spiritual life. Every cross has its particular mission to accomplish. May no cross ever be wasted on any of us!

When Christians become affectionately attached to the Lord, they are usually experiencing a life of feeling. At this phase of their spiritual walk, they assume this kind of emotional experience is a most spiritual one, because it affords them great pleasure. However, this causes a problem for many, because the delight it bestows is so satisfying, they find it difficult to cut loose and move on any further into a deeper walk with the Lord.

Many Christians mistake a life of feeling for spiritual experience. But real spiritual life is neither dominated by, nor lived in, feeling. On the contrary, it is the spiritual life within that should regulate one's feelings.

To live for the Lord means to reserve nothing for self. One who accepts everything that comes his way with gladness, as being from the Lord—including darkness, dryness, and flatness—is one who is living for Him.

Those who live by feeling are worthless when it comes to spiritual warfare. This is because battling the Enemy in prayer is truly a self-denying work. Spiritual warfare accordingly demands an attitude of death to feeling and an absolute trust in God.

Fifty-Nine

The Spiritual Man
(Volume Three)

According to the Bible, the mind of man is the battlefield where Satan and his evil spirits contend against the believer. Man's will and spirit are like a citadel that evil spirits crave to capture. (See 2 Corinthians 10:3–5.)

Satan's *modus operandi* is to introduce thoughts into the mind of a believer. Should they be accepted, Satan now has a footing for future operation in the mind of this one. For this reason, every vain idea, unproven theory, unknown thought, casually read line, and overheard word should be tested to see if it exalts itself above God (2 Cor. 10:5).

Passivity is to refrain oneself from movement and instead allow oneself to be moved by outside elements. A passive state is most advantageous to evil spirits on the prowl. It affords them the opportunity to occupy not only the believer's mind, but his will and body as well.

There is a crucially important distinction between allowing either the working of evil spirits or the working of the Holy Spirit in one's life. Evil spirits are at work when man fulfills their working conditions, while the Spirit is at work when man fulfills His working conditions.

Christians today do not perceive that their minds need to be saved (Eph. 4:23; 6:17). They fail to recognize that if they are to be saved to the uttermost, all of their abilities have to be renewed and made fit for His use. The salvation God imparts includes not only a new life, but the renewal of every part of our souls as well (2 Cor. 5:17).

As Christians, if we expect to mature, we must begin to face the fact that a war is on. Unless we learn to fight, how can we expect to retake the fortresses held by the Enemy?

The more spiritual a child of God becomes, the more conscious he is of the significance of walking according to the spirit and the dangers of walking according to the flesh.

What do we follow after? Whatever we set our minds on. If we set our minds on the things of this world, we are occupied with the flesh. And if we always set our minds on spiritual things, we are following after the spirit (Rom. 8:5).

Following after the spirit produces life and peace, while following after the flesh produces death (Rom. 8:6). By this we can see that a believer is capable of living in death though he still possesses life.

If our minds are not governed by the spirit, they must be governed by the flesh; if not guided by heaven, they must be guided by earth; and if not regulated from above, then regulated from beneath.

Our union with the Lord has two steps: the union of life and the union of will. Aside from God's giving us a new life, the turning over of our will to Him is the greatest work in salvation. Hence, the ultimate goal of the Gospel is to facilitate the union of our will with God. Anything short of this is a failure of the mission.

There are two measures necessary for one to be joined to God in will. First, God has to subdue the activities of our will. Second, the life of our will must be conquered. Quite often our volition is subservient to the Lord only in the few particular areas we have turned over to Him. But the greatest blessing and highest privilege we have lies in our rejecting all the corrupted volition of our flesh and being wholly united with God's will for the accomplishment of His heart's desire.

Today many grasp the truth of being crucified with the Lord on the Cross, yet few exhibit its reality. Sadly, the truth of co-crucifixion is only a teaching to many saints, and they wonder whether the reality of practical salvation can ever be experienced on a daily basis. Yet unless believers totally abandon themselves to God and trust completely in the power of the Spirit to lay to rest the deeds of the body, the truth they profess to know will always persist as mere theory.

How could we ever think that God is pleased with a people who praise Him in prosperity but complain against Him in adversity? He is looking for a people who love and obey Him even unto death.

It is widely believed that the life of Christ is for our spirits and not for our bodies. Few realize that the salvation God gives us is intended to reach to the soul and body after He has given life to the spirit.

It is God's aim to bring His children into the experience of victory over sin, self, the world, and Satan. However, few in our day are willing to tread that far with God. Yet for those who have, there remains one more enemy God wants us to overcome: death. If we wish to enjoy complete and total victory, we must destroy the last enemy (1 Cor. 15:26).

Sixty

The Church and the Work
(Volume One: Assembly Life)

God's purpose from the beginning to the end is to obtain a corporate Christ—the church. To substitute other work for the church of God is what Satan tempts people to do today.

God gathers together all who are saved in a local region and makes them a local assembly. This is His miniature New Jerusalem in each locality that is to manifest His eternal purpose. In this way, the will of God is manifested to the world around them. Sadly, few people ever give attention to this miniature expression of God's eternal purpose. We instead stress personal victory and works.

No Christian student should boycott a class; no Christian laborer should strike; no Christian son or daughter should be undutiful; and no Christian should speak with disrespect against any of the authorities that God has placed over him. For since these authorities are appointed by God, they represent God and His authority (Rom. 13:1).

The biblical word usually coupled with authority is *submission*. In the Bible, authority and submission are interrelated. If a person is submissive, he is in subjection to God's authority. If not, he is one who is trying to overturn God's authority (Rom. 13:2).

The purpose of God for His people is that they obtain united life in the body of Christ and abstain from all independent action.

Irrespective of how well the authorities God has placed over us represent His divine authority, a Christian must nevertheless learn to submit to them, because all authorities are of God (Rom. 13:1).

Who is unfit to be an elder? He who hopes to be an elder when he hears about elders. Who is fit to be an elder? He who considers himself unfit when he hears about elders. All who aspire to rule are unfit to rule; no authority should be placed in their hands. Only those who do not think of ruling may rule.

There are two inherently weak sides of the flesh: it either boasts or shrinks back. Never take the boasting of the flesh as courage or the withdrawing of the flesh as humility. Why? Because if we look at our strong points, we will be inclined to be proud, and if we look at our weaknesses and failures, we will tend to shrink back and do nothing.

What is humility? It is not looking at the good as well as not looking at the bad in oneself. Hence, true humility is not looking at oneself at all.

One accord is the work of the Holy Spirit, while the majority vote is man-made.

He who serves is greater than he who is served. Every time we come to a meeting, our attention should be focused on how we can serve the brothers and sisters.

A matter that has not been thoroughly prayed through at home shows neither the need nor worth for corporate prayer. Only after private prayer has been offered, and a sense of inadequacy still lingers, should the matter be mentioned publicly in a prayer meeting.

The Cross abolishes all elements of social distinction: in the Lord there is neither rich nor poor, noble nor humble, master nor servant, male nor female, parent nor child (Gal. 3:28; Col. 3:11). These social and class distinctions simply do not exist in the body of Christ. Accordingly, we should not bring into fellowship things that the Cross has abolished and laid in the tomb.

The Scriptures speak often of praying with hands lifted up. (See, for example, Exodus 17:11 and 1 Timothy 2:8.) This is indicative of one who is asking of God; it serves the purpose of attracting God's attention.

Sixty-One

The Church and the Work
(Volume Two: Rethinking the Work)

God not only reveals truths concerning our inner life; He also reveals truths concerning the outward expression of that life. Though God may prize the inner reality, He does not ignore its outward expression.

God has one objective: to increase His Son. His purpose is to have people come under the name of His Son as children and then learn to share in the life of His Son so that they too, by maturing, can become full-grown sons.

In the Bible, there is not only the personal Christ in view, but also the corporate Christ. The first has the total victory; the second has yet to experience this victory. The triumph of the Head has yet to be fully experienced by the body.

Ministry is nothing less than to supply Christ to the church.

The Son came to accomplish the will of the Father; the Spirit came to accomplish the will of the Son. The Son came to glorify the Father; the Spirit came to glorify the Son. The Father appointed Christ to be "the Apostle"; the Son, while on earth, appointed the Twelve to be apostles. Now the Son has returned to the Father, and the Spirit is on earth, appointing men to be apostles.

The objective of our work is not to produce an evidence of our ministry, but evidence of the resurrection of the Lord.

The first requirement in divine work is a divine call; everything hinges on this. A divine call gives God His rightful place, for it recognizes Him as the originator of the work. The tragedy in Christian work today is that so many of the workers have simply gone out on their own; they have not been sent.

The reason for both the oneness of believers and their separation from the world—for the unity of the body and its detachment from the world—is the same: the Spirit of God dwells in believers.

To bring error into the church is carnal, but to divide a church on account of error may also be carnal.

To have constant and close association with people whose interpretation of Scripture does not agree with our own is hard for the flesh, but good for the spirit. God does not use division to solve these problems—He uses the Cross.

All distinctions in Adam have been done away with in Christ. Any distinctions according to race, gender, or social status have no recognition in the Word of God. Hence, in the church we are all one in Christ (Gal. 3:28).

If the work is of God, it will be spiritual. And if the work is spiritual, the way of supply will be spiritual. If supplies are not on a spiritual plane, the work will speedily drift down to the plane of secular business. If spirituality does not characterize the financial side of the work, the spirituality of its other departments is merely theoretical.

In God's Word we read of no servant of God asking for or receiving a salary for his services. A settled income does not foster trust in God or fellowship with Him, but utter dependence on Him for the meeting of one's needs certainly does. The nature of the work and the source of the supply are always closely related.

Whenever our trust is in men, our work cannot help but be influenced by men. If we are supported by men, we will seek to please men. Unfortunately, it is often impossible to please both God and men at the same time.

It is a dishonor to the Lord for any representative of His to disclose needs that would promote pity on the part of others. If we have a living faith in God, we will always make our boast in Him, and we will dare to proclaim under every circumstance: "I have all things and abound." (See Philippians 4:18.) As representatives of God in the world, we are here to prove His faithfulness.

The spontaneous growth of the work of God does not necessitate any activities of human nature to raise funds, for God meets all the demands that He creates.

You will not have any anxiety if the sovereignty of God is a reality to you. You will only see indifferent people, haphazard circumstances, and the opposing hosts of evil being harnessed to accomplish His will. Unrelated forces will all become related as one in order to serve His purpose through those whose will is one with His.

The local church is the life of the body in miniature. Ministry is the functioning of the body in service, and work is the reaching out of the body in growth. Neither church, ministry, nor work can exist as a thing by itself; all three are from the body, in the body, and for the body.

Sixty-Two

The Church and the Work
(Volume Three: Church Affairs)

In the New Testament, apostles, often accompanied by other believers, would go forth and establish new churches. Here is an important secret of God's working: after this year's harvest, wheat will grow again, and it will grow just as richly next year. But for this to occur, you cannot remain stationary. You must move on and make room for other believers, for it is the measure of the outgoing that determines the increase. As many will be added as have moved out. But if there is no moving out, there will be no adding.

Once there was a believer who had twenty years of executive experience in business. Many people in the church asked me why he had not been invited to be an elder. My reply was this: twenty years of executive experiences in the world does not even count for one single year of experience in the church.

If the church were a worldly institution, we would need only to choose capable people. But since the church is a spiritual organism, the primary qualification is one of spirituality; then, after this, comes ability and so forth.

The spiritual growth of the body lies in the whole church serving, but most Protestant churches today place the emphasis on Sunday preaching. Yet if preaching takes precedence at our gatherings, not all of the body is serving. I would rather there be no preaching if then the body would be motivated to serve.

As we have inherited the priestly system of Roman Catholicism and the pastoral system of Protestantism, the problems in the church lie within us. Only when all the members of the body rise up and function will we see the reality of the body of Christ.

In the current history of the church, you and I are the people who must rise up to rebuild the temple. Like Zerubbabel, Ezra, Nehemiah, and the remnant who rose up and rebuilt the wall and the city of Jerusalem, we must learn to bring forth God's church and its testimonies in our time.

Generally, a church that is carnal is permissive and allows anything to be done in any way. Moreover, the tighter the grip of a *"strong man"* (Matt. 12:29) on a church, the more uneventful spiritual life will be. On the other hand, a spiritual church tends to have many difficulties, because it has so many things to consider; the more life there is, the more matters it will have that need to be solved.

The first principle in the body of Christ is that of authority, while the second is that of fellowship. While the use of the body lies in fellowship, the supply of the coordination is based on the amount of authority that exists within it locally.

What comes from the Head is authority; what comes from the body is fellowship. Today, if there is any failure in the church, you will see that such failure falls either into the area of authority or into the area of fellowship.

Why is it that the authority of God cannot be established among His children? It is because His children are always criticizing those in authority and demanding perfection. They refuse to submit to the authority God has established, without realizing that God does not give authority to a perfect man.

What is individualism? It means that a person cannot submit to authority, for once anyone submits to authority, his individualism vanishes.

What is obeying authority? It is certainly not choosing whom to obey. If you choose, it is apparent you do not know what authority is. A person who knows authority will recognize it wherever he goes. As soon as he meets authority, he knows whom to submit to, and if he cannot submit, it is proof that he never knew authority.

Sixty-Three

Revive Thy Work

The book of Acts is the only unfinished book of the Bible. The reason is this: the Holy Spirit is still working to bring about the completion of the task assigned to Him on the Day of Pentecost. He is to create the *"perfect man"* (Eph. 4:13)—the fullness in stature of the Head and His body (v. 13, 15). The work will be finished when this has been accomplished. In our day, we are in the midst of the final stages of that glorious work.

What a believer obtains upon receiving the salvation of God is positional gain. But henceforth, the purpose or goal of one's walk is experiential gain. And in order for one to gain, one must suffer loss. Therefore, unless we forsake what we hold so tightly, we will not gain more of God experientially in our lives.

As members in a body, we need to see that being part of the body and being a coordinated part of the body are two separate things. Independent action is most unbecoming. For this reason, we must come to recognize who is in authority above us and who is below us if we are to function as members connected to a Head.

The act of wearing a covering is an expression of one's willingness to submit to authority. The ability to recognize the authority God has placed around us and to submit to that authority constitutes our covering. The very nature of the life within us demands that we always be familiar with those to whom we are to submit. The fact that ninety-eight percent of the authority we are to submit to has been delegated by God (Rom. 13:1)—parents, government, bosses, husbands, elderly—reveals to us a principle that is absent among the members of the body. This principle is that we must be willing to submit to authority.

What God expects of men is testimony. The conduct that can express this was given to man, by God, through the law. If man keeps the law, it becomes a testimony, not only of God, but of man's obedience to God. Yet, as can be seen in much of the church today, what God demands, men fail to respond to in obedience. Thus the testimony is lost. When this occurs, divisions and factions within the body are the inevitable result.

The ability that one has been given by God is authority for ministry. To exceed the ability is to exceed one's authority. Those who see have authority to be the eyes, and others must submit to what is seen; those who speak have authority as the mouth, and others must listen to what is said. The problem today is that many think they must receive all directly from God, whereas God works His will through the various members of the body.

Both the tabernacle and the temple of the Old Testament typify the New Testament church, which is the body of Christ. They represent the riches available to the body when it is shown to be in submission, member to member, and each to the Head, as a body. Such submission is always manifested as a strong testimony.

As in the days of Ezra and Nehemiah, and their work of restoring what had fallen down, the church today is in the midst of a recovery that has been occurring since the Middle Ages.

In order to have the kingdom—to occupy territory for God—there must be warfare. Therefore, any restoration of the kingdom necessitates that there first be a resurgence of spiritual warfare.

Kingdom reality for the church is where and when people spiritually occupy a specific territory for God. Wherever the kingdom of God is, there is God's occupation of that land.

The Gospel does not merely cause people to be delivered from sin, the world, and self; it also enables us to be liberated from individualism, wealth, and everything else, so that we can enter into the full reality of the body of Christ.

Today, the Gospel lacks authority because there are so few manifestations of what a normal church is. In a normal church, as soon as one gets saved, he is fully committed to the body; there is total consecration from the start. But due to a lack of this example by those already in the local assembly, we are unable to show the newly saved what the normal expression of the body of Christ is.

I think, in God's eyes, there is nothing better than obedience, and nothing more beautiful than order. Yet even among God's people, we can see rebellion and insubordination. People desire to be free and independent, having their own opinions and subjective views, even though, in God's kingdom, none of these exist.

The problems within the church today rest on us, if only we would realize the great responsibility we have. If we are to preach a Gospel that transforms, we ourselves must first be transformed. If we expect others to be consecrated, we must first be fully consecrated. If we are not faithful, God will look to the next generation, rather than to us, to fulfill His need.

In our day, there is an abundance of preaching and little testimony. This is apparent by the resulting lack of fruit. In the early church, there was not much preaching, yet their martyrdom spoke out as the most powerful of testimonies. Because of this, fruit abounded, and the church spread like a blazing fire.

Whenever there is a company of people walking with the same commitment and consecration as that of the men of Acts 2 (see Luke 18:28), there will be a similar appearing of the manifestation of God's power.

The reason people do not believe us is that we ourselves lack faith. If we have sufficient spiritual weight, not only will we have the courage to speak, but people will also dare to believe the full Gospel.

Many do not realize that the church is in ruin on the one hand, and is progressing steadfastly toward her completion on the other hand.

In the early church, as soon as people believed in the Lord, they renounced the world. Thereafter, all their occupations were for the church, not for their own gain and satisfaction.

In the church today, the principle of Cain is rampant. Without any consciousness of the curse that was upon the soil, he felt quite satisfied going out each day to toil and till in it. And when the harvest was in, he was even content to offer the fruits of it as a sacrifice to God. In like manner, as if there is no concern that the world is at enmity with God, many believers seek the attainment and enjoyment of what the world has to offer while they labor in the Lord's work. And then, after having labored in their flesh by the sweat of their brow, they offer up the fruit of their efforts to God.

In viewing the church over the last twenty centuries, the example of Jacob comes readily to mind. Though he fell and rose many times throughout his life, before his departure from the world he could lean on his staff and worship (Heb. 11:21). All that he had lost was ultimately returned to him. Thus he could return to God as one saved to the uttermost (Heb. 7:25).

The church today is a paradox of two opposite states or conditions. Outwardly, she is becoming more and more corrupted by the world; yet inwardly, there are those who are moving on deeper with, and closer to, God.

The issue for people who wish to seek God in our day is this: will you stand on God's side and accept His riches? Those who would do so must be willing to pay any cost to obtain them.

The life we have in Christ is a shared life, not a complete life. Only as we learn to experience the riches of the other members is the body truly established.

If the reality of the Holy Spirit is present, there will not be the necessity of centralization. In contrast, the absence of the reality of the Holy Spirit is evident through the passing of proposals, the drawing up of work plans, and an abundance of committees and meetings.

When the body is healthy, life will flow freely; but when life is lacking, organization is bound to occur. The appearing of centralization is due to a lack of life and is symptomatic of sickness within.

When organization is found in the body of Christ, it is indeed a heavy burden for the individual members to bear.

Why is truth referred to as a pillar in God's Word (1 Tim. 3:15)? Because a pillar is something immovable. Those who refuse to let God deal with self cannot know what truth is, because when they are wrong they lower the truth, and when they are right they raise the truth. Forcing the truth to follow us is the main reason for the darkness that is in the church.

There is a basic difference between Protestant and Catholic churches in their approach to understanding the Bible. The latter consider the Pope and church hierarchy to be the only ones who can interpret God's Word, while the Protestants believe that all Christians can read and interpret God's Word. Yet both are wrong because, in the body, only certain members whom the Lord sets forth have been given authority by God to interpret His Word correctly.

In our day, most who preach the Gospel are concerned with saving souls from hell. Yet the Bible seldom speaks of being saved from hell. Mostly, it speaks of being saved from the world. Perhaps the reason this is not preached is that people do not want to hear it.

Regarding submission, only a few places in the Scriptures refer to our offering obedience directly to God. Most places actually speak of how we are to submit to those in authority over us. Perhaps this is because we as Christians need to learn that submission to God is not possible if we are not in submission to those He has placed over us (Rom. 13:1–2).

Coordination among the members of the body is learned through obedience and submission. An insubordinate and independent person cannot be a coordinated part of the body. The result of this is that the body will be lacking. For this reason, Christians must learn to be in subjection to one another (Eph. 5:21).

Within most of the denominations of our day, there is one weakening tradition that must be recognized and done away with by those who desire to move on to maturity: the pastor arrangement. In other words, whether it be an individual or a group, there should not be one group serving and one group not serving. All must learn to serve, and the emphasis should not be on either learning or serving, but on learning while serving.

God wishes to restore the church of Christ to her early state. Throughout the Scriptures, He can be seen working ceaselessly to this end, starting first in the Garden of Eden, then in the period of the tabernacle and the temple, and thereafter in our day through the church. His work will culminate with the appearance of the Holy City—the eternal dwelling place of God.

A person may be busily occupied, and yet from God's viewpoint he may be seen as being very much at leisure. Why is this? Because being engaged in works that one thinks are pleasing to God, yet are not, is reckoned as if one is idle.

The Bible does not teach majority rule, and this should not be present in His church. But it does teach one heart and one mind (Phil. 2:2). The fundamental principle of the church is that its members be of one accord. If this is not present, we need to seek healing and forgiveness.

Though individual lamps might not give off enough light to draw much attention, a city of lights set upon a hill cannot be hidden (Matt. 5:14). Likewise, when the body associates in fellowship, with unity, and is of one accord, the world around the body will take notice.

The prevailing concept of the Christian life is as follows: at the beginning, I am saved through His grace, by His blood. After a while, as I advance, I should forsake the world. Then sometime later, I should forsake all and serve God. Yet this is the teaching of a fallen church. On the very first day of salvation, a believer should meet the tomb, and, on that very same day, also forsake the world.

The blind are not those who cannot see, but those who do not wish to see.

Salvation is more than the saving of our souls; it is also deliverance from former things.

For a time, the believers in the church at Rome were killed under terrible persecution. Later, they were exiled because of the tremendous public impact the martyrs were having. Today, Christianity has no power on others because it has no power on Christians. The testimony of the early believers frightened the spectators on the one hand, but attracted them to such a Gospel on the other. Should there be any wonder that our lukewarmness has so little effect on those around us?

If I were a well-rounded individual, I would become the entire body and have no need of coordination with the other members. Yet, since I am only one member, I cannot therefore consider myself as having all. If there is to be coordination within the body, each member must accept the limitation that comes with being only one part of the whole body.

When the church is strong, it can stand on the ground of voluntary poverty. Thus, the church is protected from false brethren, for they dare not enter at the cost of giving up all that they have. Consequently, the church is kept clean.

In making an offering to the Lord, it is not a question of one-tenth or two-tenths. It is a matter of giving everything beyond one's necessary personal requirements. Any consecration less than this is below the Lord's standard.

One problem of the church is our desire to beautify the earthen vessel, instead of manifesting the treasure within the earthen vessel. (See 2 Corinthians 4:7.)

The salvation of the Lord is in manifesting Christ before men—in presenting to them the Lord who is within us. We should not attempt to draw attention to the earthen vessels, but to the Christ that is within.

The more we know of Christ, the simpler our lives become. Human ways always make us, and our lives, more complicated.

The basis of ministry is one's knowledge of God. Whether this ministry is effective or not depends on the breaking of the outer shell of our flesh.

Spiritual growth is far beyond the ability of human energy. The Lord places us in situations of utter powerlessness and impossibility, so that He can have His way with us. Then, as we learn to depend on Him, He shows His mercy to us by carrying us through them. In this process of repeatedly being struck down, we learn to know Him. Over a period of time, as our knowledge of Him increases by these daily blows to our outward man, we are able to see how the life of the Lord replaces our life. Yet it is not the increase of life, but the increase of our knowledge of His life—for His life we already have!

Bibliography*

Aids to "Revelation." New York: Christian Fellowship Publishers, 1983.

Assembling Together. New York: Christian Fellowship Publishers, 1973.

Back to the Cross. New York: Christian Fellowship Publishers, 1988.

Balanced Christian Life, A. New York: Christian Fellowship Publishers, 1981.

Body of Christ: A Reality, The. New York: Christian Fellowship Publishers, 1978.

Changed into His Likeness. Wheaton, IL: Tyndale House Publishers; Fort Washington, PA: Christian Literature Crusade, 1978.

Character of God's Workman, The. New York: Christian Fellowship Publishers, 1988.

Christ: The Sum of All Spiritual Things. New York: Christian Fellowship Publishers, 1973.

Church and the Work, The. Vol. 1, *Assembly Life.* New York: Christian Fellowship Publishers, 1982.

Church and the Work, The. Vol. 2, *Rethinking the Work.* New York: Christian Fellowship Publishers, 1982.

Church and the Work, The. Vol. 3, *Church Affairs.* New York: Christian Fellowship Publishers, 1982.

"Come, Lord Jesus." New York: Christian Fellowship Publishers, 1976.

---

* All titles by Watchman Nee.

Communion of the Holy Spirit, The. New York: Christian Fellowship Publishers, 1994.

Do All to the Glory of God. New York: Christian Fellowship Publishers, 1974.

Finest of the Wheat, The. Vol. 1. New York: Christian Fellowship Publishers, 1992.

Finest of the Wheat, The. Vol. 2. New York: Christian Fellowship Publishers, 1993.

From Faith to Faith. New York: Christian Fellowship Publishers, 1984.

From Glory to Glory. New York: Christian Fellowship Publishers, 1985.

Full of Grace and Truth. Vol. 1. New York: Christian Fellowship Publishers, 1980.

Full of Grace and Truth. Vol. 2. New York: Christian Fellowship Publishers, 1981.

Gleanings in the Fields of Boaz. New York: Christian Fellowship Publishers, 1987.

Glory of His Life, The. New York: Christian Fellowship Publishers, 1976.

God's Plan and the Overcomers. New York: Christian Fellowship Publishers, 1977.

God's Work. New York: Christian Fellowship Publishers, 1974.

Good Confession, The. New York: Christian Fellowship Publishers, 1973.

Gospel Dialogue. New York: Christian Fellowship Publishers, 1975.

Grace for Grace. New York: Christian Fellowship Publishers, 1983.

Interpreting Matthew. New York: Christian Fellowship Publishers, 1989.

King and the Kingdom of Heaven, The. New York: Christian Fellowship Publishers, 1978.

Latent Power of the Soul, The. New York: Christian Fellowship Publishers, 1972.

Let Us Pray. New York: Christian Fellowship Publishers, 1977.

Life That Wins, The. New York: Christian Fellowship Publishers, 1986.

Living Sacrifice, A. New York: Christian Fellowship Publishers, 1972.

Love Not the World. Fort Washington, PA: Christian Literature Crusade; Eastbourne, Sussex, England: Kingsway Publications, 1968.

Love One Another. New York: Christian Fellowship Publishers, 1975.

Messenger of the Cross, The. New York: Christian Fellowship Publishers, 1980.

Ministry of God's Word, The. New York: Christian Fellowship Publishers, 1971.

Mystery of Creation, The. New York: Christian Fellowship Publishers, 1981.

Normal Christian Life, The. Wheaton, IL: Tyndale House Publishers; Fort Washington, PA: Christian Literature Crusade, 1977.

Not I but Christ. New York: Christian Fellowship Publishers, 1974.

Practical Issues of This Life. New York: Christian Fellowship Publishers, 1975.

Prayer Ministry of the Church, The. New York: Christian Fellowship Publishers, 1973.

Release of the Spirit, The. Indianapolis: Sure Foundation Publishers, 1965.

Revive Thy Work. New York: Christian Fellowship Publishers, 1996.

Salvation of the Soul, The. New York: Christian Fellowship Publishers, 1978.

Sit, Walk, Stand. Wheaton, IL: Tyndale House Publishers; Fort Washington, PA: Christian Literature Crusade, 1977.

Song of Songs. Fort Washington, PA: Christian Literature Crusade, 1965.

Spirit of Judgment, The. New York: Christian Fellowship Publishers, 1984.

Spirit of the Gospel, The. New York: Christian Fellowship Publishers, 1986.

Spirit of Wisdom and Revelation, The. New York: Christian Fellowship Publishers, 1980.

Spiritual Authority. New York: Christian Fellowship Publishers, 1972.

Spiritual Knowledge. New York: Christian Fellowship Publishers, 1973.

Spiritual Man, The. 3 vols. New York: Christian Fellowship Publishers, 1968.

Spiritual Reality or Obsession. New York: Christian Fellowship Publishers, 1970.

Take Heed. New York: Christian Fellowship Publishers, 1991.

Testimony of God, The. New York: Christian Fellowship Publishers, 1979.

What Shall This Man Do? Fort Washington, PA: Christian Literature Crusade; Eastbourne, Sussex, England: Kingsway Publications, 1961.

Whom Shall I Send? New York: Christian Fellowship Publishers, 1979.

Word of the Cross, The. New York: Christian Fellowship Publishers, 1995.

Worship God. New York: Christian Fellowship Publishers, 1990.

Ye Search the Scriptures. New York: Christian Fellowship Publishers, 1974.

Reference Index*

Chapter 1: The Normal Christian Life

12; 14; 29; 34; 37; 42; 48; 49; 53–54; 54; 54; 60–61; 72–73; 73–74; 75; 79–80; 80; 81; 88–89; 93; 101; 103; 104–105; 105; 106; 117; 128; 140–141; 144–145; 145; 150; 155; 156; 157–159; 159; 164–165; 165–166; 167; 167; 172–173; 176–177; 179; 180; 182; 185; 191; 205; 219; 224; 230–231; 235; 241; 242; 259; 261; 277; 283–284

Chapter 2: Changed into His Likeness

21; 39; 44; 59–60; 66; 72; 74; 78–79; 80–81; 101; 103; 104; 107; 112; 113; 117; 153; 153

Chapter 3: Sit, Walk, Stand

18; 23; 38; 39; 41; 43; 66; 66; 67; 69

Chapter 4: Love Not the World

13; 52–53; 62; 63; 70; 81; 103; 125

Chapter 5: Back to the Cross

1–2; 2–4; 4; 6; 7; 10; 11; 11; 12; 15–16; 19; 20; 21; 24–25; 27; 28; 28–29; 34; 36; 37–38; 38–39; 46; 46; 49–50; 57–58; 60–61; 61; 62; 67; 67; 70; 71; 80; 108; 115; 136; 140; 147; 149–150; 152; 152; 156–157; 166; 171

Chapter 6: Let Us Pray

3; 3; 4; 4–5; 6; 7–8; 8; 8; 9; 9; 10; 11; 16; 20; 20; 22; 26; 34; 35; 35; 38–39; 39–40; 41; 44; 46; 56; 57; 58–60; 66; 69; 71; 79–80; 83

---

* This reference index provides the original source and page number(s) for each excerpt used in this compilation. Please see the bibliography for full publication information on each source.

Chapter 16: Whom Shall I Send?

Chapter 17: The Prayer Ministry of the Church

Chapter 18: Practical Issues of This Life

Chapter 19: A Living Sacrifice

Chapter 20: The Good Confession

Chapter 21: Assembling Together

Chapter 22: Not I but Christ

Chapter 23: Do All to the Glory of God

Chapter 24: Love One Another

Chapter 25: The Life That Wins

Chapter 26: The Release of the Spirit

Chapter 27: A Balanced Christian Life

Chapter 28: The Character of God's Workman

Chapter 29: Christ: The Sum of All Spiritual Things

Chapter 30: The Finest of the Wheat (Volume One)

Chapter 31: The Finest of the Wheat (Volume Two)

Chapter 32: The Glory of His Life

Chapter 33: The Salvation of the Soul

Chapter 44: The Spirit of Judgment

4; 13; 17; 19; 26; 27; 30; 30; 30–31; 31; 31; 33; 35; 42; 47; 49; 48; 50; 50; 50; 53; 60; 61; 62; 63; 71; 99; 103–104; 107; 111–112; 113–114; 117; 123; 124; 124–125; 125; 125; 127; 128; 128; 129; 134; 135; 136; 138; 139; 140; 141; 144; 144; 144; 145; 146; 152; 156

Chapter 45: The Testimony of God

6–7; 7–8; 13; 17; 18–19; 27–28; 30; 31; 32; 33; 34; 34; 37; 49–50; 57–58; 58; 59; 59–60; 61; 61; 61–62; 62; 62–63; 63; 64; 65; 73; 80; 89; 91; 92; 95–96; 95; 99; 101; 106; 114; 115, 118–119

Chapter 46: Spiritual Knowledge

11; 11; 12–13; 20; 25; 27; 39; 40; 42; 47; 47; 69; 48; 51; 53; 53; 54; 57; 59–60; 60; 61; 61; 62; 66; 66; 73; 75; 78; 79–80; 82; 100–101; 113; 112; 116–117; 118; 118

Chapter 47: Ye Search the Scriptures

15; 17; 19; 22; 24; 26–27; 27; 28; 29; 29–30; 30; 30; 32; 33; 43–44; 60; 73; 74–75; 74; 75; 77; 80; 80; 81; 144

Chapter 48: Spiritual Authority

11; 12; 13; 13; 16; 16; 16–17; 20; 21; 22; 22–23; 23; 23; 23–24; 28; 30; 33; 37; 37–38; 38; 48; 49; 50; 59; 73; 78; 81; 81; 81; 89; 90; 97; 102–103; 105; 106; 109; 109; 110; 115–116; 121; 122; 126; 127; 129; 129; 137; 152; 152–153; 163; 163; 166; 167; 175; 176; 185

Chapter 49: The Ministry of God's Word

10; 24; 29; 29; 33–34; 39; 45; 53; 62; 83–84; 92; 96–97; 99; 109; 113; 115; 118; 120; 124; 125; 126; 137–138; 138; 138–139; 153; 186; 189–190; 192; 192; 193; 207; 207; 214; 214; 214; 215; 216–217; 218; 219; 224; 224; 226–227; 229; 231; 241; 241; 242; 249; 250; 253; 255; 273; 276; 279–280

Chapter 50: "Come, Lord Jesus"

31; 39; 44; 141

Chapter 51: Interpreting Matthew

13; 13; 14; 16; 17; 29; 31; 32; 33; 42–43; 50; 65; 68–69; 70; 98; 105; 121; 129; 146; 152; 152; 155; 164–165; 181; 191; 200; 240; 240–241; 244; 247; 261; 262

Chapter 52: The King and the Kingdom of Heaven

Chapter 53: The Word of the Cross

Chapter 54: The Communion of the Holy Spirit

Chapter 55: Worship God

Chapter 56: What Shall This Man Do?

Chapter 57: The Spiritual Man (Volume One)

Chapter 58: The Spiritual Man (Volume Two)

Chapter 59: The Spiritual Man (Volume Three)

Chapter 60: The Church and the Work (Volume One: Assembly Life)

1; 4–5; 10; 12; 14; 14–15; 43; 44; 44; 61; 79; 83; 87–88; 92

Chapter 61: The Church and the Work (Volume Two: Rethinking the Work)

6; 11; 13; 32; 37–38; 44; 52–53; 113; 126; 127; 129; 182; 182–183; 184; 193–195; 200; 204; 236

Chapter 62: The Church and the Work (Volume Three: Church Affairs)

6–7; 18; 19; 51–52; 57; 71; 122; 148; 148; 195; 196; 196–197

Chapter 63: Revive Thy Work

5, 9; 9; 17–18; 20; 34–35; 37–38; 42; 45–72; 59; 59; 61; 60–61; 64; 66–67; 67; 72; 72; 73; 76; 76–77; 78; 79; 81; 92; 93; 97; 113–114; 126–127; 131; 135; 136; 143; 148; 154; 156; 158; 171–172; 174; 175; 176; 188; 221; 222; 228; 230; 231; 235; 237–238